The Bystander

The Bystander

Behavior, Law, Ethics

Leon Shaskolsky Sheleff
Tel Aviv University

Lexington Books
D.C. Heath and Company
Lexington, Massachusetts
Toronto

Library of Congress Cataloging in Publication Data

Sheleff, Leon Shaskolsky.
    The bystander.

    Includes index.
    1. Crime prevention—Citizen participation. 2. Assistance in emergencies.
3. Helping behavior. 4. Social ethics. I. Title.
HV7431.S53   362   77-18577
ISBN 0-669-02110-5

Copyright © 1978 by D.C. Heath and Company

Published simultaneously in Canada.

Printed in the United States of America.

International Standard Book Number: 0-669-02110-5

Library of Congress Catalog Card Number: 77-18577

To Sy Dinitz—a very special person

Contents

Preface

My initial interest in the study of the bystander started during my graduate studies in the 1960s at the Ohio State University. I was fortunate to receive much encouragement then from my professors, Walter Reckless and Simon Dinitz, as I searched out the possibilities contained in this topic, which was just beginning to arouse general academic interest. My master's thesis was written on this theme under their guidance. Later, I published several articles on the subject, and at the first International Conference on Victimology, held in Jerusalem in September, 1973, I presented a paper on the "criminal triad," summarizing the key aspects of bystander studies.

Although other commitments and other academic interests sometimes turned my attention away from this topic, it continued to intrigue me. A sabbatical year spent at the University of California in Irvine finally afforded me the time and the impetus for a concerted effort aimed at presenting a comprehensive picture of the role of the bystander. During this period, Gilbert Geis provided me with much help, and with characteristic generosity gave me access to some of his own material in this area.

I have also benefited from my correspondence, and one all-too-brief visit, with Janez Pecar of Lublijana, Yugoslavia, and from a work project during which Russell Dynes and Enrico Quarantelli introduced me to the many aspects of bystander activity in disaster work. My thanks also to Michael Markowitz, who pointed out to me that Chinese legal history in citizen involvement contained some interesting parallels with that of England. Parts of the manuscript were read by David Shichor and Ted Huston, whose comments have been most useful and are much appreciated.

There have been other bystanders along the way who in diverse, and sometimes intangible ways, have helped: students who have responded positively to many of the ideas presented in class; colleagues who have contributed to a collegial atmosphere conducive to work, particularly David Libai at Tel Aviv and Ellen Greenberger at Irvine; several typists at both these institutions, who have efficiently and pleasantly prepared the manuscript; and my wife and children—Rinah, Kinor and Ariel—who have vicariously shared with me both the agonies and the joys that are a part of writing.

And always, over the years, with friendship, understanding and advice, there has been Sy Dinitz, to whom I dedicate this book.

Acknowledgments

Some of the basic ideas for this book first appeared in research papers and journal articles which I have published in the past few years. I wish to thank editors and publishers for allowing me to use short extracts from these articles:

"Volunteerism in Disaster Situations," Preliminary Paper No. 1, Disaster Research Center, The Ohio State University.

"The Innocent Bystander: Socio-Legal Aspects," in *Israel Studies in Criminology*, edited by Shlomo Shoham, 1973, vol. 2 (Jerusalem: Jerusalem Academic Press).

"The Criminal Triad: Bystander, Victim, Criminal," *International Journal of Criminology and Penology*, 1974, vol. 2; also appearing in *Victimology: A New Focus*, edited by Israel Drapkin and Emilio Viano, vol. 1 (Lexington, Mass.: Lexington Books, D.C. Heath, 1974).

I wish also to thank Alfred A. Knopf, Inc., for permission to use an extract from *The Fall* by Albert Camus, translated by Justin O'Brien, copyright 1957.

1

Introduction: The Bystander's Dilemma

Few social interactions so illuminate the nature of the social bond within a society as the manner in which an innocent bystander responds to the plight of a stranger in need of assistance. The emotions evoked and the actions elicited by the cry for help of a fellow being in distress serve as the touchstone for expressing the obligations that one member of a society owes another by virtue of their shared humanity.

The dyadic connection between two strangers—a victim in distress and his potential rescuer—offers a glimpse into the network of human relationships. The complexities of social life are clearly etched out in the two-way interaction that comes into existence when one individual turns to another for aid. The way that any individual reacts to a cry for help reflects not only his own personal attributes or passing mood, but also mirrors, to a large extent, the mores of the society in which he lives. The varying ways in which societies organize themselves—in law and education, in declared intent and practical policy—with respect to the problem of the innocent bystander are a consequence of the way each society feels about some of its most cherished values.

There are moments of crisis in the life of every individual, and in the history of every society, when they stand exposed to certain truths about themselves—truths which may be hidden behind the artificial trappings of normal social intercourse, but which are bared when the smooth path of social equilibrium is upset by an unanticipated event which thrusts itself into consciousness and forces the need to take stock.

Such a moment of truth occurred on the night of March 13-14, 1964, when thirty-eight New Yorkers were awakened in the early hours of the morning by the frenzied cries for help of a young woman, Kitty Genovese, the victim of a savage physical assault perpetrated by a man who had accosted her within the proximity of her apartment while she was on her way home. Over a period of about forty minutes, the assailant made several separate attacks on her, while she struggled, battered and bleeding, to reach the sanctuary of her apartment. Her screams of anguish and her calls for help were heard by at least thirty-eight neighbors, who, in the privacy and anonymity of their own homes, witnessed her struggle, yet offered no assistance in any form, whether through direct intervention or through the simple expedient of telephoning the police. A neighbor finally summoned the police, after first calling a friend to seek advice as to what to do. A patrol car arrived on the scene within two minutes but this prompt response was too late to be of help to the young woman, who died on

1

the way to the hospital. It is clear that Kitty Genovese was a victim not only of her assailant's viciousness but also of her neighbors' inaction.[1]

When the facts of the Genovese case became known to the general public, the event became a cause célèbre as newspapers in the United States and elsewhere inundated the public with the full details, and columnists and editors pondered the quality of a society in which such apparent callousness could have been shown by so many people. In the soul-searching that followed, awkward and anxious questions were posed about the failure not only of those thirty-eight witnesses but of society at large; attacks were made on the anonymity and alienation of urban life and the dehumanization of modern society. The witnesses themselves might have been seen as aberrants, devoid of normal feelings, but it soon became apparent that they were more probably a representative sample of their society, ordinary men and women with the normal range of human emotions, for whom the memory of their inaction was to haunt their future. In the words of one witness a year later, "Every time I look out now, it's like looking out at a nightmare."[2]

The Genovese case was not unique, for such indifference and inaction by the neighbors had many precedents—and later replications. Yet somehow it touched a deep chord and aroused a great deal of publicity; it has served ever since as an oft-quoted example epitomizing the problem of the bystander. In the wake of the publicity engendered, academic research began to focus for the first time on the behavioral, legal, and philosophical aspects of bystander response. In 1965, the year following the death of Kitty Genovese, the first conference on these topics was held in Chicago,[3] and a special session at the 1966 annual meeting of the American Psychological Association was devoted to the new theme of the "unconcerned bystander."

While it was the negative behavior of the bystanders in the Genovese case that prompted the deeper studies, it was apparent that the issues involved were far more complex than would allow for rote condemnation of the bystanders' indifference and society's alienating tendencies. On the one hand, there was the callous behavior of the witnesses to this tragedy and to many other similar cases; on the other hand, there were the many moments of equally critical situations which, for some reason, evoked diametrically opposite behavior—constructive, sometimes courageous, occasionally even self-sacrificial. A reference to the sinking of the *Titanic* notes eyewitness accounts that point to the full spectrum of human behavior, ranging from heroic self-sacrifice to narrow selfishness elicited by the very same crisis.[4]

Indeed, some of the more tantalizing paradoxes and contradictions in the innocent bystander situation become even more explicit when focus is shifted from the bystander who remains aloof from, or casually indifferent to, a crisis situation, to the bystander who becomes actively involved in an attempt to extricate the victim from his plight. Once the bystander voluntarily places himself at the disposal of the victim, a number of critical questions loom large:

Are any reciprocal connections set up? What is the nature of the social nexus, the legal link, the moral obligation that come into existence? What motivates the bystander to act? What is the constellation of rights and duties that arise when a bystander comes into direct contact with the victim? What if the active bystander should be injured through his activity: what kind of obligation would devolve upon the victim to compensate the bystander? Alternatively, what would happen if the bystander's intervention were inadvertently to exacerbate the situation and to cause more damage to the victim? In such a situation, should the victim be entitled to claim damages? What should be the legal position in each of these circumstances? Should society encourage bystander response? If so, how?

Such larger social and legal questions are intrinsic to the Genovese case itself. Deplorable as the behavior of the bystanders may have been, shocking as the consequences undoubtedly were, the results of active efforts to save the young woman might have caused other disturbing reactions. A potential rescuer might have been killed, or conversely, found, to his surprise, that the presumed assault was no more than a family squabble. In fact, two other, lesser-known incidents, which also occurred in metropolitan New York a little before and after the Genovese case, highlight the possible fate which may befall an innocent bystander who attempts to respond to the call for help.

Bystanders Who Help

In October 1965, a passenger on a New York subway train began molesting some women passengers. When another passenger, Arthur Collins, remonstrated with the molester, the latter stabbed him to death in the presence of his wife and fifteen-month-old baby. The dependents did not institute any legal proceedings against the criminal, the woman whom Collins had been trying to protect, or any public body—but later the New York Transit Authority announced that, purely as a matter of good will, they had guaranteed to provide ex gratia payments for the dependents of the deceased.[5]

In another case, a citizen was indicted on a charge of third-degree assault as a result of his intervention to protect a young boy from two adult men who were apparently beating him. In the course of freeing the boy, injury was caused to one of the men, who, it later transpired, was a plainclothes policeman intent upon arresting the boy for delinquency. The citizen was convicted of assault, the judges admonishing him for action which they deemed to be not "conducive to an orderly society."[6] Basing this decision on a whole series of cases from many jurisdictions in the United States, the judges concluded, "The weight of authority holds that . . . one who goes to the aid of a third person does so at his own peril." In a dissenting opinion, a different interpretation was placed on the citizen's action. The basic moral, social, and legal issues are clearly drawn, in the dissenting judge's rhetorical question: "What public interest is promoted by a principle which would deter one from coming to the aid of a fellow citizen whom he has a reasonable ground to apprehend is in imminent danger of personal injury at the hands of assailants?"

These cases dramatically illustrate the dilemmas facing the bystander. The dangers and inconveniences of intervening may often lead to serious, unintended consequences for the active bystander, while the passive bystander is released from all further complications. Thus, in an analysis of the indifference of the public, Menninger recounts how "two medical students of my acquaintance were walking in a park . . . when they saw an elderly man stretched out on the ground. They successfully resuscitated him by mouth and with massage, called an ambulance, and took him to the hospital. The next day he died. The students found themselves in deep trouble over having tried to help."[7]

Such dilemmas are not of recent origin. Montaigne, writing in the seventeenth century, relates an incident which points out the earthy wisdom of a group of peasants who judged discretion to be the better part of their valor—and their values:

> Some peasants have just informed me hastily that a moment ago they left in a wood that belong to me a man stabbed in a hundred places who is still breathing, and who begged them for pity's sake to bring him some water and help him to get up. They say they did not dare go near him and ran away, for fear that the officers of the law would catch them there and hold them accountable for the accident—as is done with those who are found near a murdered man—to their total ruin, since they had neither ability nor money to defend their innocence. What could I say to them? It is certain that this act of humanity would have got them into trouble.[8]

Montaigne does not relate what his own reaction and response was to the plight of this stranger found on his property. However, the reasoning of twentieth-century Anglo-American legal thinking would have bade him to be cautious in his response.

The problem of the innocent bystander, then, is far more complex than would appear on the surface. For a bystander involving himself in the dangers confronting a stranger, the personal consequences may be dire, the legal position obscure, and the moral and social implications problematical. On the personal and psychological levels, the considerations may be a mixture of self-seeking and self-sacrificing motivation.

Sometimes an apparently altruistic act may be performed for base reasons—more out of vindictiveness toward the culprit than from any empathy for the victim. Sometimes the consequences of intervening may be actually more detrimental than the harm it was presumably intended to prevent. Sacrificial behavior may be motivated by suicidal tendencies: the hero may be a fool or a villain.

A United Nations symposium on the prevention of crime drew attention to the overzealous responses of some bystanders, noting evidence of people taking the law into their own hands, and sometimes even lynching offenders.[9] Likewise, the vigilante tradition in the United States often led to harsh sanctions meted out by vigilante groups to people considered deviants.[10] In ancient Rome, the Twelve Tables provided formal condonation of this type of behavior, making it permissible to call in one's neighbors to apprehend a thief. Almost no limitations were put on the procedures, and in some cases the thief might even be put to death. Indeed, in certain circumstances (for example, where the thief was armed or came in the night), "If he was not killed in the struggle to seize him, it would be possible to execute the thief after a hearing before a crowd of neighbors."[11] The bystander situation must thus take due cognizance of these and other examples of supposedly helpful behavior and of the perversions which may be perpetrated in the name of "good citizenship."

The academic studies which have come in the wake of the Genovese case fall into three distinct categories:

1. Those that have attempted to understand the actual *behavior* of bystanders: the dilemmas that confront them; their perception of the crisis situation; the role-playing capacities they are capable of activating; the pragmatic considerations that influence their response; the motivations for action or inaction.

2. Those that analyze the *legal* position of the bystander: the obligation to act; the sanctions, if any, for inaction; the rewards if any for intervention; the legal protection offered for harm inadvertently caused to others; the compensation provided should bystanders suffer harm as a result of their intervention; the role that law can play in encouraging legitimate and effective bystander intervention.

3. Those that relate to the larger *social, moral*, and *philosophical* issues: the nature of the social bond; the demands a society may reasonably make upon its members for altruistic and prosocial behavior; the role and importance of altruism as a factor in social life; the practical manner in which society may, apart from the legal provisions, create the conditions for fostering altruistic behavior.

During the past decade much information has been accumulated; creative research has provided us with heretofore unknown data about the sociological and psychological dimensions of bystander behavior in crisis situations; legal scholars have inquired into the desirability of the present legal situation and have challenged the failure, particularly of the Anglo-American legal systems, to deal adequately with the rights and duties of the bystander; and philosophers and theologians have returned with renewed vigor to the age-old question of the responsibility all human beings share toward one another.

Bystander Studies and Victimology

The question of the bystander touches upon many disciplines, yet, for the most part, the three major trends of research have remained isolated from each other. This may be a consequence of the lack of an overall and recognized academic framework within which a synthesis of these trends may be formulated. Such a framework does potentially exist, and the first tentative moves in its direction have already been made. At the First International Conference on Victimology, held in Jerusalem in 1973, several resolutions were adopted accepting the study of the bystander as an integral part of the discipline of victimology, which incorporates many of the behavioral, legal, and philosophical aspects enunciated above.[12]

Victimology is a relatively new discipline and is still seeking a definition of its legitimate parameters. It is firmly rooted in the field of criminology, as much of its concern has to do with the victim of a crime. In the 1940s the study of crime was given a new dimension by the parallel, yet independent, pioneering work of von Hentig[13] and Mendelsohn,[14] both of whom drew attention to the fact that the criminal act generally involved some degree of interaction between the criminal and his victim, and that a full understanding of crime could only be attained when the behavior of victims was examined to determine whether their actions had perhaps provoked or precipitated the crime. In the years since the initial presentation of this argument, the discipline of victimology has emerged as a comprehensive field of study, embracing not only the role of the victim in causing crime, but a far wider range of related issues: the victim's right to compensation for harm caused; the definition and significance of the concept, "crime without victims"; specific types of victims, such as battered children and wives; the creation and expansion of specialized services for aiding victims; analyses of historical situations within a victimology perspective, concentrating on the victimization of racial, religious, ethnic groups; and the incorporation of other noncriminal situations, such as natural disasters and human accidents, which take their toll of victims as well.

While some of the academic research and practical involvement would probably have taken place in any case, there can be little doubt that the concept of victimology has helped considerably in giving greater substance and cohesion to such work.

It would seem that victimology is also the logical area within which bystander studies might develop, since the basic question of bystander studies is the attitude adopted, and the action taken, by a bystander in response to the plight of a stranger in distress as a victim of circumstances. Victimology provides, then, a framework for integrating the work of bystander studies into a coherent and comprehensive unity.

A full study of the bystander cannot be limited only to studies of crime. In both of the parent disciplines, criminology and victimology, ample references are made to other disciplines. Thus, criminology has taken the broadest possible approach to issues of deviant behavior and social control, incorporating mental illness and marginal political and social behavior, as well as the legal and extralegal means used by society to control such forms of behavior.

The same is true of victimology. While its origins were in criminology, and the bulk of work in this area has been carried out by criminologists, consideration is also paid to noncriminal situations in which there are victims. Mendelsohn, in particular, has argued consistently for the recognition of victimology as a discipline in its own right, separate from criminology, and concentrating on human suffering per se, irrespective of the specific causes of that suffering.

The possible bystander situations, too, are many and varied. The cry for help may emanate from the lips of one individual or be a concerted plea uttered by large masses. The event may be a minor incident or a major calamity, a crime or a natural disaster, a momentary, fleeting event affecting a handful of people, or a momentous, continuous act embracing an entire community or society. The perilous situation may have arisen through the culpable behavior of the victim himself, or through purely fortuitous circumstances. Victims may make direct demands upon the bystanders, or be totally unaware of their presence. The bystander may be in the immediate proximity of the perilous situation, or be linked by proxy to the victim's suffering, through hearsay or reportage in the mass media. The cry for help may be only metaphorical, finding expression in a silent prayer or a pleading look, a gesture or a sign. The bystander may be the only witness to the scene, or part of an audience embracing untold numbers.

The bystander situation may thus be of varied types—the help sought and the response evoked cover a wide spectrum of possibilities. Although superficially it might appear that the problem of the bystander is of only peripheral concern for society, the total impact of bystander activity touches on the very essence of a society, and helps both to form and reflect much of its true nature and the quality of its life. The cry for help poses a dilemma not only for the particular individual directly involved. Its echo reverberates on and poses a problem for all of society.

Notes

1. For a detailed account of this case, see A.M. Rosenthal, *Thirty-eight Witnesses* (New York: McGraw Hill, 1964).

2. See article in the *New York Times*, published on the first anniversary of the event, March 12, 1965, p. 35.

3. See James M. Ratcliffe, ed., *The Good Samaritan and the Law* (New York: Anchor Books, 1966).

4. See Martha Wolfenstein, *Disaster: A Psychological Essay* (London: Routledge and Kegan Paul, 1957).

5. See the *New York Times*, October 11, 1965, p. 41.

6. *People* v. *Young*, 310 N.Y.S. 2d. 358 App. Div. (1962) rev. New York, 2d. 274, C.T. App. (1962).

7. Karl Menninger, *The Crime of Punishment* (New York: Viking, 1969), p. 148.

8. Montaigne, "Of Experience," in Ephraim London, ed., *The Law as Literature* (New York: Simon and Schuster, 1960).

9. Report, "Preparatory Meeting of Experts in Social Defense (African Region) for the Fourth United Nations Congress on the Prevention of Crime and the Treatment of Offenders," *International Review of Criminal Policy*, 1969, *27*, p. 66.

10. See articles by Joe Frontz, "The Frontier Tradition: An Invitation to Violence" and Richard Brown, "The American Vigilante Tradition," in Hugh Graham and Ted Guss, eds., *Violence in America* (New York: Bantam, 1969).

11. A.W. Lintott, *Violence in Republican Rome* (London: Oxford University Press, 1968), p. 16.

12. For resolutions passed see Israel Drapkin and Emilio Viano, eds., *Victimology: A New Focus* (Lexington, Mass.: Lexington Books, 1974), *1*, p. 209. See especially resolution 1:3: "Focus should be expanded from the 'two-dimensional' person-to-person interaction to the three or multidimensional one, thus including the bystander and other relevant persons." See also my article presented at the conference, "The Criminal Triad—Bystander, Victim, Criminal," pp. 111-126; also published in *International Journal of Criminology and Penology*, 1974, *2*, pp. 159-172.

13. Hans von Hentig, *The Criminal and His Victim—Studies in the Sociobiology of Crime* (New Haven: Yale University Press, 1948).

14. For a survey of the origins and development of victimology see Beniamin Mendelsohn, "The Origin of the Doctrine of Victimology," *Excerpta Victimologica*, 1963 *3*, pp. 239-241.

Part I
Behavior

2 The Bystander's Response

In the wake of the Genovese incident, and the shock and dismay that it engendered, researchers in many branches of the social sciences began to inquire into the nature of bystander behavior. They found a fertile field for investigation, one that allowed full rein for creative research designs—generally in laboratory settings, occasionally in artificially contrived real-life stress situations.

Gradually, a clearer picture of the bystander has emerged than that which had been formerly fostered by unsystematic stereotyped thinking based largely on chance mass media coverage of extreme behavior (whether selfish or sacrificial). Some old ideas have been partly deflated or totally demolished; some new concepts have been introduced, with varying degrees of acceptance, into the scientific lexicon. Yet, much uncertainty still remains, and many factors have to be more extensively probed.

It is still not clear, for instance, what the nature is of the relationship between the normative and legal rules of a society, the personal attributes of a particular bystander, and the patterns of a specific distress situation. It is not even clear how to determine who can be considered a bystander in a given set of circumstances. There are problems in knowing the relevance of laboratory research for extrapolating to real-life situations. The sheer diversity of bystander situations—crime and accidents, sudden natural disasters and ongoing victimization—poses further problems as to the possibility of attempting to draw connections between different types of bystander situations.

Part of the limitation in the research is a consequence of many researchers ignoring those aspects of bystander behavior that lie outside the range of their immediate research project, or their larger academic interests. Thus, for instance, the extensive work on disaster situations, an unusual, but total, event causing a breakdown in normal social functioning, has not been incorporated into the work on the more regular but limited interpersonal stress situation of a crime or accident, though a comparison between disasters and other stress situations may lead to mutual advances in these areas, with the possibility of some synthesis being sought.

In addition, there has been almost no cross-cultural comparison which might provide some indication of the manner in which general societal norms have a direct impact on the individual responses to a crisis situation.

Major factors complicating the efforts at clarification of bystander behavior are the problem of determining the degree to which behavioral responses in stress situations are a reflection of inner attitudinal sentiments, and the possibility of clearly checking, in a meaningful manner, attitudinal concepts which are not easily amenable to research. The concept of altruism is probably the most widely recognized factor, and runs as a constant thread through much of the work. Yet, there is no means of categorically demonstrating that it is the existence of altruistic sentiments that leads to the enhancement of prosocial behavior in stress, or in dangerous situations. Indeed, it is possible that a propensity for risk-taking, or a sense of narcissistic involvement with oneself, may be often instrumental in motivating prosocial behavior.

At the practical level, the very dimensions of the problem remain a constant unknown. Criminologists have for long struggled with the problem of the "dark figures," the mass of unreported criminal behavior that takes place. Techniques of self-reporting, or victim reporting,[1] have been developed in an attempt to move beyond the limited picture provided by the official figures for crime, but the results have served perhaps more to accentuate the inaccuracy of the official figures than to remedy the defects. The problem of knowing who are the criminals, or who are the victims, becomes magnified tenfold in trying to assess with any degree of accuracy who the bystanders are, how many people have gone to the aid of others, and, even more so, how many people have been exposed to a stress situation and failed to take action.

Given this background of diversity of bystander situations, of paucity of firm data, of the newness of the area, of the compartmentalization of much of the research, the findings that have thus far accumulated should by no means be seen as definitive, but rather as laying down tentative directions approximating to social reality. Whatever the limitations, however, the field is rich in insights and originality.

The Research of Latané and Darley

Some of the most significant work in this area has been the series of research projects on the unresponsive bystander carried out by Latané and Darley in the 1960s.[2] Their work was precipitated by the Genovese case, and became an attempt to move beyond the superficial level of rote responses to bystander situations, where behavioral scientists along with laymen would talk in general terms of the problems of modern urban society with its anonymous, apathetic, and alienated masses.

On the basis of several experiments, mainly in the laboratory, in which subjects were exposed to potentially dangerous and crisis situations, they challenged these rather widespread notions and suggested that bystander responses were far more closely related to the actual circumstances of a particular situation, in which, for instance, the number of persons present and potentially available to render assistance, might be a far more significant factor than the overall values of the society, or the personal characteristics of the bystander.

Eschewing theoretical perspectives—such as Freudian concepts of a superego internalizing society's values, or reinforcement ideas of the anticipated good feelings that the approval of others will arouse—they have delved through to the heart of an emergency situation, suggesting that the crucial variables for determining altruistic, other-oriented behavior lie within the situation itself. Thus, for them, intervention becomes a consequence of a sequential, cognitive process where the innocent bystander is faced with a series of choices in which his ultimate involvement or abstention will depend on "whether he notices an event or not, perceives it as an emergency or not, feels personal responsibility or not, is able to think of the kinds of intervention or not, and has sufficient skills to intervene or not."[3]

However, as a backdrop to the social psychological setting, there is a further overriding factor to be considered—the presence of others within the emergency scene in which, paradoxically, the more bystanders there are, the less likely it is that anyone of them will respond. Under the rubric of a theoretical concept termed the "diffusion of responsibility" and the "diffusion of blame" Latané and Darley explain, firstly, "If only one bystander is present in an emergency, he carries all of the responsibility; he will feel all the guilt for not acting; he will bear all of the blame that accrues from non-intervention. If others are present, the onus of responsibility is diffused, and the finger of blame points less directly to any one person. The individual may be more likely to resolve his conflicts between intervening and non-intervening in favor of the latter alternative."[4]

Secondly, in a process of searching for clues, each bystander measures his emotive reaction and practical response against those of other strangers, and affects and is affected by, every other bystander. From this perspective, Latané and Darley claim that the inaction of bystanders can be better explained on the basis of incorrect and selective perceptions of a particular situation than through any intrinsic apathy or widespread alienation. Where several bystanders are present, each concerned, but not immediately reacting, "it is possible for a state of pluralistic ignorance to develop, in which each bystander is led by the *apparent* lack of concern of the others to interpret the situation as being less serious than he would if alone."[5]

According to them, apparently, given the right circumstances the coward may respond positively; given another constellation of facts, the hero will abstain. "Anybody can be led to help or not to help in a specific situation."[6] The failure of the thirty-eight witnesses to the Genovese case may thus be explained in terms of a diffusion of responsibility and a diffusion of anticipated blame.

Much of the rationale behind the work of Latané and Darley is based on the considered premise that there is a large fund of goodwill and other-oriented activity present in society, ranging from a willingness to be involved in charitable work on behalf of others, often unknown and amorphous, to more, direct, minimal and transient activities, such as helping a young child to cross the road.

A key factor in any study of bystander behavior thus becomes the need to analyze the specific qualities of an emergency situation. For most people it is an irregular, even unique, event for which they have no prior direct knowledge as to its nature, or prior training as to their possible responses. The situation in which the bystander finds himself is, according to Latané and Darley, a "grim one. Faced with a situation in which he can gain no benefit, unable to rely on past experience, or the experience of others, or on forethought and planning, denied the opportunity to consider carefully his course of action, the bystander to an emergency is in an unenviable position. It is perhaps surprising that anyone should intervene at all."[7]

From the perspective of an untoward, developing situation, Latané and Darley show how, at each of the five separate stages that they have delineated, a series of factors makes for a selective narrowing down of those likely to be involved. Their research was designed to measure the bystander behavior at each of the five stages.

In the first two stages the bystander must notice the event, and then realize that he is confronted by some crisis or stress situation demanding a response on his part. In one experiment[8] they showed that, even in situations where the bystander was liable to be a victim of an emerging crisis situation, there would be a marked tendency to ignore the indications of any emergency requiring a reaction.

Each subject was exposed to smoke being infiltrated into a room. Although most of the subjects did stop what they were doing and leave the room to look for someone to whom they could report what had happened, a sizable minority (six out of twenty-four) ignored the smoke for as much as six minutes, at which stage the experiment was terminated, partly on the assumption that there was little likelihood that they would respond at all—and partly to save them from further discomfort, as by this time the amount of smoke in the room was obscuring vision, producing a mildly acrid odor, and interfering with breathing.

The inhibiting impact of the presence of other bystanders is clearly noted as the response became even less when the subject was in the room together with two confederates whose task it was to remain implacably passive (only one out of ten subjects reporting the smoke), or when there were several subjects in the room (only three people out of twenty-four in eight separate groups reporting the smoke).

In another experiment,[9] where a theft was committed in full view of a bystander (money taken from a cash register in a shop), many subjects claimed in a postexperiment interview that they had not noticed the crime. Of course, in these latter situations it is possible that the subjects denied having been aware of the theft in order to justify their own inaction; nevertheless, their passivity in the "smoke" experiment shows how reluctant people are to acknowledge a threatening situation, even when it threatens them; this is a common experience found by many researchers in disaster situations, where widespread warnings as to imminent dangerous conditions are ignored. Williams notes that unconscious and irrational factors may lead to "repressive denial and even perceptual distortion of incoming information. . . . Most people would rather believe they are safe than in danger . . . the definition of the situation is likely at least to lead to delay in action while further information is sought. Often it leads to no action."[10]

The third stage of Latané and Darley's schema involves the decision process as to whether the bystander can attribute any personal responsibility for the emergency situation that has been identified. In many respects this is a key stage, certainly in terms of the manner in which the bystander perceives of his relationship to other people. Many factors enter into consideration, including the nature of the crisis, and the nature of the relationship between the victim and the bystander, such as sex, age, physical condition, socioeconomic class, and race.

In order to neutralize the effect of the ambiguity of the first two stages, Latané and Darley designed an experiment[11] in which there would be almost no chance not to be aware of what was happening, or not to recognize it as an emergency situation. In addition, their design had many points of similarities with the Genovese case, as the bystanders were, in some of the cases, aware of the presence of other bystanders, but unable to know what their reactions were.

The subject, sitting alone in a room, was linked by intercom to another person in an adjoining room (or other persons in separate adjoining rooms) with the intercom being their only means of communication. The ostensible purpose of the experiment was to allow the participants the opportunity to talk freely about their personal problems; the subjects were told that the experimenter would not be a party to the discussion, but would subsequently obtain the subjects' reactions (to eliminate the possibility that the subject would presume that the experimenter was also listening). Finally the intercom was set up in such a manner that each participant would be given two minutes to talk, during which time microphones of the other participants would not be functioning (which would avoid direct communication by the intercom during the staged emergency).

During the discussion one of the participants, the confederate in the experiment, staged an epileptic fit, which involved inter alia unambiguous requests for help, the emission of choking sounds, and frenzied statements of fear of death. The ramblings continued for just over two minutes, with the voice becoming increasingly louder and the sentences more disjointed.

One of the major independent variables that the researchers wished to examine was the impact of the presence of other bystanders in the vicinity, as a test of their hypothesis of the diffusion of responsibility. Three different-sized groups were used—a two-person group (consisting of the subject and the confederate-victim who was to simulate the fit), a three-person group (the subject, and two confederates, one of whom was the victim), and a six-person group (with subject, victim, and four other confederates).

The findings indicate, according to Latané and Darley, that the number of bystanders had a major effect on the likelihood that the emergency would be reported. Of those in the first group (with only the subject and the victim, and no additional confederates) 85 percent of the subjects reported by the end of the fit, while the remainder reported within the next few minutes (up to maximum of six minutes from the onset of the fit). Where there was one confederate the figures were 62 percent reporting by the end of the fit and 85 percent before the experiment was terminated, while in the case of four confederates, the respective figures were 31 percent and 62 percent. Even though the total sample was rather small and selective (fifty-two students in an introductory psychology course), these findings provide strong support for the concept of diffusion of responsibility.

However, other aspects of the researchers' conclusions seem much more problematical. Latané and Darley conclude that their subjects "showed few signs of the apathy and indifference thought to characterize unresponsive by-standers."[12] According to them those subjects who failed to respond were caught up in a conflict that they were unable to resolve, "a situation of an 'avoidance-avoidance' type. On the one hand, subjects worried about the guilt and shame they would feel if they did not help the person in distress. On the other hand, they were concerned not to make fools of themselves by over-reacting, not to ruin the ongoing experiment by leaving their intercoms, and not to destroy the anonymous nature of the situation which the experimenter had earlier stressed as important."[13]

The extent of the conflict they were undergoing is indicated, according to Latané and Darley, by their inquiries as to the welfare of the victim at the conclusion of the experiment and to the physical signs of "trembling hands and sweating palms. If anything, they seemed more emotionally aroused than did the subjects who reported the emergency."[14]

While this explanation might have some validity, their research still seems to leave many questions unanswered, and in fact, in some respects, to raise new issues. If the subjects were truly concerned about the victim, it is not at all clear why they failed to respond. After all, the serious aspect of the Genovese case was not simply why the bystanders were unconcerned about the plight of the victim (in fact some of them were so concerned), but why they did not actively respond. In the epileptic fit experiment, a sizable number in the three groups did not respond—over a third during the two minutes of the fit, (a disturbingly high total to which the researchers make no reference); this, despite the recognition of the existence of a problem, the urgency of the situation, the certainty of the danger, their professed concern for the victim, the relative ease with which they could have rendered aid (merely by leaving the room and calling the experi-menter), and even their absolute inability to shirk responsibility under the cloak of anonymity (for instance, most bystanders can subsequently deny any knowledge of what had happened even if they did have knowledge, but in the experiment the conditions were such as not to allow such a possibility).[15]

The reasons that Latané and Darley provide for their inaction do not seem adequate to explain the nonintervention, given the dire and direct need of the victim. Indeed, the stress that they place on being faithful to the requirements of the experiment, is reminiscent of the results obtained by Milgram[16] in his well-known experiments where the subjects were willing to administer electric shocks of a lethal capacity in blind obedience to the dictates of the experimenter. These results are generally interpreted to indicate negative characteristics which, in their implications, are considered to be no less disturbing than the apathy of the Genovese bystanders.

Although the research of Darley and Latané seems to indicate the relevance and importance of the concept of diffusion of responsibility in inhibiting prosocial behavior, it is still not clear why the degree of responsibility potentially sensed should be so fragile as to become eroded merely through the presence of others. Although Latané and Darley tried to minimize the influence of social factors, it would seem that only through analyzing overall societal values and interactions would it be possible to know why the presence of others has such a negative effect; and this fact may be as indicative of alienation as complete unconcern would have been.

The final two stages of Latané and Darley's model deal with the capacity of the bystander, who has assumed responsibility, to conceive of an effective form of intervention, and the ability to undertake such intervention. They provide little direct empirical data on these problems, but their analysis seems to be well founded. It is quite possible that many well-meaning intentions become aborted at this stage. It does not seem helpful for a nonswimmer to jump into deep water to save someone from drowning; a bystander lacking the rudimentary knowledge of first-aid techniques would often do well not to attempt any first aid to a victim of an accident; direct intervention in an armed robbery or serious battery case may lead to serious adverse consequences. Nevertheless, in all these cases, there generally is an alternative to direct action—in the form of what Latané and Darley term "reportorial" intervention or detour intervention,[17] in which all that is required is that the emergency be brought to the notice of somebody who is qualified to handle it.

In most cases where direct intervention would have endangered the bystander, the alternative of reportorial intervention was available, at little cost or inconvenience. In fact, where there is a real commitment to help, and where the responsibility for the victim has been firmly assumed, bystanders, lacking in skills, often find means of successfully improvising assistance, a phenomenon noted in many natural disasters.

Latané and Darley have done much to arouse an awareness of the importance of social psychological factors—the circumstances of the emerging situation, the problems of perception, the inhibitive impact of other bystanders in the vicinity, the competence of the bystander; yet, their work may have led to an overemphasis on these social psychological factors, with too little attention being paid to the larger societal factors. Their final conclusion at the end of their book is that situational factors may be of greater importance in determining an individual's reaction to an emergency than such broad motivational concepts as "apathy" or "alienation due to urbanization." ... the failure to intervene may be better understood by knowing the relationship among bystanders rather than that between a bystander and a victim.[18]

What Latané and Darley tend to ignore is the fact that all these situations take place within a larger framework of norms, values, and prior patterns of behavior, which determine the nature of the relationship among the bystanders.

However, before relating to these larger questions of the total environment, it is necessary to investigate whether their research, for all the apparent decisiveness of their results, has received sufficient support from independent researchers.

Later Research

Huston and Korte have directly challenged some of their findings by suggesting that helping behavior may be so prevalent, even in unanticipated situations, as to warrant the obverse question, "The Responsive Bystander: Why He Helps?"[19] They argue that bystander response to emergencies seems to be more complicated than the analysis by Latané and Darley implies, and they quote a series of reports from the mass media to indicate active bystander response, though not all of it is constructive. They note that, in some cases, bystanders intervene in order to foment trouble or hand out immediate retribution to a criminal caught red-handed in the act.

Huston argues also that the emergency scenario of most research lacks the "mob quality" of many real-life situations, where bystanders are not as "easily identifiable and personally accountable for their actions"[20] as in the research situations; nor does research note the possibility of bystander intervention not being constructive, but being the product of "an apparent callousness, a devaluation of life."[21]

In later research, Huston, together with Geis and Wright,[22] have shown that some bystanders apparently intervene more out of hostility for the harm-doer and a desire to mete out immediate "justice" than out of any feelings of empathy for a victim, or even any effort to help him. Examining bystanders who had been injured in their rescue attempts, they note that, contrary to their original assumptions,

> our impression now ... is ... [the active bystanders are] made up of a larger number of risk-takers, persons for whom violence, and the potential of violence, is something with which they are on familiar and rather amiable terms. We have also been struck by the number of Samaritans who derogate others who tried to help during the incidents in which they were involved. ...

[We are also beginning to sense that it is often primarily anger toward the offender rather than concern for the victim which induces intervention.[23])

In support of their research findings they quote a newspaper report of a motorist, who chased after a hit-and-run driver, catching and holding him at gunpoint until the police arrived.[24] The bystander was so intent on catching the offender that he left the victim at the site of the accident in a serious condition—and she died an hour later at the hospital. It may be surmised that the delay in getting her to the hospital could have been a material fact in her death.

The subjects in this research were a very select sample, consisting only of those who had actually been harmed and had then submitted claims for compensation. But, while in no way exemplifying the typical prosocial behavior or motivations of helpful bystanders, they do indicate that personal attributes may often outweigh situational variables.

This is true not only of those with aggressive tendencies, as noted in the Geis-Huston research, but also in other cases where prosocial behavior was constructive. Huston and Korte analyzed several such research reports, some of them dealing with political issues, including concern for human rights, and suggested that they provide a basis for sketching a tentative profile of the good samaritan as a person who has a "strong sense of moral and social responsibility, a spirit of adventurousness and unconventionality, sympathy for others, and a tendency to reduce his or her own distress by social actions designed to reduce the distress of another."[25]

Other research also indicates fairly widespread willingness to help, especially where there is no ambiguity as to the need of the victim, and minimal inconvenience as to the nature of the required intervention.

In a research attempt that resembled very closely the "epileptic fit" research project of Latané and Darley, Clark and Word[26] set up a situation where a maintenance man, working in an adjoining room, fell off a ladder, and cried out in agony for help. Five different research groups were investigated—a subject alone, two subjects who were strangers to each other, two subjects who were friends, a subject with a stranger who was a confederate, and a subject with a friend who was a confederate. In every situation at least one subject took action to help the victim.

Clark and Word suggest that the major reason for the categorical nature of these results was the unambiguous nature of the experiment. They tested this hypothesis in a later experiment, in which bystanders were confronted by a similar situation of a maintenance man falling, except that this time they created an ambiguity in some of the instances, when the victim did not cry out. They noted that, in this latter situation, far fewer bystanders went to his aid. Similar results were obtained in a different experimental situation, where a technician appeared to receive an electric shock.[27] Clark and Word summarize their work by noting that "whether the victim received help or not depended directly on the level of ambiguity presented in the emergency situation."[28] Of course, this was a factor that Darley and Latané had stressed, and in this respect, there is strong support for their work. Where they differ is in finding a far greater degree of bystander intervention on behalf of a victim than was found by Darley and Latané.

Similar results of helping behavior were also obtained by the Piliavins and Rodin.[29] Their research involved a real-life contrived incident, of a man collapsing in a crowded express subway train—in New York—where at least seven minutes would elapse from the moment of the onset of the emergency until arrival at the next station. The results showed that, in most cases, at least one of the passengers, and in many cases several of them—went to the aid of the victim. It is of course possible that here too the situation did partly contribute to the positive responses, since all of the passengers were, for the seven minutes of the ride, a "captive" group. Research by Staub[30] suggests that when the bystander has an easy means of avoiding the victim he may well choose such an alternative. In his research the bystander came onto a street deserted except for the "victim," who walked toward him and collapsed about forty feet from him—in one condition on the same side of the street and directly in his path, in the other situation on the opposite side of the street from the bystander. A far greater number of bystanders helped in the former condition (what Staub calls the "difficult escape" condition) than in the latter condition of "easy escape." It should be noted though that the lack of response in a fairly high proportion of cases tends to undermine another aspect of the Latané and Darley thesis, namely of the diffusion of responsibility, since, in Staub's experiment, the bystander was alone in a deserted street [Staub notes that there seemed also to have been little ambiguity about the situation as those who failed to respond gave indications of having noticed the victim and then carefully refrained from looking in his direction again.]

Further, in the experiments by Clark and Word and the Piliavins it would seem that, where there are a number of bystanders, the diffusion of responsibility, inasmuch as it is operative, works in a less drastic manner than indicated by Latané and Darley, leading not to inaction as much as to a delay in the response. In these experiments, the presence of other bystanders seemed to cause initial hesitation in the reaction of the involved bystander. The more ambiguous the situation, the more likely that the diffusion of responsibility will have an effect as people search out, in the reactions of others, for a clue to attach meaning to the ambiguous situation. However, the mere inaction of other bystanders is not sufficient to prevent response. Some of the initial hesitancy may be so as to allow others to get involved. Where such response is lacking, one of the bystanders may eventually act on his own.

Models of Bystander Behavior

On the basis of their research the Piliavins and Rodin have suggested a five-part model of bystander behavior that has points of both similarity and difference with that of Latané and Darley:

1. Observation of an emergency creates an emotional arousal state in the bystander.
2. This state will be differently interpreted in different situations as fear, disgust, sympathy, and so on, and possibly a combination of these.
3. This state of arousal is higher according to the empathy one has with the victim, the closer one is to the emergency, and the longer the emergency persists without intervention by others.
4. The emotional state created can be reduced either by offering help (direct or reportorial), leaving the scene, or rejecting the victim as undeserving of help.
5. The response that will be chosen is a function of a cost-reward matrix that includes costs associated with helping or not helping, and the rewards associated with helping or not helping.[31]

They stress that the "major motivation implied in the model is not a positive 'altruistic' one, but rather a selfish desire to rid oneself of an unpleasant emotional state."[32] Yet it seems clear that the unpleasant emotional state arises out of concern for the victim. It is possible that, in acting, the bystander relieves an unpleasant emotional state; but this seems to be begging the question—for this state arises out of empathy for the victim, and out of awareness and acknowledgment of the norms of helping. It is the perception of an inequitable situation, and the desire to remedy it, that underlies the prosocial behavior of the Piliavin model. This is clearly borne out by the joint work that has been done with Walster to combine their model of prosocial behavior with an equity model.[33]

Schwartz has dealt specifically with the factors that make for the emotional arousal in the bystander. He writes that the "experience of this arousal is labeled empathy, and it is thought to derive from a learned or genetic capacity to view events from the perspective of those to whom one feels similar."[34] Schwartz goes on to note that there are extreme situations where the "source of empathetic arousal is helped in order to reduce the helper's *own* distress,"[35] in which case there would be no true altruism. But this is only in an extreme situation. For the most part, the emotional arousal and the subsequent prosocial behavior arise from prior feelings of empathy. Indeed it may be specifically the feelings of empathy which enable the bystander to perceive the act in distress terms or to define it in a more serious and demanding manner.

Schwartz has devoted much of his research to analyzing the manner in which prosocial behavior can be understood in terms of the norms which motivate the involved bystander. He suggests a three-step decision-making process which underlies and precedes prosocial behavior, embracing: 1) recognition of another's dependence, and the possibility of contributing to the welfare of that person or persons by a particular action; 2) knowledge of pertinent norms; and 3) ascription of some degree of personal responsibility for action.[36]

While Schwartz takes due account of situational and personal factors, the influence of social norms at the second stage is crucial. It is "social specifications of desirable behavior in particular situations [which] provide the actor with potential directions for his action to take."[37]

Berkowitz,[38] too has stressed the fact of another's dependence as an important variable in helping behavior, and has argued strongly that the perceptions of dependence and the willingness to act on these perceptions are closely bound up with the social and moral norms that people hold. He claims that many people have "acquired strong standards of conduct which prescribe that they aid those who are dependent upon them. These persons will therefore often help someone in need . . . not for tangible gain or social approval, but supposedly primarily for approval from themselves. They presumably act unselfishly for the good feeling they anticipate and in order to avoid the guilt that would arise if they violated their moral standard."[39]

In his latest work Schwartz has attempted specifically to "tie internalized norms to altruistic behavior," based on three underlying propositions:

1. Altruistic behavior is influenced by the intensity of moral (personal) obligation which an individual feels to take specific helping actions.
2. Feelings of moral obligation are generated in particular situations by the activation of the individual's cognitive structure of norms and values.
3. Feelings of moral obligation may be neutralized prior to overt action by defenses against the relevance or appropriateness of the obligation.[40]

From these basic propositions, and related corollaries, Schwartz develops a nine-stage model which "spells out a process moving from the original perception of need through the activation of the normative structure and the generation of feelings of moral obligation to the eventual overt response."[41]

Having stressed the need for altruism, Schwartz notes that there are situations where, contrary to expectations, prosocial behavior may not be forthcoming. He claims that due consideration has to be given to what he calls "boomerang effects on altruism."[42] He suggests that in certain cases bystanders may be reluctant to offer help, or more particularly, as emerged in his research, to continue to help or to increase their help, because of the fear that they might be exploited and that their initial prosocial behavior might expose them to further unjustifiable demands. For instance, "Trust in the purity of need may . . . be undermined by actions implying undue pressure or manipulativeness on the part of the person seeking help."[43] Thus, "If the critical threshold of pressure is traversed, feelings of moral obligation will be reduced and altruistic helping will decrease because: (1) the reality or the seriousness of need may be denied; 2) the desire to retain one's behavioral freedom by resisting pressure may be stimulated; and 3) external pressure may be experienced as replacing internalized motivation."[44]

Other researchers have related to each of these factors; inasmuch as altruistic norms might, as Schwartz argues, be a decisive factor in prosocial behavior, the lack of such behavior may require precise explanation for the overall thesis to be accepted. In fact, the denial of the victim's need is an approach that has been strongly argued by Lerner.[45] He claims that social norms oriented to a desire for justice are so deeply ingrained that, where an injustice is *Accused.* perceived, bystanders will attempt to rationalize the victim's predicament as a consequence of his own fault; and under such circumstances the demand for prosocial behavior becomes lessened. Lerner noted that bystander response to crisis situations is a mixture of contradictions. "People can be both cruelly indifferent and compassionately concerned about the suffering of others. How does one make sense out of this apparent contradiction? . . . Most people exhibit both kinds of reactions from time to time."[46]

Lerner claims that, for all the apparent contradiction in these diverging reactions, the reason lies in the fact that both indifference and concern stem from "the same underlying psychological process."[47] Struggling at the psychological level with questions as to unjust suffering in the world, that have puzzled philosophers and religious leaders down the ages, Lerner claims that it is precisely our belief in a just world that leads to concern for the victim. However, where there is apparently undeserved suffering, the belief is threatened. Two alternatives are then open to the bystander. He may act to aid the victim, or he may persuade himself that the victim deserved to suffer, thereby automatically reducing the desire to offer help.

On the basis of this perspective, where people are able to help, they will gladly do so; but, where unable to help, "the observers may construe the victim as the kind of undesirable person who 'deserves' to suffer. The greater the injustice of the victim's fate the greater the efforts at condemnation and rejection."[48]

Lerner's line of thinking is an interesting one, and has parallels in the work of other theorists. At the abstract level Rawls[49] has written of the deep human aspiration for a just world. In criminology Matza and Sykes[50] have argued that many delinquents know and acknowledge the norms and rules of the society, and therefore undergo a thought process of denying the victim's rights in order to neutralize the demands of society's norms, and in order to justify the performance of the criminal act.

Ryan[51] has dealt with the manner in which those living deprived lives in society are often blamed for their plight. By attaching responsibility and blame directly to the victim, other groups are released from the need to redress the grievances. Blaming the victim becomes, for Ryan, an important factor in the perpetuation of the victim's condition.

Other factors dealt with by Schwartz leading to neutralization of altruistic impulses involve the attempt by the bystander to maintain control over his fate. Where a person unquestioningly allows his altruistic motives to be tapped, he might sense that he has foregone his freedom of action. Schwartz here refers to an interesting theory by Brehm[52] on psychological reactance, in which he explains the need for people often to act in a contrary fashion for the main purpose of retaining their freedom of action. In some cases they may refuse to perform an altruistic act (perhaps especially where the request for such act is based on a prior voluntary act), but reactance may also be applied in other cases—for example, where a person rejects good advice that he is given merely in order to show his independence. In Schwartz's research[53] a group of blood donors was asked to volunteer also for a bone marrow transplant. Most of them agreed under nearly all the circumstances described; but there was one situation where the plea for help included also a story of the hardship of the victim's family if the help should not be forthcoming. Schwartz suggests that the decrease in volunteering in this situation was a consequence of the sensed perception that the goodwill in offering blood was now being unfairly exploited. "The emotional intensity and pathos of the appeal may therefore have been viewed as manipulative pressuring."[54]

The original social psychological research by Latané and Darley claimed that, despite the existence of norms of helping in the society at large, the key factor for understanding helping behavior in an emergency situation was not the norms, but the specific circumstances. They downgraded the possibility that the norms were themselves a factor in the way in which bystanders would perceive a situation, define it, and conceive of a role for themselves.

But later research has been tending with increasing vigor and empirical substantiation to recognize that much helping behavior could only be understood in terms of altruistic motives. Even inaction could be explained within the framework of such norms, where the bystander, reluctant to act, would have to find some legitimate way to negate the relevance of the applicability of norms of prosocial behavior.

In fact no other variable seems to provide a firmer basis for understanding helping behavior. The most significant and clear-cut finding by Latané and Darley as to the diffusion of responsibility has not been fully replicated, and seems to have more of a delaying effect than outright negation. A host of other variables have been tested, but as most of the review articles on the subject indicate, the results are far from conclusive. Midlarsky,[55] in a careful survey, has discounted the relevance of factors such as intelligence, age, and social class because research has yielded no clear differences, and the results are often contradictory. One factor that does appear consistently to be relevant is the competence of the bystander to act, a fact that was considered by Latané and Darley, as well as by several other leading researchers. But in those instances where lack of competence was a factor in the lack of response, this would not, in and of itself, diminish the impact of moral and altruistic norms. It only indicates that, in a specific situation, the norms were not applied for pragmatic reasons. For while the concept of altruism does conjure up the idea of sacrificing behavior, it involves sacrifice within the framework of one's competence, and not sacrifice arising directly from one's incompetence.

Pomazal and Jaccard,[56] in their more recent survey of the social psychological research, are critical of the fact that the manipulation of the variables by the researcher are often of prime importance. The researchers tend to concentrate too much on the specific variable they have chosen for testing and to ignore other factors.

Whatever the impact of the situation, or of personal background, it seems clear that an overall understanding of the nature of helping behavior must take due account of the relevance of the norms of altruism and helping. Inasmuch as the research has given evidence of helping behavior it may well be that the norm of helping has been relevant; inasmuch as the needed helping behavior has been lacking, it may well be that there is a need for a reevaluation of normative standards.

Just as the bystander must act within the framework of the situation, so the situation takes place within the larger societal framework. It is this which, in the final analysis, may well determine the individual's behavior in the emergency situation.

Notes

1. For studies on self-reporting, see J.S. Wallerstein and C.J. Wyle, "Our Law-abiding Lawbreakers," *Probation*, 1947, *25*, pp. 107-112, and F. Ivan Nye and James F. Short, Jr., "Scaling Delinquent Behavior," *American Sociological Review*, 1957, *22*, 326-331. For reporting by victims see R.F. Sparks, Hazel G. Genn, and D.J. Dodd, *Surveying Victims* (London: Wiley and Sons, 1977).

2. For an overall presentation of their major research projects see Bibb Latané and John M. Darley, *The Unresponsive Bystander: Why Doesn't He Help?* (New York: Appleton-Century-Crofts, 1970).

3. Ibid., p. 36.

4. Ibid., p. 90.

5. Ibid., p. 110.

6. Ibid., p. 120.

7. Ibid., p. 31.

8. Ibid., Ch. 6, "Where There's Smoke . . . ," pp. 43-55.

9. Ibid., Ch. 8, "The Bystander and the Thief," pp. 69-78.

10. Harry B. Williams, "Human Factors in Warning and Response Systems," in G.H. Grossler, H. Wechsler, and M. Greenblatt, eds., *The Threat of Impending Disaster: Contributions to the Psychology of Stress* (Cambridge, Mass.: The M.I.T. Press, 1964), p. 94.

11. Latané and Darley, Ch. 11, "An Epileptic Seizure," pp. 93-113. See also J.M. Darley and B. Latané, "Bystander Intervention in Emergencies: Diffusion of Responsibility," *Journal of Personality and Social Psychology*, 1968, *8*, pp. 377-383.

12. Ibid., p. 100.

13. Ibid., pp. 100-101.

14. Ibid., p. 100.

15. The connection between victim and bystander is so close that the question of legal liability might even have arisen. The legal situation will be dealt with in greater detail in chapter 6.

16. See Stanley Milgram, "Some Conditions of Obedience and Disobedience to Authority," *Human Relations*, 1965, *18*, pp. 57-75, and *Obedience to Authority: An Experimental View* (New York: Harper and Row, 1974).

17. Latané and Darley, pp. 34-35, 103-104.

18. Ibid., pp. 127-128.

19. Ted L. Huston and Chuck Korte, "The Responsive Bystander: Why He Helps," in T. Lickona, ed., *Moral Development and Behavior: Theory Research and Social Issues* (New York: Holt, Rinehart and Winston, 1976), pp. 269-283.

20. Ted L. Huston, unpublished paper, presented at annual meeting of The American Psychological Association, Washington, 1975. Some parts of this paper were incorporated into the article by Huston and Korte cited in note 19.

21. Huston, unpublished paper.

22. Gilbert Geis, Ted L. Huston, and Richard Wright, "Compensating Good Samaritans," *Crime Prevention Review*, 1976, *5*, pp. 28-35.

23. Ibid., p. 33.

24. Ibid.

25. Huston and Korte, p. 281.

26. Russell D. Clark and Larry E. Word, "Why Don't Bystanders Help? Because of Ambiguity?" *Journal of Personality and Social Psychology*, 1972, *24*, pp. 392-400.

27. Russell D. Clark and Larry E. Word, "Where Is the Apathetic Bystander? Situational Characteristics of the Emergency," *Journal of Personality and Social Psychology*, 1974, *29*, pp. 279-287.

28. Ibid., p. 285.

29. Irving M. Piliavin, Judith Rodin, and Jane Allyn Piliavin, "Good Samaritanism: An Underground Phenomenon?" *Journal of Personality and Social Psychology*, 1969, *13*, pp. 289-299.

30. Ervin Staub, "Helping a Distressed Person: Social Personality, and

Stimulus Determinants," in Leonard Berkowitz, ed., *Advances in Experimental and Social Psychology* (New York: Academic Press, 1974), 7, pp. 305-308.

31. "Good Samaritanism," p. 298.

32. Ibid.

33. See Elaine Walster and Jane Allyn Piliavin, "Equity and the Innocent Bystander," *Journal of Social Issues*, 1972, *28*, pp. 165-190.

34. Shalom H. Schwartz, "Normative Influences in Altruism," in Leonard Berkowitz, ed., *Advances in Experimental Social Psychology* (New York: Academic Press, 1977), *10*, pp. 222-280, at p. 224.

35. Ibid., p. 224.

36. Shalom H. Schwartz, "Moral Decision Making and Behavior," in J. Macaulay and L. Berkowitz, eds., *Altruism and Helping Behavior* (New York: Academic Press, 1970), p. 132.

37. Ibid., p. 130.

38. See, for instance, L. Berkowitz and L.R. Daniels, "Responsibility and Dependency," *Journal of Abnormal and Social Psychology*, 1963, *66*, pp. 429-437.

39. Leonard Berkowitz, "Social Norms, Feelings, and Other Factors Affecting Helping and Altruism," in L. Berkowitz, ed., *Advances in Experimental Social Psychology* (New York: Academic Press, 1972), *6*, p. 68.

40. Schwartz, 1977, p. 227.

41. Ibid., p. 241.

42. Ibid., pp. 263-268.

43. Ibid., p. 264.

44. Ibid.

45. Melvin J. Lerner, "The Desire for Justice and Reactions to Victims," in Macaulay and Berkowitz, pp. 205-229. See also M.J. Lerner and C.H. Simmons, "Observer's Reactions to the 'Innocent Victim': Compassion or Rejection," *Journal of Personality and Social Psychology*, 1966, *4*, pp. 203-210; C.H. Simmons and M.J. Lerner, "Altruism as a Search for Justice," *Journal of Personality and Social Psychology*, 1968, *9* pp. 216-225; M.J. Lerner, "All the World Loathes a Loser," *Psychology Today*, June 1971, pp. 51-54.

46. Ibid., p. 207.

47. Ibid.

48. Ibid.

49. John Rawls, *A Theory of Justice* (Cambridge: Harvard University Press, 1971).

50. Gresham M. Sykes and David Matza, "Techniques of Neutralization: A Theory of Delinquency," *American Sociological Review*, 1957, *22*, pp. 664-670.

51. William Ryan, *Blaming the Victim* (New York: Vintage Books, 1972).

52. J.W. Brehm, *A Theory of Psychological Reactance* (New York: Academic Press, 1966). For an experimental substantiation of the theory see Russell A. Jones, "Volunteering to Help: The Effects of Choice, Dependence and

Anticipated Dependence," *Journal of Personality and Social Psychology*, 1970, *14*, pp. 121-129.

53. Schwartz, 1977, pp. 248-249.

54. Ibid., p. 265.

55. Elizabeth Midlarsky, "Aiding Responses: An Analysis and Review," *Merrill-Palmer Quarterly*, 1968, *14*, pp. 229-260. See also her article "Aiding Under Stress: The Effects of Competence, Dependency, Visibility and Fatalism," *Journal of Personality*, 1971, *39*, pp. 132-149. Much of the social psychological research has been limited to testing the correlation between different variables and helping behavior. I have not dealt with all of these research projects, partly because of the limited nature of the research with only minimal theoretical implications, partly because there are a number of excellent survey articles of these research findings, in addition to the article by Midlarsky. See especially Dennis L. Krebs, "Altruism: An Examination of the Concept and a Review of the Literature," *Psychological Bulletin*, 1970, *33*, pp. 258-302; J.H. Bryan and Perry London, "Altruistic Behavior by Children," *Psychological Bulletin*, 1970, *73*, pp. 200-211; Leonard Berkowitz, "Reactance and the Unwillingness to Help Others," *Psychological Bulletin*, 1973, *79*, pp. 310-317. See also Huston and Korte, and Staub. Much of the ongoing research in this area appears in the *Journal of Personality and Social Psychology*. For many references to social psychological research, see Harvey A. Hornstein, *Cruelty and Kindness: A New Look at Aggression and Altruism* (Englewood Cliffs, New Jersey: Prentice-Hall, 1976). See also special issue of *Journal of Social Issues*, 1972, *28*, devoted to "Positive Forms of Social Behavior," L.G. Wispe, ed.

56. Richard J. Pomazal and James J. Jaccard, "An Informational Approach to Altruistic Behavior," *Journal of Personality and Social Psychology*, 1976, *33*, pp. 317-326.

3 The Disaster Situation

While most social psychology research has focused on the behavior of the bystander in relatively limited situations—either alone or in the presence of a small group—a parallel, but separate, body of research has been formulated by sociologists working in the area of disaster research, and measuring the behavioral response of total communities to such situations. Nearly all of the work in this area has been based upon on-the-spot observations of stricken communities, coupled with in-depth interviews with members of the community.

The research in this area has grown in recent years, with several research units having staff members prepared to move into disaster areas at short notice in order to ensure immediate recording of the key events as the community struggles to cope, survive, and then recover.

Whereas it was a single event—the murder of Genovese—that served as the catalyst for the situational probes of bystander activity, the research into natural disasters was originally prompted, in large measure, by concern for the disasters caused by human actions, specifically wars.[1] Much of the early research covered mass behavior during the hardships of war conditions, especially the reactions of civilians to constant bombing attacks, and received added impetus because of the desire to have some prior indication of anticipated behavior in the event of a future outbreak of war with its all-embracing dimensions, including the possibility of the use of nuclear weaponry.

In general, the research into the behavior of the civilian population during the Second World War showed that people had a far greater resilience and capacity to cope and function, despite being subject to constant bombing attack, than had been thought likely or even possible.[2]

More recently, the research has taken on a new perspective in the light of the growing awareness that disasters are real social problems themselves, often having political implications, since they test the ability of leaders to operate in unusual circumstances; and of the awareness that there is an acute need for knowledge of human reaction in the various stages—warning, impact, and rehabilitation[3]—so as to facilitate prior planning.

While focusing on the response of total communities—and, in a few instances, of total societies, as in the research in the flooding in the Netherlands in 1953[4]—the research is rich in examples of helping behavior at the individual and group levels.

As in the social psychological research, the behavioral responses entail a wide spectrum of possibilities; nevertheless, certain key characteristics tend to recur and serve as the basis for attempting to correlate and integrate the different kinds of helping behavior. Whatever the diversities of behavior, it seems clear that the dominant theme, noted by most researchers, is one of altruism and concern for others, and of attempts to become personally and actively involved; conversely, instances of panic, flight, or exploitation, often thought to be endemic in such situations, turn out to be the exception, and not the rule.

Historical Accounts

In addition to the growing evidence as to how people react to present-day disasters, there are also some reports of the nature of societal responses in earlier times, much of it of a fortuitous nature, or of a relatively unique event, which happened to capture the imagination of historians. One disaster in which there is a surfeit of evidence is the great London Fire of 1666, partly because of the sheer dimensions of the fire, destroying much of the then largest city in the world; partly because the chronicler of London life, Samuel Pepys, played an important role in the fight to control the fire, it being he who first brought the news to the king, and then relayed messages to the mayor, all of which he subsequently recorded in detail in his diary.[5]

It may well be that the impact of natural disaster on specific societies, or even on the development of social life, is an aspect of history that has been regrettably ignored. Langer, in his presidential address to the American Historical Society, argued that the next challenge confronting historians was to delve into this area since major disasters could have a crucial effect on society; there was thus a need to examine "whether major changes in the psychology of a society and culture can be traced, even in part, to some severe trauma suffered in common."[6] This is an approach strongly supported by a sociologist, Sjoberg,[7] who notes the many occasions when a disaster served as "a trigger for alteration of the social landscape," accelerating and facilitating demographic changes and population movements and reshuffling status positions.

The disasters that have elicited the most interest by historians have been those occasioned by disease and plague, and the demoralizing impact that they had on society. In his account of the black death in 1347, Deaux notes that already in ancient Greece, Thucydides had been "the first to have depicted the corruption and demoralization of a society under the plague, and this theme is to be repeated over and over again in plague accounts."[8] Deaux notes further that in the fourteenth century "the world got worse after the Death; charity grew cold ... people everywhere were more self-indulgent and frivolous than ever. Certainly some of the responses to the Black Death reveal the very extremes of human gullibility and cruelty."[9]

Although the overall picture appears to be bleak and negative, Deaux does acknowledge that often opposite forms of behavior were to be noted: "If it brought out the worst in some men, it brought out the best in others." Indeed there is a problem in that much of the record of these past tragedies is biased: "Bad news is invariably more widely reported than good," particularly since "the source for the contemporary reports of the wickedness of the world . . . were written for the most part by clergymen who were deeply committed to the idea of Original Sin and man's essential depravity, and were always on the look-out for evidence to support their conviction."[10]

Even Thucydides's account is tempered by examples of those who, despite the dangers involved, were willing to minister to the sick. He writes that despite the general fear to visit the sick there were cases of those who went to "see their friends without thought of themselves."[11] Those who had already been stricken and recovered were particularly active in tending the sick, fortified by the knowledge that they could not be harmed again.

In the London fire too, although many people concentrated on saving only their personal goods, and many others exploited the situation (the price of hiring a coach soared speculatively as people sought means to transport their goods out of the range of the fire's devastating path), there was, as Bell notes, "ample charity extended by all the outlying places and residents within the suburbs to ameliorate the lot of the unhappy Londoners."[12] A contemporary report also tells of the personal efforts of the king and of the "great number of nobility and gentry unweariedly assisting."[13]

In more modern times similar varied responses have been recorded in a wide range of reports. One of the first detailed records is Deacon's analysis of the work of the Red Cross,[14] which since the turn of the century had committed itself to rescue operations in disaster situations. Although dealing mainly with responses of this organization the book is replete with instances of personal involvement by concerned bystanders, and Deacon acknowledges the vital importance of immediate spontaneous help, in the initial stages. In discussing one particular disaster situation—of a capsized ship which sank in a harbor with the loss of over 800 lives—he recounts a host of different activities performed by citizens as the "community responds, each person or group instinctively seeking to apply the skill or resources he happens to possess . . . there seems to be a kind of unplanned, unconscious harmony among those who spring to the immediate and obvious task of rescue and first aid."[15]

Shortly after Deacon's book, which was mainly reportorial and anecdotal, a first major sociological treatise on disasters was published by Prince,[16] in which he attempted to set out the larger societal implications of disasters and delineated the ambivalence of the reactions. His theoretical framework was built around a case-study of an explosion of a ship in Halifax harbor, in which out of a population of 50,000 over 2,000 people were killed and many more thousands injured.

Prince's work contains descriptions of a wide range of behavior. Some of it is shock, panic, passivity, looting, profiteering, and callousness in which he quotes evidence of "night prowlers among the ruins, who rifled the pockets of the dead and dying . . . hardened landlords raised the rents upon people in no position to bear it. Truckmen charged exorbitant prices for the transferring of goods and baggage . . . a small shopkeeper asked a little starving child thirty cents for a loaf of bread."[17] But there were also instances of helping, heroism, sacrifice, and fortitude, and here Prince provides many more examples, including the organized response of disciplined soldiers, the total involvement of many strangers, and the spirit displayed by the local people. He quotes outside observers who averred that they had "never seen such kindly feelings . . . never seen such tender sympathy . . . "; who reported cases of people who were "covered with burns, and whose hearts were heavy, who have not had a single night's sleep, and who go all day long without thought of food"; and that "there is not a more courageous, sane and reasonable people. Everyone is tender and considerate. Men who have lost wives and children, women whose sons and husbands are dead, boys and girls whose homes have been destroyed, are working to relieve the distress."[18]

Beyond the descriptions of the behavior Prince attempted to provide a sociological explanation for the mood of the community and for the prodigious physical efforts of the people who called on their inner resources to withstand the tragedy. He writes of the substantive transformation that was set off by the disaster and portrays Halifax as what people came to call the City of Comrades.[19] Social distinctions and various barriers to free communication and interaction became nullified as the shared tragedy and widespread victimization provided forcible proof of the essential common fate of all and the relative irrelevance of the factors making for divisiveness within the community. The disaster seemed to have had a cleansing effect, and in the destruction which it wrought, to have provided a basis for rebuilding for a better future. The themes of ambivalence and of altruism originally propounded by Prince have been echoed and embellished by many of the later researchers on disaster.

Modern Research

Recently Dynes and Quarantelli have provided a succinct summary of the contrasting pictures that people have of disasters:

> There is a duality to the image—one part focuses on damage, loss, tragedy, and destruction while the other part focuses on heroism, optimism, healing, recovery, altruism, and rebuilding. Because of this duality, disaster can become a collective projective test, providing an ambiguous form into which members of the society project their own meanings. Some see only loss; others see opportunity. Some see only the end of aspirations; others see the beginnings of hope and change.[20]

These contrasting images have touched off a debate as to various aspects of behavior in disaster. One of the major issues enjoined has focused on the degree to which people will put community needs above their own and their family's needs. In an early article that has had much impact, Killian[21] claimed that, in a clash between overall obligations to community arising out of occupational position (mayor, police, doctor, fire-fighter) and familial obligations, the latter would take precedence.

He noted that emergency situations undermine the basis of multiple-group membership which is a key factor in modern social life. In normal circumstances the conflicts between the different groups are kept to a minimum; however, in an emergency these conflicts are often irreconcilable, and there is no alternative but to choose priorities. Killian claims that, in four disasters that he analyzed, "the choice required of the greatest number of individuals was the one between the family and other groups, principally the employment group or the community."[22]

Killian provides several examples of people placing the needs of their family above their community and occupational obligations, and cites instances of people neglecting their duties until such time as they had taken care of their family, and, in some cases, even of their neighbors and friends.

These conclusions have been directly challenged by White.[23] Basing her argument on research in several disaster-struck communities, she claims, in a manner similar to the thesis of Latané and Darley,[24] that the situational factors are a key to the behavior of people in disaster situations. Given the uncertainty engendered by a disaster situation, the awareness of a narrow brush with death, the guilt felt as survivors toward those who had perished, people seek a course of action in which there is a clearly defined problem to which they can respond. In these circumstances the individual will choose from among community, occupational, and family obligations that action which will provide the best opportunity to become involved immediately; and once having done so, will likely show a single-minded dedication to the particular course of action chosen, blocking out any distractions that might lead to any wavering or hesitancy in performing the chosen action.

If the choice is for the family, the occupational role will be downplayed or even denied; if the occupational role is chosen, the person will ignore the family. In White's words, ". . . the individual will jump at the first chance to do something to help. . . . Once he has made his choice he will try to dismiss from his mind disturbing thoughts of other courses of action he might have chosen, other responsibilities he might have met instead. Thus, whether he chooses to serve family or organization, he will tend to minimize internal conflict by dismissing thoughts of the other."[25]

Dynes, developing White's analysis, is even more critical of Killian's presentation. Noting that Killian himself had conceded that, even though most people favored their family over the community, there were no adverse consequences for the community, Dynes argues that the reason Killian noted no disastrous consequences was because "abandonment of organizational roles simply does not occur. While such conflict is theoretically possible and while individuals are obviously confronted with the choice of alternative actions, it seems clear that they do not abandon their role in *disaster-relevant organiza-*1970*tions*."[26] White, for instance, claims that, in the three communities she studied, "not a single person abandoned ongoing disaster work to be with his family."[27] Dynes adds that both community pressures and the strength of primary group loyalty assure the adequate response.

This is true not only for those with clearly defined and badly needed occupational roles, but also where organizational affiliation is only peripheral, as in the case of volunteer organizations, where there is generally an overwhelming response, with few people reneging on their voluntary commitments. Beyond this, many people who have no prior connection with disaster-oriented groups offer their services. Of course, in many cases, they may do this only after ensuring that their own families are safe and being cared for. But, even in such conditions there is no inconsistency between caring for both family and community, realizing, and fulfilling, the possibility of sequentially serving both family and community obligations.

Another key debate has revolved around the extent to which the community is rendered paralyzed and incapacitated. Quarantelli[28] 1954 has shown the misconceptions that exist as to panic patterns of behavior. He notes that not only mass media presentations but sometimes even academic and professional literature stresses such negative behavior associated with the "disaster syndrome";[29] 1957 he argues that it is an unusual reaction, generally manifested in unique situations. In most disasters, where panic does occur, it is generally of short duration, during a stage of loss of orientation, and recovery is usually rapid.

Nor is there much passive dependency, while victims and others wait for formal organizations and government agencies to solve the myriad of new and unanticipated problems. On the contrary, as Form and Loomis note:

> Almost immediately after the impact of the destructive agent, a disaster system arises spontaneously to meet the human problems created and to restore a social equilibrium. Far from having a condition of social *anomie*, social systems continue to operate through *all* of the disaster stages, new systems emerge, and continuity is found between the old and the emergent social system.[30] 1956

In Form and Nosow's analysis of a tornado, the small local community, suffering over 100 dead and close to 1,000 injured, continued functioning. In the initial stages of the emergency, before any help was forthcoming from the outside, those who had not been incapacitated became immediately involved in rescue activities:

People tended to look around and appraise what had happened. They took stock of property damage but they did not stop there. They began looking for victims whether they knew them or not. They performed first aid, transported victims to first aid stations, and did other things to facilitate rescue. The feverish, purposive activities, the lack of shock, and the constructive organized behavior of both victims and rescuers are difficult to conceive. Perhaps what was most remarkable at the time was that the activities were selflessly directed toward others.[31] 1958

There are differing conceptions also as to the response of those who live in the proximity of the disaster but are not directly affected. Almost unanimously, observers have noted the phenomenon of convergence on the afflicted area—here too the images are conflicting, some seeing the outsiders as enticed by, at the least, curiosity, or worse, the chance of looting or even deriving satisfaction from the plight of others; others see them as being motivated by a desire to be of assistance.

Thus, in research articles published during the Second World War, Glover[32] 1942 claimed that people who entered bombed areas did so in order to gloat whereas Matte[33] 1943 stressed that the outsiders were seeking a means of meaningful communication with the victims. According to him, the facial expressions of the outsiders seemed to reflect an "emotional working-through" of air-raid experiences, perhaps resulting in increased understanding and acceptance of the realities of the threat.[34] 1957

Fritz and Mathewson[35] have described the nature, and stressed the importance, of convergence behavior, acknowledging that some of this is problematical, raising serious problems as to control, particularly of the curious and exploitative. As to the curious, they state that "current evidence suggests that most curiosity convergence in disaster does not arise from neurotic impulses or 'ghoulish glee' in witnessing destruction or suffering but, rather, arises from the need to assimilate happenings which lie outside the viewer's frame of reference or realm of experience, and which may affect his future safety. In this sense, at least, curiosity may be viewed essentially as an adaptive future-oriented response to disaster."[36]

As to those who enter the area to exploit, Fritz and Mathewson claim that, despite the opportunities for exploitation, "in actual fact . . . the extent of exploitation . . . is usually grossly exaggerated in popular thinking. Certainly the dire predictions of widespread looting, stealing, profiteering, mob violence and crime that frequently have been made in the past have rarely, if ever, been fulfilled."[37]

On the other hand, much of the convergence is of people who wish to participate actively in aiding the stricken community; while much of this help will be directed to those with whom the helper has prior contact—family, friends, acquaintances—a significant amount is also oriented to the community as a whole. Fritz and Mathewson[38] quote the case of a tornado in Arkansas where over 25 percent of the total adult population of a nearby community of 6,000 people rendered some form of medical assistance during the first night following the tornado. As Dynes and Quarantelli note, in discussing the same disaster, "Those who did engage in rescue work tended to work with others, primarily strangers and/or acquaintances, rather than with kin or close friends."[39]

Extreme Situations

While there seems to be emerging a clear consensus among researchers as to the prevalence of altruistic behavior in large-scale disasters, no such overall positive appraisal exists as to the conduct of people caught up in particularly severe disaster situations—either because of the sheer dimensions of the damage or the extreme circumstances, where people are isolated in conditions of stress.

Whereas most evidence indicates a totally unexpected capacity to withstand the terror of conventional aerial bombardment, it is generally considered that the nature and scope of an atomic bombing is so devastating as to totally overwhelm the population and destroy the will to initiate any constructive response or to display any altruism whatsoever.

Several reports have detailed the passivity and apathy of the survivors of Hiroshima and Nagasaki, some of these eyewitness accounts, others recorded later by journalists and social scientists. Among the best known are Hersey's book,[40] which consists mainly of six case studies, and Lifton's work,[41] which includes an attempt to set forward a theoretical explanation for the atmosphere engendered by the devastation. Both of these works indicate that much of the positive behavior which had been noticed in conventional air raids was not in evidence after the devastation of Hiroshima and Nagasaki. Yet Janis[42] has argued that the evidence is by no means conclusive, and claims that, despite the total and sudden nature of the attack, the people were not completely overcome by the malaise attributed to them by many writers,[43,46] but succeeded in displaying the same kind of helping behavior widely noted in cases of conventional bombing.

Janis wrote before Lifton, but Lifton's work contains no evidence of the behavior at the time of the air attack that was not available when Janis wrote. Lifton's book deals mainly with the long-range impact and the existentialistic meaning of the first nuclear blasts;[44] inasmuch as he deals with behavior at the time of the attack he relies on and repeats some of the very evidence that Janis had previously criticized.

Janis argues that there is confusion as to the real nature of the behavior displayed. People did flee from the center of the city, but this was not necessarily in panic; it was a rational mass exodus to be clear of the immediate danger of the conflagration. He also notes that much had been made of the fact that people trapped in buildings were often left to their fate and cried out in vain for help. In most of the recorded instances a closer indication reveals that generally there was a clear danger to the bystander and very little chance of saving the victim. Referring specifically to Hersey's book, Janis claims that, contrary to the total impression evoked of a lack of helping behavior, "there were so many examples of rescue work, of spontaneous co-operative effort, of mutual aid and care of the wounded that it is difficult to believe that these were the exceptions rather than the general rule."[45]

Similarly, in an account by a survivor of the bombing in Nagasaki,[46] 1969 despite the overall negative portrayal Janis points out that there are "numerous references to spontaneous relief activities and mutual aid."[47] He also draws attention to a research project which noted that one-third of the interviewees "referred to rational, practical actions carried out in order to assist other people, whereas no one spoke about any form of neglect."[48] Even in the long-term effects, a later research project[49] carried out after the war indicated that there was no difference in the morale of the people of Hiroshima and Nagasaki as compared to the rest of Japan.

It is doubtful if there is any completely reliable evidence as to what precisely occurred in the immediate aftermath of the atomic explosion, but Janis's balanced analysis suggests that the altruism generally evoked by more moderate disaster situations was forthcoming to a certain extent even under these most debilitating of conditions.

Another disputed area as to human behavior under conditions of extreme stress concerns accounts of groups of isolated people—survivors of shipwrecks adrift at sea, travelers lost in the endless desert sands, miners trapped underground, stranded mountaineers.

In terms of the bystanders, in these cases there are generally very clear norms adhered to by subgroups that are connected with the victims. Rescue operations are often mandatory in such circumstances, such as the rule of the sea obliging a ship to go to the rescue of another ship in distress;[50] yet, in many instances, the work of rescue is accomplished through the willingness of others to go beyond the call of duty and to risk their lives in treacherous and dangerous conditions in order to save strangers, linked to them in this instance not only by a shared humanity and chance proximity, but also by the identification with a common profession or endeavor. Interestingly there has been almost no research into the sentiments of people involved in such rescue activity.

On the other hand, there have been several reports on the behavior of victims under such conditions—with a fair amount of evidence of selfish, aggressive behavior. Wolfenstein,[51] 1957 in noting that disasters bring out the best and the worst in people, felt that it was the extreme conditions of a shortage of life-sustaining resources which often led to the latter response, specifically noting the struggle by passengers and crew on the *Titanic* for a place in one of the few lifeboats that were available (though even here others evinced sacrificial behavior, some voluntarily giving up a place).

However, there is a tendency in these cases for the emphasis to be placed on the bizarre and the unnatural. One of the best-known instances is the sinking of the *Medusa*, and the trials and the tribulations of some of the survivors, particularly the 150 crowded onto a hastily improvised makeshift raft, in which there was, in the beginning, standing room only, because of cramped conditions and because the water was waist deep. The agony of the survivors has been immortalized by Géricault's famous painting; a more detailed account was provided by the ship's doctor,[52] who was on the raft and, after his rescue, described the horrors undergone as fights broke out, some people were forced overboard, the raft itself was left to its fate by other crew and passengers in safer lifeboats, and the cannibalism, where those who had died were eaten by the remainder.

In a recent reassessment of this tragedy, McKee[53] has given a more sympathetic treatment of behavior under such circumstances. He calls for more scientific research to seek means for enhancing the prospects of survival in such conditions and also suggests that at least some of the biazarre behavior, such as eating human flesh, may be understood and approved as a legitimate way to provide sustenance where few alternatives are available. He points out that in similar dire circumstances in recent times the survivors of a plane crash in mountainous regions in the Andes had resorted, albeit reluctantly, to similar actions.[54] In this case, unlike in the case of the *Medusa*, all the members of the surviving party were known to each other, so that there was at the beginning an even greater reluctance and revulsion to use their flesh as meat. But the sheer exigencies of the situation left them no reasonable choice.

In some instances, given the problems of maintaining a reasonable level of liquids in the body, there has been a resort to the use of urine; provided the quantities are drunk in moderation, this could be a key factor in sustaining life. Lucas[55] sensitively deals with this issue in this analysis of the behavior of two groups of men isolated in a mine for nearly two weeks. He recreates the dilemma in which the miners found themselves forced to face a choice of violating a social taboo by imbibing human waste. But this dilemma was only one of a series of moral issues that confronted them, and have confronted other groups striving together to survive, torn between their need to cooperate and sacrifice for one another, and their drive to look after their own needs.

Lucas's work is a penetrating and sensitive analysis of the human interaction of a group of men cut off from society, with only limited and dwindling life-sustaining resources, and within a dark and confined environment, dependent on their own willingness and ability to preserve the norms of social interaction, mutual respect, and psychological support, and the willingness and ability of their fellow workers to pursue to the utmost their struggle to rescue them.

Of course, groups of fellow workers isolated in such situations do not constitute a normal form of natural disaster; those trying to rescue them were not bystanders in the full sense of the term since they knew the people whom they were trying to rescue and some of them had undergone special training for rescue work. Even so, it would still seem that in this small, specialized world of coal-mining there is some meaning for the larger problems of society.

However diverse the types of problems and the response, often these artificial and isolated human groupings provide, in stark form, further proof of altruism in operation, where sharing and mutuality become key factors in coping with the situation. Limited supplies of water and food are rationed equally, fostered by faith in the efforts of others to overcome all obstacles in order to effect a rescue.

These situations are unique; they cannot provide any direct precedent for bystander behavior in other situations. But they do provide a model of the kind of conditions under which it is possible—and desirable, perhaps essential—to maintain altruistic norms.

The Altruistic Community

Disasters of all types, then, evoke, to a greater or lesser degree, in one form of another, the need for, and the possibility and desirability of, altruistic behavior. Whatever confusion and disorientation exist at the moment of impact, most communities and groups show a remarkable capacity for recovery and almost immediately undertake the work of rescue in an "emotional climate" of "almost complete selflessness and great generosity."[56] 1956

A deep chord in human nature is apparently touched; the damage wrought by nature's wrath is met by humanity's cooperative endeavors.

Barton, in a survey of all the available research, has characterized the behavior in most disaster-struck communities as being that of an "altruistic community."[57] This does seem to be the ultimate picture that emerges from his delineation of seventy-one propositions which, he claims, are the essence of the behavioral response to disasters.

Barton and others refer also to a therapeutic community or therapeutic social system based partly on the norms of altruism, and a minimization of social conflict. Fritz[58] has explained this therapeutic framework in both individual and social terms. He sees clear tendencies: 1) to resolve and ameliorate preexisting personal and social conflicts that could endanger the viability and continuity of social life; 2) to attenuate or prevent disorganizing individual and social response which could emerge in conditions of loss, danger, and deprivation; 3) to reduce or prevent self-aggressive and antisocial behavior arising from the losses imposed by the disaster; and 4) to remotivate individuals within the community system to devote their energies to socially constructive and regenerative tasks.

Dynes,[59] in his study of the performance of organizations in disasters, notes the high degree of supportive behavior which most disasters evoke, and contrasts this with the lack of similar helping behavior when conditions are those of a chronic or ongoing nature—people who will willingly contribute to the weak of the community in moments of extreme stress caused by disaster will wittingly ignore the plight and suffering of their fellow beings at other more normal times.

In discussing the various types of organizational activities, Dynes differentiates among four forms of organization,[60] the differentiation being based partly on the degree and the manner in which volunteer helping behavior finds its expression through organizations. The first type of organization is an established framework, and carries on its regular tasks in intensified form without any appreciable volunteer help—for example, the police. The second type of organization discussed by Dynes is termed an expanding organization, where its basic work force is augmented by volunteers—for example, the Red Cross. The third type is an extending organization, and refers to organizations which are activated in nonregular tasks in order to help cope with the emergency—for example, a construction company making its workers and material available for rescue and rehabilitation activities. The fourth type of organization is an emergent group which is generally an ad hoc group set up to deal specifically with the emergency, and may consist of an officially constituted emergency committee of leading officials and citizens in the community or may comprise a group of individuals coming together in order to accomplish volunteer rescue and rehabilitation work. In the expanding, extending, and emerging organizations, it is obvious that the role of the voluntary bystander is crucial for the effective operation of the group.

It is becoming increasingly clear that often it is volunteers, even of a spontaneous type and outside of formal agencies, that provide much of the relief. Fritz and Mathewson[61] even warn against too great an emphasis on the role of organizations in coping with disaster. Most of the work performed by official organizations is carefully recorded and often selectively publicized. Yet, "Recent disasters repeatedly have shown that, with the possible exception of first aid and medical care, a significant proportion of the emergency relief and restorative activity can be and actually is handled on an informal, unofficial basis . . . most of the critical work done during the emergency period—rescue, transportation to hospital, provision of emergency shelter, assistance in cleaning debris, traffic direction, salvaging property, and providing emotional support—has come from informal rather than formal sources."[62]

A close study of a formal relief organization reveals the extent to which even such organizations are dependent for their ultimate success on spontaneous volunteerism. In a report on a hurricane that hit New Orleans it appears from numerous interviews that the success of the Red Cross in offering its aid was partly a consequence of unaffiliated volunteers who placed themselves and their skills at the disposal of the organization. As one of the Red Cross workers put it, "One of the real highlights . . . was that never before have we seen such a spontaneous response from the general public in terms of volunteer help. . . . I don't know what we would have done without these volunteers."[63]

Barton[64] notes that so significant is the volunteer response that organizations would do well to take into account the fact that not everything can be planned in advance, and that they should pay due attention to the fact of mass spontaneous volunteerism, and take this factor into account by seeking means to utilize the spontaneous mass response in the most effective manner.

From diverse research reports it seems, then, that, in sharp contrast to much behavior noted in instances of accidents and crimes, and, in some of the social psychology research, empathy is a predominant emotion and helping behavior is a predominant response. A number of differing reasons have been advanced for this outpouring of altruism.

Wolfenstein,[65] concentrating on the individual psychological aspect, argues that the normal negative feelings "deriving from a variety of frustrations and annoyances" are dissipated as an expression of relief at having escaped from the worst of the danger. Inasmuch as people have a regular component of hostility toward others, they "receive unusual vicarious satisfaction from the disastrous event."[66]

Fritz and Mathewson[67] focus more on the value system of the society as a whole. They note that while disasters *"increase the opportunities* for exploitation, they often *reduce the motivation*."[68] Disasters generally have the effect of indiscriminately eradicating inequalities of status and wealth, and therefore minimizing the sense of frustration and deprivation of those at the lower end of the social and economic scale. People who feel rejected and ignored might find a new role for themselves in creative and constructive work on behalf of the community. The norms of the society accordingly undergo an extreme and rapid transformation. Selfish motives are relegated to a minor aspect of life as community needs take precedence. Titmuss[69] also shows how the egalitarian nature of a war-torn society enabled the British to withstand the strains of war and particularly bombings from the air, with great equanimity and self-assurance, and without any breakdown of social organization.

Turner[70] has attempted to provide a theoretical explanation for the change in society that takes place consequent upon a disaster. He points out that there are two basic phenomena that regularly occur: 1) an intolerance toward outsiders (even the well-meaning), and 2) a heightened solidarity experienced by members of the community. Turner suggests that the intolerance toward outsiders is a function of the in-group-out-group distinction first remarked on by Sumner,[71] and which is more typical of simple societies. The second, a heightened solidarity, "the manifestation of a common—a uniform—sentiment,"[72] Turner explains in terms of Durkheim's concept of mechanical solidarity.[73] Durkheim had explained that, in simple societies lacking a division of labor, social cohesion was based on the similarities among people.

According to Turner, when the division of labor breaks down, as he claims is the case in disaster situations when the normal functioning of society is disrupted, "there is often a resurgence of *mechanical solidarity*, based upon the vital sense of shared sentiment among the victims and other persons directly or indirectly involved in the disaster."[74]

Turner's model is intriguing, and, though lacking in direct empirical evidence, has been given some retroactive ratification in an almost tailor-made example subsequently provided by Zurcher,[75] who describes, from his own personal experience, the stages through which a spontaneous volunteer work group passed as it groped its way from the initial confusion of the disaster into a cohesive, functionally effective entity, with each member having a clearly established role to perform within the rudimentary system of division of labor that developed. According to this thesis, the original motivation was apparently the feeling of solidarity engendered by their common position as members of a stricken community. Later, over a period of several days, the work group took on routinized forms, including a growing division of labor paralleled with the community's recovery as it returned to its original organic solidarity. Toward the end the group became more intensified and sophisticated with hierarchical structure until it finally disbanded after the community was well on the way to normalcy.

However, it is possible that Turner has been too hidebound by Durkheim's model. The collapse of the division of labor is not an inevitable, or even likely, result of a natural disaster. In most cases the division of labor does not disappear; it may even increase as persons utilize their skills as doctors, law-enforcement officials, public utility workers, and so on, usually foregoing the general aspects of the occupation so as to devote their time and energy completely to disaster-related activity.[76]

It would seem that it is not the breakdown of the division of labor or even the presumed hostility to outsiders that can adequately explain the heightened social solidarity from a sociological perspective. Tönnies's approach,[77] accentuating the nature of the social relationship, seems more applicable. He spoke of two types of social organization, the *Gemeinschaft*, characterized by affective and intimate contacts among its members based on natural will rooted in custom, and the *Gesellschaft*, characterized by impersonal and segmented contacts based on rational will rooted in law.

From a sociological perspective, a disaster destroys many of the artificial impediments to social interaction. It is not the breakdown of the division of labor that is critically significant in causing this change, but rather the inroads made into the structural embellishments of a modern society. The impact of a disaster disrupts the outer facade of a society and removes the props which sustain it, bringing people face to face with their environment and with each other without the mediating influence of artificial social factors. The community undergoes a deep and traumatic experience. To this new situation, and within this new environment, the members of the community and those in proximity must react.

Simmel has written of the metropolitan person who ". . . develops an organ protecting him against the threatening currents and discrepancies of his external environment which would uproot him."[78] People are enabled thereby to ignore, deny, or reject many of the social demands that are made upon them. However, these protective devices are no longer available during disaster; a structural transformation takes place, not only in the physical world, but also in the social environment. The old patterns of behavior and the old frameworks of social organization are no longer relevant, and new patterns and frameworks must be improvised. It is from this perspective that the role of the volunteer must be understood and analyzed.

A new normative structure arises in which altruistic acts based upon deep emotions of concern for the welfare of fellow citizens, and grounded in sentiments of empathy, become the normative standard. The sense of close community ties becomes pervasive at the same time as the community seeks to recover from the physical destruction.

Bonds of Empathy

What I am suggesting is that it is not the personal tragedies and the physical damage alone nor even feelings of relief and/or guilt by the survivors/bystanders that is the key to understanding the nature of the altruistic actions which seem to be the predominant pattern of behavior in the wake of a natural disaster. In the normal course of events people are liable to encounter such instances of deprivation to others without sensing a similar need to become personally involved. It is not even the dire circumstances alone that can explain the behavior, since, as has already been noticed, the plight of individual victims of accidents or crimes is often as critical yet ignored, while much of the helping behavior in disaster continues into the recovery stages when the urgency of immediate danger to life and property has abated. The altruism displayed seems to flow from far deeper, almost primeval, sources. Altruism seems to become, as Durkeim once picturesquely argued, more than just an ornamental aspect of social life.[79] It seems to be embedded deeply in the collective psyche of community life; while often dormant and unnoticed, it is revealed fully as the societal framework becomes shorn of its various appertunances.

Fritz reflects well this dual layer of social life. He notes:

widespread sharing of danger, loss and deprivation produces an intimate, primary group solidarity among the survivors, which overcomes social isolation, and provides a channel for intimate communication and expression and a major force of physical and emotional support and reassurance. The capacity of human societies under severe stress to construct from a highly elaborated set of secondary group organizations to a kind of universal primary group existence is probably their central built-in protective mechanism. This mechanism seems to account for the resiliency of groups and society in the face of disaster and their ability to regenerate a more complex social life. The reversion to the primary-group mode of existence might be likened to the antibodies which are formed in the human body to attack disease and return the body mechanism to a state of homeostasis; but Charles H. Cooley's analogy of the primary group as the nucleus from which all social organization grows is probably a more useful metaphor.

The social disorganization that occurs in disaster is essentially a social disorganization of secondary-group life—a disruption of the complex structure of social differentiation and culturally defined communication networks among human beings. Except momentarily, it does not disorganize primary group life. On the contrary this is strengthened, and this in turn constitutes the nucleus out of which the society can once again reconstitute itself and develop a new complexity of organization. . . . The quality of interaction . . . in the entire community of survivors approximates more closely the characteristics of intimate, personal, informal, sympathetic, direct, spontaneous and sentimental interaction set forth in the concept of the primary group.

The breakdown of culturally prescribed barriers to intimate communication and interaction provides some major gratifications to survivors. People are able to confirm the fact that others are basically like themselves. That people respond in like manner to the fears, dangers, deprivations, and anxieties posed by the disaster, largely regardless of previous station in life, is greatly reassuring—especially for those who have previously felt marginal, detached, isolated, or uncomfortably different from others. The "outsider" becomes an "insider," the "marginal man" a "central man." People are able to perceive with a clarity never before possible, a set of underlying basic values to which all subscribe. They come to see that collective action is necessary for these values to be maintained. Individual and group goals and means become merged inextricably. This merging of individual and societal needs provides a feeling of belongingness and a sense of unity rarely achieved under normal circumstances. . . .

Thus, while the natural or human forces that created or precipitated the disaster appear hostile and punishing, the people who survive become more friendly, sympathetic, and helpful.[80]

Often the feelings of empathy take on an added dimension, and the disaster, for all its tragedy, leads to the creation of a special kind of atmosphere. A number of writers have remarked on this phenomenon. Crawshaw notes that "there was a reaction of excitement which was expressed in a carnival, camping out atmosphere. Unshaven men quickly bought out all camping supplies in the community, while housewives stacked up at local stores with essentials of food, flashlight batteries, and charcoal, chattering gaily with strangers about their personal 'good fortune.' Many sightseers and amateur photographers made the rounds, stopping at badly damaged houses for social visits and to commiserate with the owners. . . . Much help was given to the owners of seriously damaged houses. People pitched in with power saws to clean trees off homes, while others nailed down temporary paper roofs on the homes of people they hardly knew."[81]

The philosopher and psychologist William James[82] described his own reaction to the 1906 San Francisco earthquake in similar terms. Although about thirty miles from the center of the quake, he was still in an area that absorbed some of the upheaval. He notes that "everybody was excited, but the excitement, at first . . . seemed to be almost joyous. Here at last was a *real* earthquake, after so many years of harmless waggle! Above all, there was an irresistible desire to talk about it, and exchange experiences."[83]

James sums up the overall atmosphere in terms that he finds "reassuring as to human nature,"[84] noting firstly the rapidity of the improvisation of order out of chaos, and the universal equanimity. James suggests that the key to understanding the positive nature of human behavior in such adverse and unpropitious conditions is the fact that "private miseries were merged in the vast general sum of privations and in the all-absorbing practical problem of general recuperation."[85]

Research carried out during the war indicates similar feelings. Vernon[86] found that the common plight of being subjected to constant bombing led to increased interaction while Gillespie[87] and Titmuss[88] draw attention to the community spirit prevailing in the public air-raid shelter, and in the stations of the underground railway, where many people would come every night, finding not only physical security but also emotional support.

In the widespread flooding in England in 1953, Spiegel remarked upon similar experiences where, even at the height of the emergency, "while the flood waters filled the town, morale was extremely high in spite of the great threats to life . . . "[89] while Wallace wrote of the "euphoria" that seemed to grip the population of a disaster after recovery from the initial shock, a euphoria "marked by thankfulness for survival and by intense public spirit and eagerness to work for the community's welfare."[90] In describing the community's efforts to comprehend, and respond to, the damage done, Wallace draws a parallel with revitalization movements[91] and the search for meaning on the part of communities whose social framework had been seriously undermined. The community, realizing that there are survivors and that there is hope for the future, celebrated, in essence, its rebirth.

Despite the near consensus as to these positive aspects there is one recent research report which contains information and an analysis at variance with the picture generally portrayed. Erikson,[92] in his sensitive study of the flood that swept through the Appalachian communities in Buffalo Creek in 1972, describes a society that, two and a half years later, had not recovered from the tragedy, and that knew none of the sense of cohesion and excitement that so many other writers have ascribed to disaster-stricken communities. His study raises many pertinent questions, since the community that he described was one specifically characterized by a sense of inner cohesion and intimate interaction in the predisaster period.

Erikson claims that the community underwent a collective trauma, which he categorizes as a "loss of communality,"[93] communality being used to describe not merely a physical connection of people living in proximity but the deeper dimension of a network of relationships with neighbors "with whom one shares bonds of intimacy and a feeling of mutual concern. The people of Buffalo Creek are 'neighbor people,' which is a local way of referring to a style of relationship long familiar among social scientists. Toennies called it 'gemeinschaft,' Cooley called it 'primary,' Durkheim called it 'mechanical,' Redfield called it 'folk,' and every generation of social scientists have found other ways to express the same thought, one of the most recent being Herbert Gans's concept of 'person orientation.' "[94]

Erikson describes in some detail, with extensive quotation from, and in the language of, the people in Buffalo Creek, the nature of community life, in which each person is an integral part of a larger, living, unified framework. This communality does not have specified qualities; it is "a state of mind shared among a particular gathering of people, and this state of mind by definition, does not lend itself to sociological abstraction. It does not have a name or a cluster of distinguishing properties. It is a quiet set of understandings that become absorbed into the atmosphere and are thus part of a natural order."[95]

It was this framework that was destroyed in the disaster. The people were so much bound up in this larger entity that they were left defenseless when it was destroyed. ". . . not only are you diminished as a person when that surrounding tissue is stripped away, but . . . you are no longer able to reclaim as your own the emotional resources you invested in it. To 'be neighborly' is not a quality you can carry with you into a new situation like negotiable emotional currency; the old community was your niche in the classic ecological sense and your ability to relate to that niche is not a skill easily transferred to another setting."[96] Inasmuch as rescue and recovery operations were undertaken, they were performed by outside officials of rescue organizations and government agencies. The people of Buffalo Creek, while grateful, were also acutely aware of their own dependence and loss of control over their own lives.

In taking note of Erikson's analysis it should be borne in mind that there were a number of unique aspects in this disaster, including the totality of destruction in which whole villages were swept away by the storm waters, and in which the company for whom many of the inhabitants worked, and whom they had trusted, bore direct responsibility for the disaster caused by the collapse of a makeshift dam that it had built.

In addition the community itself had, even before the flood, been the "victims of one long, sustained disaster brought about by the pillaging of the timber reserves, the opening of the coal fields, the emergence of the Depression, and the introduction of welfare as a way of life."[97] The disaster, according to Erikson, came at a time when the community was on the point of reversing these negative trends. Being poised for recovery from the accumulated pressures of these larger, overpowering problems, they were unable to gather up their resources again for yet another struggle against the superior forces of nature and society arraigned against them. Writing before this event, Sjoberg had suggested the circumstances which might be essential for the recovery of a community from a disaster. "Heightened integration and morale," he wrote, "emerge only where the population has confidence in the eventual restitution of the *status quo*."[98] It was this confidence that was apparently lacking at Buffalo Creek, and that probably caused the unusual negative response noted by Erikson.

In fact, it is not only the possibility of restoring the status quo that is the key to disaster response, but the ability to capitalize on the rare opportunity that a disaster offers for a meaningful restructuring of the community. The period of restoration is noted not only for the physical rebuilding, but for the attempts to mould anew the social framework of the society. Prince[99] was the first to have placed this aspect of the disaster phenomenon within a general sociological perspective; other researchers have constantly reiterated the theme, most notably Fritz[100] in his summary article of the sociological aspects of disaster.

For Fritz, "Disasters provide a realistic laboratory for testing the integration, stamina, and recuperative power of large-scale social systems."[101] Fritz maintains that, because of the need to improve the measures for coping with disasters, most research tends to stress the disruptive nature of the occurrence and makes only minimal reference to "significant positive effects of disaster on social systems,"[102] including most notably the fact that disaster often serves as a unifying force, provides the "possibility of introducing desired innovations into the social system," causes a "democratization of the social structure" as all perceive the random manner in which the harm is generally distributed over all sections of the population, and facilitates a reassessment and, if necessary, a reformulation of society's values, norms, and goals.[103]

In many instances there is an " 'amplified rebound' effect, in which the society is carried beyond its pre-existing levels of integration, productivity, and capacity for growth."[104] Fritz uses Toynbee's concept of challenge and response[105] to suggest that disaster may often provide just the right amount of challenge to act as a precipitating factor for a rejuvenation which may well rebound to the benefit of the affected society and enable it to make advances it might otherwise have failed to do.

Notes

1. These aspects of the research are clearly and strongly emphasized in two of the first collections of articles devoted to the topic. See *Human Organization*, "Human Adaptation to Disaster," Nicholas J. Demerath and Anthony F.C. Wallace, eds., Vol. 16, 1957; *Annals of American Academy of Political and Social Sciences*, "Disasters and Disaster Relief," DeWitt Smith, ed., Vol. 309, 1957.

2. See especially Richard M. Titmuss, "Problems of Social Policy," in *History of Second World War* (London: His Majesty's Stationery Office, 1950); Irving L. Janis, *Air War and Emotional Stress: Psychological Studies of Bombing and Civilian Defense* (New York: McGraw-Hill, 1951); Fred C. Ickle, *The Social Impact of Bomb Destruction* (Norman: University of Oklahoma Press, 1958).

3. For articles on each of these three phases see: George H. Grosser, Henry Wechsler, Milton Greenblatt, eds., *The Threat of Impending Disaster: Contributions to the Psychology of Stress* (Cambridge, Mass.: M.I.T. Press, 1964), George W. Baker and D.W. Chapman, eds., *Man and Society in Disaster* (New York: Basic Books, 1962); J. Eugene Haas, Robert W. Kotes, Martyn J. Bowden, *Reconstruction Following Disaster* (Cambridge, Mass.: M.I.T. Press, 1977).

4. Instituut voor Sociaal Onderzoek van het Nederlandse Volk, *Studies in Holland Flood Disaster, 1953*, Washington National Academy of Sciences–National Research Council, Committee on Disaster Studies, 1955.

5. Samuel Pepys, *The Diary of Samuel Pepys*; See also Richard Ollard, *Pepys: A Biography* (London: Hodder and Stoughton, 1974), pp. 172-173.

6. William Langer, "The Next Assignment," *American Historical Review*, 1958, *63*, pp. 283-304.

7. Gideon Sjoberg, "Disasters and Social Change," in Baker and Chapman, p. 356. See also Pitirim A. Sorokin, *Man and Society in Calamity* (New York: E.P. Dutton, 1942).

8. George Deaux, *The Black Death–1347* (London: Hamish Hamilton, 1969), p. 21; see also Geoffrey Marks, *The Medieval Plague: The Black Death of the Middle Ages* (Garden City: Doubleday, 1971).

9. Ibid., p. 145.

10. Ibid., p. 146.

11. Thucydides, "Great Plague in Athens," *The Peloponnesian War*, Book 2, Sec. 51.

12. Walter G. Bell, *The Story of London's Great Fire* (London: The Bodley Head, 1920), p. 229.

13. "Account of the Fire of London: Published by Authority," *London Gazette*, Sept. 8, 1666.

14. J. Byron Deacon, *Disaster and the American Red Cross in Disaster Relief* (New York: Russell Sage, 1918).

15. Ibid., pp. 15-16.

16. S.H. Prince, *Catastrophe and Social Change* (New York: Columbia University Press, 1920).

17. Ibid., p. 50. Quoted from reports made at the time of the disaster.

18. Ibid., pp. 47-48.

19. Ibid., p. 57.

20. Russell R. Dynes and Enrico L. Quarantelli, *Helping Behavior in Large-Scale Disasters: A Social Organization Approach*, Disaster Research Center, The Ohio State University, preliminary paper No. 48.

21. Lewis M. Killian, "The Significance of Multiple-Group Membership in Disaster," *American Journal of Sociology*, 1952, *47*, pp. 309-314.

22. Ibid.

23. Medea Miller White, "Role-Conflict in Disasters: Not Family but Familiarities First," Research report, Disaster Study Group, National Academy of Sciences, National Research Council, 1962.

24. Bibb Latané and John M. Darley, *The Unresponsive Bystander: Why Doesn't He Help?* (New York: Appleton-Century-Crofts, 1970).

25. White, "Role-Conflict. . . ."

26. Russell R. Dynes, *Organization Behavior in Disaster* (Lexington, Mass.: Lexington Books, 1970), pp. 153-154.

27. White, p. 30.

28. Enrico L. Quarantelli, "The Nature and Conditions of Panic," *American Journal of Sociology*, 1954, *60*, pp. 267-275.

29. For an explanation of the term see Anthony F. Wallace, "Mazeway Disintegration: The Individual's Perception of Socio-Cultural Disintegration," *Human Organization*, 1957, *16*, p. 23.

30. William H. Form and Charles P. Loomis, "The Persistence and Emergence of Social and Cultural Systems in Disasters," *American Sociological Review*, 1956, *21*, p. 181.

31. William H. Form and Sigmund Nosow (with Gregory P. Stone and Charles M. Westie), *Community in Disaster* (New York: Harper and Bros., 1958), p. 62.

32. E. Glover, "Notes on the Psychological Effects of War Conditions on the Civilian Population," *International Journal of Psychoanalysis*, 1942, *23*, pp. 17-37.

33. I. Matte, "Observations of the English in War Time," *Journal of Nervous and Mental Disease*, 1943, *97*, pp. 447-463.

34. Ibid., p. 463.

35. Charles E. Fritz and J.H. Mathewson, *Convergence Behavior in Disasters: A Problem in Social Control* (Washington, D.C.: National Academy, Committee on Disaster Studies, 1957).

36. Ibid., p. 49.

37. Ibid., p. 50.

38. Ibid.

39. Dynes and Quarantelli, *Helping Behavior*. . . .

40. John Hersey, *Hiroshima* (New York: Knopf, 1946). See also his book *Here To Stay* (New York: Knopf, 1962), recounting personal stories of people rescued in disaster and stress situations.

41. Robert J. Lifton, *Death in Life: Survivors of Hiroshima* (New York: Random House, 1967).

42. Janis, *Air War and Emotional Distress.*

43. Janis is particularly critical of the article by Father Siemes, "Hiroshima, August 1945," *Bulletin of Atomic Scientists*, 1946, *1*, pp. 2-6.

44. This book is part of ongoing work by Lifton into the questions of life, death, and immortality; see R.J. Lifton and Eric Olson, *Living and Dying* (New York: Praeger, 1974).

45. Janis, p. 33.

46. Takashi Nagai, *We of Nagasaki: The Story of Survivors in an Atomic Wasteland* (New York: Meredith Press, 1969).

47. Janis, p. 36.

48. Ibid., p. 39. The report was carried out by the United States Strategic Bombing Survey.

49. Ibid., p. 66.

50. See chapter 6 for discussion of this legal obligation.

51. Martha Wolfenstein, *Disaster: A Psychological Essay* (London: Routledge and Kegan Paul, 1957).

52. The doctor, Savigny, wrote a report of the happenings, which was later leaked to the press and became the cause of political debate in France as the behavior on the raft, and of the ship's captain and leading officers, and of the leader of the expedition in abandoning the people on the raft, became subject to virulent criticism.

53. Alexander McKee, *Death Raft: The Human Drama of the Medusa Wreck* (New York: Warner, 1975). For further accounts of human behavior in shipwrecks, see R. Thomas, *Interesting and Authentic Narratives of the Most Remarkable Shipwrecks* (Freeport, New York: Books for Libraries Press, 1970; first published 1835).

54. See Piers Paul Read, *Alive* (New York: Lippincott, 1974). The even more extreme situation of actually killing one of the members of the group in order to eat the meat of his body, or of throwing some survivors overboard in order to increase the rescue prospects of the survivors is discussed in two classic shipwreck cases, one in the United States (*U.S.* v. *Holmes*, Wall. Jr. 1 [c.c. E.D. Pa. 1842]), the other in Britain (*Regina* v. *Dudley and Stevens*, L.R. 14 Q.B.D. 273, 1884). In these cases, there are hints that the use of lots to decide who should be sacrificed might satisfy the moral and legal demands of society.

55. Rex A. Lucas, *Men in Crisis: A Study of a Mine Disaster* (New York: Basic Books, 1969.

56. Harry Estill Moore, "Towards a Theory of Disaster," *American Sociological Review*, 1956, *21*, pp. 733-737.

57. Allen H. Barton, *Communities in Disaster* (Garden City, N.J.: Doubleday, 1969).

58. Charles E. Fritz, "The Therapeutic Aspects of Community Disaster," unpublished paper presented to Southern Sociological Society, 1961, cited in F.C. Bates et al., *The Social and Psychological Consequences of a Natural Disaster* (Washington, D.C.: National Academy of Sciences, 1963), p. 61.

59. Dynes, *Organization Behavior. . . .*

60. Ibid., chapter 6, "Ways of Conceptualizing Organized Behavior," pp. 136-150.

61. Fritz and Mathewson, p. 41.

62. Ibid., p. 41.

63. See Leon Shaskolsky, *Volunteerism in Disaster Situations*, Disaster Research Center, The Ohio State University, Preliminary Paper No. 1.

64. Allen H. Burton, "The Emergency Social System," in Baker and Chapman, *Man and Society in Disaster*, p. 252.

65. Wolfenstein, p. 93.

66. Ibid.

67. Fritz and Mathewson, p. 51.

68. Ibid.

69. Titmuss, "Problems of Social Policy."

70. Ralph H. Turner, "Types of Solidarity in the Reconstituting of Groups," *Pacific Sociological Review*, 1967, *10*, pp. 60-68.

71. William G. Sumner, *Folkways: A Study of the Sociological Importance of Usages, Manners, Customs, Mores and Morals* (Boston: Ginn and Co., 1940), pp. 12-13.

72. Turner, "Types of Solidarity . . . ," p. 61.

73. Emile Durkheim, *The Division of Labor in Society*, trans., George Simpson (Glencoe: The Free Press, 1964).

74. Turner, "Types of Solidarity . . . ," p. 62.

75. Louis Zurcher, "Social-Psychological Functions of Ephemeral Roles: A Disaster Work Crew," *Human Organization*, 1968, *27*, pp. 281-297.

76. This argument is presented in Shaskolsky, *Volunteerism. . . .*

77. Friederich Tönnies, *Gemeinschaft und Geselleschaft* (Berlin, 1887).

78. Georg Simmel, "The Metropolis and Mental Life," in *The Sociology of Georg Simmel*, Kurt H. Wolff, ed. (New York: Free Press, 1964), p. 410.

79. Durkheim, p. 228.

80. Charles E. Fritz, "Disaster," in Robert K. Merton and Robert A. Nisbet, *Contemporary Social Problems* (New York: Harcourt Brace and Jovanovich, Inc., 1961), pp. 689-690.

81. Ralph Crawshaw, "Reactions to a Disaster," *Archives of General Psychiatry*, 1963, *9*.

82. William James, "On Some Mental Effects of the Earthquake," *Memories and Studies*, 1911.

83. Ibid., p. 216.

84. Ibid., p. 321.

85. Ibid., p. 225.

86. P.E. Vernon, "Psychological Effects of Air Raids," *Journal of Abnormal and Social Psychology*, 1941, *36*, pp. 459-476.

87. R.D. Gillespie, *Psychological Effects of War on Citizens and Soldiers*, 1947.

88. Titmuss, "Problems of Social Policy."

89. John D. Spiegel, "The English Flood of 1953," *Human Organization*, 1957, *16*, p. 5.

90. Anthony F. Wallace, "Mazeway Disintegration," p. 23.

91. Anthony F. Wallace, "Revitilization Movements," *American Anthropology*, 1956, *58*, pp. 264-281.

92. Kai T. Erikson, *Everything in Its Path: Destruction of Community in the Buffalo Creek Flood* (New York: Simon and Schuster, 1976).

93. Ibid., pp. 186-246.

94. Ibid., p. 187.

95. Ibid., p. 189.

96. Ibid., p. 191.

97. Ibid., p. 250.

98. Gideon Sjoberg, "Disasters and Social Change," in Baker and Chapman, p. 370.

99. Prince, *Catastrophe and Social Change.*

100. Charles E. Fritz, "Disaster."

101. Ibid., p. 682.

102. Ibid.

103. Ibid., p. 692.

104. Ibid.

105. Arnold Toynbee, *Study of History* (London: Oxford University Press, 12 volumes, 1956-1962).

4 The Criminal Triad

Of all the bystander situations, the one that has probably caused the most concern has been in connection with crime. It was a crime—the Genovese incident—which touched off the original public reaction and academic involvement; it is crime in general—far more than disasters or accidents—that affects people's perceptions and feelings about their society. Disasters, for all the traumatic impact, are exceptional circumstances, which happen fortuitously, and may never impinge directly on a particular individual or community at all. Accidents are admittedly more prevalent, but do not normally induce fear or pose a threatening situation. Crime, on the other hand, is not only endemic in society, but the fear of being victimized looms large, and the awareness of crime as a major and troublesome social problem is pervasive.

Yet, despite the growing interest in the bystander in general, and despite the extended work that criminologists have been devoting in recent years to the position of the victim of a crime, only minimal research has been oriented to the role of the bystander in crime. The spate of social psychology research into bystander activity has dealt with the crime situation only peripherally; nearly all the laboratory and the field projects deal with noncriminal situations.

When the research does not relate to crime as such, it is not possible, in most cases, to extrapolate to a criminal situation. In the work of the Piliavins and Rodin, as discussed in chapter 2,[1] it would be interesting to know whether the widespread positive response to the plight of a person collapsing in a subway train would have been replicated had the passengers been confronted with a crime, particularly a crime of violence. One variable that they did examine—an inebriated person collapsing in contrast to someone sober—did show clear differences in the responses of bystanders. In the research project of a person falling off a ladder[2] and crying out in pain for help, it would be interesting to know if the basically positive response recorded for the staged fall would have been replicated for a staged crime.

Research on Criminal Situations

Latané and Darley specifically relate to the fact that there are unique aspects of a crime which make extrapolation inapplicable. Even so, their own research involves only a few examples of a crime—for instance the theft from a grocery store in the presence of witnesses.[3] In their preparatory remarks to the research they note that, generally, crime is differentiated from other stress situations, mainly because an individual bystander may be harmed by the culprit.

> A villain represents a danger not only to the victim, but to anybody who is rash enough to interfere with him. A single individual may be reluctant to tangle with a villain. If it comes to physical violence, his odds are at best equal. At worst, the villain will be armed and vicious. Undeterred from crime he may be undeterred from physical violence as well.[4]

Recently some initial attempts have been made to probe more deeply into the specific nature of bystander behavior in criminal situations. In cases where the work has been in the tradition of staged real-life situations, often serious problems arise in setting up the research in a meaningful manner so as to resemble real situations. On the one hand there is a possibility that the action will be perceived to be staged, and the subjects will ignore what is happening. On the other hand there is a danger of an overzealous response where the act is carried out too vividly. The research by Shotland and Straw[5] gives evidence of both situations. In one simulated incident over 40 percent of the subjects claimed that they realized that the action was staged. In another situation, the acting was so real that three subjects took measures for their own self-protection and two nearby workers who had been informed beforehand of what was about to take place tried nevertheless to intervene.

The researchers had taken care to ensure there were confederates available to avoid any unforeseen escalation of the violence, a task that was facilitated by the fact that the violence enacted took place in a building on a university campus and not in a downtown street.

This research focused partly around the specific variable of the reaction to an altercation between a male and a female. In earlier research Barofsky and his colleagues[6] had found that there was a tendency for males not to go to the rescue of a female who was being assaulted; they attributed this reluctance to the vicarious sexual and/or hostile gratification that the bystanders were deriving from the action.

In the experiment by Shotland and Straw a contrast was made between two situations—in one case the altercation was between a male and a female who were ostensibly strangers; in the other case, between a married couple. In this latter situation there was a marked trend to interpret the violence as an internal quarrel in which outsiders should not intervene.

Other reactions recorded for both situations pointed out the importance of competence to act. In many instances the subjects proceeded slowly toward the scene of the assault, clearly uncertain as to exactly what they should do; some stated afterwards that they were hopeful that their appearance on the scene would be sufficient to halt the attack. Two subjects who took firm steps to intervene directly had specialized competence which they were intent on activating; one had studied martial arts, the other, a female student, had recently been at a lecture where advice had been given as to how to repulse an assailant.

In their article Shotland and Straw discuss also the ethical and practical aspects of doing such research. Before the research was undertaken they had discussed the advisability of undertaking it with a number of their colleagues who had favored the research; after each incident they had spoken to the subjects to assess their reactions, which were positive, many of them stating that they had no objection to being exposed to the artificially induced stress.

Both the Barofsky and Shotland projects took place in a building on a university campus. Far more complicated are staged muggings in a downtown street or in a subway train.

The kind of problems that this research poses is exemplified by the opposition encountered by Stewart and Cannon[7] in their attempt to stage a theft on the streets, even though there was no violence used and due precautions were taken to ensure the safety of all concerned. They had also consulted with the police and business organizations, who had supported their endeavors and expressed their opinion that the research could be of much value. Nevertheless when the public became aware of the research there was an outcry, and the local press mounted a barrage of criticism against it, as a result of which the project was abandoned.

Other simulated crimes have involved shoplifting. Gelfland and her colleagues[8] encountered an initial problem in that only 28 percent of their interviewees noticed the theft; of these, a little over a quarter reported it.

Bickman has focused on the degree to which a casual prior contact between the bystander and the victim or the wrongdoer might affect the response. He found[9] that there was a greater tendency to report when the bystander had, immediately prior to the shoplifting attempt, been treated in a pleasant manner by a sales clerk. On the other hand, the prior behavior of the wrongdoer seemed to have no effect on the subsequent reaction of the bystander.[10] In one interaction the wrongdoer had made a friendly remark, and in the other he had behaved rudely. No marked differences were noted in the tendency to report the theft, and the researchers conclude that revenge is not a factor in the bystander's considerations.

A novel approach has been followed by Geis, Huston, and their associates.[11] Utilizing the Good Samaritan Compensation Scheme in California, they have interviewed bystanders who, after being injured in the course of their intervention, subsequently made an application to the compensation board to be recompensed for the harm caused them. This is a unique project, presenting a methodical analysis of bystander behavior, in conditions generally of violent crime.

In presenting their work they stress the fact that laboratory research can never adequately replicate the kinds of perilous conditions that confront Samaritans. Their research indicates, as already noted in chapter 2, that the motivations and the considerations of the intervening bystander may be very different from those of the bystanders in the laboratory research. They note the confidence of the intervenors, their anger, and their concern, as well as a certain recklessness and adventurousness.

They argue that because of the impossibility of fully replicating a real-life situation and particularly its dangers, researchers often come to inaccurate conclusions about intervenors.

The need for pursuing this line of research—follow-up interviews of intervening bystanders—is highly desirable, but the use of the victim compensation program as the source of interviewees has obvious limitations, dealing mainly with crimes in which there was an element of violence, and only with those bystanders who helped, were injured, and then sought compensation.

Another important and unique line of research has been that adopted by Pecar in his studies of crime in Yugoslavia.[12] In the course of analyzing the nature of criminal-victim relationships in homicide along the lines originally laid down by Wolfgang,[13] Pecar noted that the interaction between these two principal parties to the crime was often influenced to a significant degree by the behavior of third parties—whom Pecar terms "involved bystanders." In many instances it was their behavior in the initial stages that served to precipitate or to provoke the crime. Whereas Wolfgang in his study had made a notable contribution to victimology by empirically showing that in many murder cases the victims bore major responsibility for the interaction preceding and leading up to the crime (it was they who tended to be drunk, who escalated a verbal argument into physical violence, who refused to be calmed), Pecar showed that by extending the investigation of the pertinent interaction it could be seen that in many cases the basis for the crime was laid in some prior provocation by a third person, who subsequently assumed only a minor role as a bystander. In some instances he provides examples of homicides committed within the home in which the original provocations which led to the final act of violence were initiated by a member of the family who was neither victim nor wrongdoer but whose behavior touched off a more violent interaction between other members. Pecar argues convincingly that if the aim of victimology is to expand our awareness of crime as an interactive phenomenon then there is a need to investigate also the role of the involved bystander in crime, not only for possible prevention but also for possible precipitation.

Pecar seems to have touched on a major unexplored area of criminological and victimological research, but so far there has been no follow-up to his pioneering approach.

While the California experiment deals with the role of the bystander as a Good Samaritan in trying to prevent crime, and the Yugoslavian research deals with the "involved bystander" as a precipitant agent in causing the crime, a third area remains the most elusive—the behavior of bystanders who are witness to actual criminal cases but fail to intervene. There seem to be few means of resolving this problem, for such bystanders are by the very nature of their inaction not easily accessible to the researcher.

Newspaper Reports

Meanwhile, given the paucity of criminological knowledge at this stage, it would seem useful to gain some kind of idea—admittedly selective and not entirely reliable—of the nature and dimensions of bystander behavior in criminal situations from sources such as the mass media and impressionistic recollections of those involved in law enforcement and criminal justice administration. No conclusions can be drawn on the basis of such facts, but useful leads for further research might easily be found.

While it is true that often it is the unusual and sensational case that attracts particular attention by the mass media, or that remains etched in the memory, it should not be forgotten that many social scientists have pointed out that the extreme or unusual case may serve to clarify aspects of human behavior. While the cases reported in the paper may be atypical they do indicate the broad lines of possible behavioral responses that could be subjected to further in-depth investigation.

It is also advisable to take note of the type of responses that attract public attention, because, just as in the case of the Genovese murder, they have a cumulative effect on the manner in which the general public regard the problems of crime and anticipated bystander behavior.

Thus, for instance, one story in a widely circulated magazine[14] describes the heroic action of two teenagers who chased after a robber, one of the two being killed in the process; the article then details the subsequent reaction of the survivor to the incident; the guilt at the death of his close friend; the harrowing experience of the hours immediately after the murder, where, instead of being given the emotional support that he so badly needed, he was subjected to a lengthy interrogation for several hours, including a visit to the scenes of the robbery and the murder; the tension of giving evidence in court where he spent an unpleasant hour on the witness stand being cross-examined by the defense attorney; the depressed state that he was in for many months afterwards, including the development of a stammer.

Both the youths were rewarded for the action (the dead friend posthumously), but the overall impression of the article is of the regret of the survivor at having become involved, his retroactive wisdom that had he known that the robber was armed he would never have intervened, and his resolve never to become involved again. "Does it pay to be a hero?" is the rhetorical question underlying the theme of the story.

On the other hand a newspaper report[15] tells of other Good Samaritans who had no regrets as to their action, despite the fact that they had themselves suffered serious and permanent injury. In one case a woman had been involved in a shoot-out between a gunman and two policemen. She had grabbed the gunman's arms, deflecting the bullet, and thereby possibly saving the lives of the policemen. However, she had herself been hit by a police bullet, and had been paralyzed from the waist down. On being awarded a prize for her bravery, she had stressed that, despite her injury, she had no regrets, and had merely done what was necessary under the circumstances.

This particular victim is an example of a special group of victims—small in number, but awesome in the implications—of bystanders killed or maimed in the course of a shoot-out between police and criminals. Sometimes this even occurs merely by the unhappy circumstance of their fortuitous presence in the vicinity, without any active intervention on their part at all. Tappan notes that, on some occasions, the bystander may actually be a victim of incorrect identification by the police, who open fire in the mistaken belief that they are confronted by a criminal.[16] Sometimes the bystander falls prey to the criminal's error. Wolfgang[17] noted in his study of homicide in Philadelphia that six out of 550 victims in his sample were bystanders, having no connection with either the criminal or the intended victim.

Yet most cases of harm to bystanders probably result from their involvement as a result of their own volition, in a desire to express tangibly their role of good citizenship.[18] In some instances the intervention is a calculated risk, as a violent response may be anticipated, such as in the case of an armed robbery. In these cases the robbers are ostentatiously armed, explicitly warn against trying to thwart them, have planned their campaign thoroughly, and have undertaken clear risks with the intention of brooking no interference with their operation. In other cases relatively innocuous incidents have serious repercussions for the unsuspecting Good Samaritan.

In one incident,[19] a young sixteen-year-old high-school student joined in a chase after two bicycle thieves and captured them. While helping to surround and hold the thieves in anticipation of the arrival of the police, the youth was suddenly attacked by one of the thieves, who stabbed him in the body, delivering a fatal wound. The dead youth was described as quiet and scholarly; his motivation for helping to apprehend the criminals may well have been the fact that two weeks earlier he too had been the victim of a bicycle theft.

The facts of this case touch on a potentially important point for future research—the degree to which prior victimization might be an important factor affecting bystander response. In their ongoing research, Geis and Huston[20] have found that a significant number of involved bystanders had previously been victims themselves and are at present probing this aspect further. There are obviously important implications for the extent to which empathy with a victim is a major consideration for a bystander.

Incidents of physical harm, occasionally fatal, or of conscious risk-taking behavior, are extreme examples of bystander intervention. However, in the realm of crime it is not only such precarious situations for bystanders that are of importance—it is also the nature of bystander behavior in other, less threatening, situations which constitute a problem of major proportions; for the capacity to ensure public security and confidence through efficient and equitable law enforcement and judicial administration is, to a large extent, a function of the willingness of people—victims and bystanders—to report crime to the police and to make themselves available to give evidence in a subsequent criminal trial.

There is growing evidence of a general dissatisfaction with the existing position; there are references in the mass media to the reluctance of people to cooperate with the police and the prosecution, because of the inconveniences imposed on them subsequently; of police interrogation, of giving evidence before a grand jury or preliminary investigation, and finally of testifying in court.

The Criminal Justice System

In the 1930s Sellin[21] had addressed himself to the problem and suggested a number of reasons that might influence people's reluctance to report a crime, including inconvenience of reporting to the police and then testifying in court, the force of public opinion which may not favor the enforcement of certain laws, indifference or ignorance, or personally knowing the wrongdoers and being reluctant to incriminate them.

A pertinent factor sometimes is the attitude toward, and the interaction with, the police; and the perceptions that people have as to the efficiency and fairness with which the police operate. Where there is little hope that the police will succeed in resolving the case, or where there is little prospect that the police will respond promptly to an emergency, people may ignore them altogether.

The police have for some time been aware of the importance of negative reactions and some police forces have set up special police-community associations to improve the image of the police and the nature of their relationship with the community. Where positive relations exist, there will be a far greater propensity to assist the police and to keep them informed as to suspicious activities.[22]

Another factor is the problem of the bystander as witness in the criminal justice system. Law books give detailed reports of the intricate rules of evidence and procedure; sometimes specialized guide books are written on the art of cross-examination.[23] Yet very rarely are the specific perspective and problems of the witness presented.

Here, too, however, there are incipient indications of growing awareness of the problem, and a recognition of the need to seek a solution, lest the criminal justice system be rendered impotent. A number of writers have, in the last few years, begun addressing themselves to the human aspect of testifying in court, trying to set out the factors militating against full citizen cooperation, while seeking means of making the system more efficient and responsive to citizen's needs.

The accumulated dissatisfaction at the treatment generally accorded bystanders is finally being accorded some attention, with attempts being made to assess the overall damage done to the system because of unpleasant experiences of witnesses, all imperceptibly eroding public support and, in specific cases, adversely affecting the bystander's future response to a criminal situation.

It is clearly difficult to show with any degree of certainty the nature of the impact that such general, often inchoate, dissatisfaction with the operation of the criminal justice system has on bystanders. It is not possible to know how many bystanders ignore the pleas for help of a victim because of their rapid analysis of the consequent inconveniences of court appearances.

Yet the awareness, whether clearly perceived or only dimly sensed, of the many impositions that a bystander may be subjected to as a witness, is surely partly responsible for the reluctance of bystanders to become involved, perhaps most noticeably in situations where the crime itself does not entail any sacrificial or risk-taking action. Thus, although the concept of the altruistic bystander conjures up the idea primarily of aid extended to a victim in stress circumstances—and much of the research has been focused on such situations—the actual concern for another's plight and the altruistic action in support may be tested under other, far less critical, circumstances. Though less discussed in the literature, the willingness of people to help victims and report criminal activities and suspicious acts to the police in nonemergency situations is also an important feature of bystander behavior.

Ash[24] has set out many of the problems liable to be encountered by witnesses in the course of their involvement with the criminal justice system, noting in particular that injudicious treatment of witnesses "has a deleterious impact on the prevention and deterrence of crime . . . [discouraging] countless numbers of witnesses in our criminal justice system from ever 'getting involved' again, that is from reporting a crime, from cooperating with investigative efforts, and from providing testimony crucial to conviction."[25]

Ash describes the series of annoyances a witness is liable to encounter at the hands of an indifferent bureaucratic structure that shows little concern for the witnesses as they suffer through continuances of a trial to a later date or long, tedious waits before being called to give evidence. Where fees are allowed for court appearances these constitute no more than token recompense for lost earnings; and even then, many courts do not bother to apprise the witnesses of their rights in this regard.

After generally describing the hardships of the witness, Ash notes that "nowhere is there hard data on witnesses in criminal cases. This absence is part of a larger pattern of blindness and neglect. In a real sense, our system does not 'see' witnesses in their human dimension. Consequently we are neglectful of their interest and problems."[26] In fact, Ash argues that the additional rights accorded to the accused in recent times have often led to further problems for witnesses, for instance, often causing them to repeat their evidence on a number of occasions; he argues that the judges never considered the impact on witnesses of their decisions extending the rights of the accused.

Banfield and Anderson,[27] in an empirical investigation of the operation of one jurisdiction, have come to similar conclusions. They remark upon the casual and informal manner in which judges accede to defense lawyers' requests for continuances, and argue that some continuances are requested as part of a strategy to wear out the witnesses in the hope that they may fail to appear again. Lawyers, they stress, often insist on all the witnesses being present for all hearings.

Penegar has also noted that the inefficient operation of the criminal justice system "could quite conceivably have detrimental effects on the rate of crime. Seen as a form of communication between the system and the general public, particularly potential violators, the syndrome of delay tells these audiences in effect that crime and its participants are not really urgent public business."[28] Thus witnesses—not just bystanders but even the victim—become resentful of wasted time and lose interest in the trial, and there is constant slippage, in which nonappearance by witnesses, after several wasted days, leads to the case being dismissed.

Komesar,[29] in discussing specifically the victims of crime, attempted to assess the real costs of being victimized, pointing out that such costs were not limited to the pecuniary loss for damages inflicted or goods stolen. A full and true accounting of the price of crime, or more accurately, the price of victimization, must include factors such as the inconvenience of a whole series of subsequent activities—reporting the crime to the police, informing the insurance of the loss or damage, visits to the doctor for treatment, time spent in searching for a replacement of the goods stolen or damaged, backlog in work, and general pain and suffering.

Similar analysis could be made of the secondary losses sustained by the bystander/witness. The most obvious loss would be, as already noted, the time spent waiting to give evidence—at the police station, in discussion with the prosecutor, in the courtroom—often aggravated by the fact that the witness is kept waiting while behind-the-scenes negotiations take place for plea-bargaining, so that the evidence may, finally, not even be required.

Recently a major attempt was made by Cannavale and Falcon[30] to probe empirically the various dimensions of the problem of witnesses. In a novel research project witnesses were questioned as to their attitudes to the court system and the reasons for any dissatisfaction that they might have felt; finally a number of possible solutions were offered for making the system more responsive to the needs of the witnesses, and for facilitating future cooperation in efforts at crime prevention.

They note that prosecutors are often aware of the problems of witnesses, attributing the lack of cooperation by witnesses to some of their difficulty in winning a conviction. Yet, they are unable to offer reasonable remedies for a situation that troubles them. In their book, Cannavale and Falcon argue that a substantive change could be achieved by a consistent effort to introduce better management techniques into the criminal justice system. In their view greater consideration for the very real human problems of the witnesses is the key to ensuring witness cooperation.

They have set out a detailed list of improvements that could be instituted in order to make the court appearance a more pleasant experience. These relate to such issues as allaying the witnesses' apprehensions of reprisals from the defendants or their friends and family, the preparation of guidelines for witnesses, adequate witness fees and efficient payment procedures, prompt notification to witnesses of delays, counseling for reluctant witnesses, and obtaining feedback from witnesses through follow-up interviews to learn of their experience as witnesses in order to detect weaknesses in the existing facilities and procedures and to improve them.[31]

Ash also suggests that there is a need for witness liaison and support squads to represent the interests of witnesses, to make any necessary representation on their behalf, and in general to "act as advocate for legitimately aggrieved witnesses who themselves may be too timid or inarticulate to complain."[32] He suggests also that such an agency might even handle more prosaic details of witness concerns such as having witnesses on telephone standby or arranging for transport to and from the court for handicapped and elderly witnesses, or babysitting services where necessary. In addition he adds that there is a need to give more attention to the provision of better facilities in the court buildings, including free coffee, reading material, television, and gymnastic facilities.

Ash himself is dubious as to the possibility of most of these ideas being introduced, because of the extremely limited lobbying power of the witnesses, who constitute an amorphous group, which is constantly changing, having little contact among themselves, each believing that their own personal experiences are somehow unique and not likely to be repeated, rarely realizing how widespread the negative phenomena encountered are.

Most of the discussion by Ash and by Cannavale and Falcon revolves around the technical issues of court appearances; they only touch marginally upon the problems of actually testifying in court. Here, too, serious problems confront witnesses and should be given due consideration in any attempt to improve their position and to encourage their participation in the criminal justice system.

Marshall[33] has set out the wide range of problems confronting a witness when appearing in the unusual atmosphere of a courtroom. Little consideration is given to the very real psychological difficulties involved in perception of the event, memory, recall, and the capacity to recount the event lucidly. The legal fraternity has only marginal knowledge of these problems, and only in isolated instances is an attempt made to bridge the gap between the strict legal rules of evidence and procedure, and the practical problems that witnesses face in trying to describe what they remember.

Frank,[34] an American judge, has been particularly critical of the judicial system, since it accentuates what he calls the fight theory, based on adversary competition, and not the truth theory, based on a systematic piecing together of the actual facts. The consequences of accentuating the competitive aspects of the trial as opposed to a more objective and cautious search for the truth are that witnesses are caught up in a struggle in which they really have no part. In cross-examination they may be exposed to the verbal onslaughts of the lawyer, who has all the advantages afforded by the rules of evidence.

Outside the courtroom other problems may occur, and the witness may be subjected to threats by the accused or his friends and family. In some exceptional circumstances the witness may be held in custody as a material witness until after completing evidence.[35] Sheleff and Shichor[36] have outlined these and other aspects of witness behavior, suggesting that often the bystander/witness may end up by becoming the victimized party.

Crime Prevention in the Community

However important the need to improve the situation of bystanders in terms of their exposure to the police and the courts, the real issue of bystander involvement will nevertheless more likely be resolved in the community. At the practical level, probably most effort has been expended at this level, much of it out of a growing realization that direct concerted efforts on the part of the community provide the best protection and there is thus a need to foster a willingness to cooperate both among the members of a community and between the community as such and the police.

Sometimes frustration and anger lead to spontaneous reactions on the part of the public. In the early 1970s a number of reports appeared in the mass media of instances where angry bystanders had responded to a crime, not merely to protect the victim but also to vent their rage at the criminal.[37] It was noted then that it was quite possible that perceptions of the breakdown of law and order were leading, as often occurs, to vigilantism, in which enraged citizens would protect themselves by immediate lynch-type law.[38]

The possibility of overzealous reactions by concerned and enraged citizens is a recurring and troubling phenomenon. A recent analysis of violence in America[39] contained a presentation of the semilegitimized expression of violence in the form of vigilantism, posses, and lynching, often providing no more than a thin cover for the expression of deeper political and ideological beliefs.

In some instances official bodies have shown a reluctance to encourage too much citizen involvement in crime prevention, in the knowledge that such encouragement might lead to abuses. The United Nations Social Defense group has gone on record with its concern at the fact that in some countries citizen contributions to crime prevention often escalate into serious infringements of the suspected criminals' rights, with immediate lynch justice being meted out.[40]

On the other hand, there are also attempts being made to channel these sorts of citizen concerns into acceptable activities. In many cities special citizen groups are set up to serve as an auxiliary force, fulfilling various protective functions in the community.

Washnis, in a recent survey of citizen involvement in crime protection,[41] prefaces his book with the statement that police officials and criminologists believe that organized citizen involvement is essential if crime is to be contained and if there are to be any real possibilities of substantially reducing the crime rate. He writes that "out of necessity the general public has been stimulated to assist undermanned, overtaxed, and often non-community oriented police forces in the development of healthy and secure communities."[42] He adds though that "considerable uncertainty exists about the extent to which the public should be involved, about what the public is capable of doing, and about the degree to which public participation can affect the reduction of crime and fear."[43]

Washnis discusses the various kinds of programs that have been instituted and critically analyzes their effectiveness. The most widespread is probably the block association. Washnis describes the major considerations which led to their establishment, including the "fear of crime, dissatisfaction with law enforcement and the criminal justice system, and the desperate feeling by some citizens that they have to get actively involved in order to force crime down."[44] Any efforts of this nature often have a cumulative effect; the knowledge that the citizens of a particular neighborhood are sufficiently concerned to set up a protection association often evokes greater concern on the part of the police for the welfare of that neighborhood. In fact, one of the major aims of block associations is to seek closer communication and contacts between the community and the police. In cities where there has been a determined effort to activate the populace, the number of block associations may even run into the thousands, as in large cities such as New York or Los Angeles.

The block association is usually set up as a response to increased concern with rising crime rates, and the ensuing apprehensions that people have. Among the major functions of the association is to act as "eyes and ears" for what is happening on the block, to encourage citizens to be prepared to report crime and to be witnesses at the subsequent trial, to work in cooperation with the police, to lobby for better police service, to educate the public about the basic crime prevention techniques, and to provide aid to the victims of crime.

Care is taken to avoid any use of violence, and in particular to prevent the development of an aura of vigilantism. Stress is placed on neighborly interaction, where neighbors come to accept responsibility for watching over each other's homes, and to commit themselves to call the police should they see any suspicious activity in the neighborhood. Generally it is made clear that the members of the block association are not expected to intervene personally against a criminal, but are trained in the most efficient and rapid means of calling the police. Often use is made of ear-splitting whistles, sirens, or horns when help is urgently required. On hearing their high, piercing sound, other neighbors are expected to take appropriate action—calling the police, switching on lights, or adding their own noise to the din to help attract attention, and to frighten the would-be criminals. A further activity is community walks, in which two or more people will walk through the neighborhood, generally in the evenings at times considered high-risk for crime, ever on the alert for any untoward activity in the vicinity. In some cases, mobile patrols may be used, using cars that may also be equipped with citizens-band radios for rapid communication. Although almost no academic research has been done on these activities, police statistics indicate that often there is a marked drop in the crime rate.

Apart from the reduction in the crime rate and the sense of security afforded, often a qualitative transformation takes place in the community with the block association acting as a catalyst for further positive social interaction.

> In regard to developing a sense of community, block associations have been one of the most effective ways of bringing people together. In city after city, the majority of block members report that they had never known most of their neighbors and that only through the block club coffee sessions and regular meetings and the door-to-door contact had they really gotten to know each other and to appreciate mutual problems. In many cases, prior to block organizing, even neighbors next door to each other communicated infrequently. Crime prevention provided the motivation to get together and block association offered the mechanism for doing it. The simple factor of adults and youth knowing each other has helped to reduce fear. Familiarity has developed friendly attitudes and an increased concern for ones neighborhood.[4 5]

Outside of the neighborhood, special citywide programs are sometimes set up, with occupation often being the link. Thus, the specific problems facing night-shift employees have, in some cases, led to a special service being instituted for their benefit. The Service Employees Union, which represents mainly cleaning women, many of whom work at night, has set up a special body in New York—the Maintenance Employees Night Protection Alert Cooperation—to help such employees, many of them older women who travel to and from work in the night hours. One of the features of the work of the Cooperation is the institution of a buddy system, whereby members travel to and from work together, thereby radically reducing the chance of becoming a mugging victim.

An interesting means of using citizen resources is the taxi patrol. Civilian Radio Taxi Patrol has also been set up in New York, in which taxi drivers voluntarily commit themselves to informing their dispatchers of any emergency situations, with the dispatcher then passing on the information to the police (or any other relevant authority such as hospital or fire department). The idea for such extensive use of readily available facilities was originally put forward by a taxi owner in New York who had been disturbed by the Genovese case and wished to make some positive contribution to avoid such happenings in the future.

As the program has grown, drivers have been given special training and have discussed techniques for effectively helping to combat crime. For instance, one of their policies is to wait until passengers get safely inside their houses before pulling away.[46] Even without an official organization, instances have been increasing where people with CB radios have used them to submit a report of a crime, accident, or suspicious activity, often in situations where, without radio, the particular person may not have bothered, or been able, to report.

This is not the only circumstance in which specialized knowledge and/or facilities may be conducive to helping behavior. The papers often carry reports of bystanders utilizing their training in first aid or in self-defense techniques to provide critically needed help under emergency conditions. It would seem that as concern for rising crime grows, so is there a greater enrollment in such courses.[47]

Both at the local and at the national level, there are increasing instances of clinics or organizations being set up to cater to the needs of special classes of victims. Both professionals and volunteers may offer their services, thereby finding a means of providing constant aid to those in need. In some cases, where there are considerations of anonymity or distance, the help may be offered through telephone calls. In Britain, there is a national organization known as The Samaritans, with some 17,000 volunteers, linked in 150 centers, who are available at any time to talk on the telephone to people in need of help, advice, or just simple human communication.[48]

Yet, in the final analysis, all these and similar attempts to provide a greater degree of protection by mutual responsibility and readiness are really hinting at a far deeper phenomenon. Block associations are basically ex post facto attempts to recreate a spirit of community—in the realization that only such a spirit can guarantee that intricate and delicate web of human community which turns a random and loose conglomeration of people living in proximity with each other into a meaningful relationship based on personal acquaintance, common interests, and mutual trust.

The Urban Environment

Recently a number of urban planners, architects, social scientists, and criminologists have been researching the correlation between the human environment and social problems. As Jeffery has argued, "The way we design our urban environment determines the crime rate and type of crime to a great extent." He goes on to bemoan the fact that till recently "we have never considered crime prevention an integral part of urban planning." He argues that manipulating the environment to prevent crime "offers new avenues of thought and development for those who are attempting to thread their way effectively and sensitively between two undesirable extremes—high crime rates . . . and a police state, besieged mentality, fortress society response."[49]

In essence this approach seeks a physical structure which will be naturally conducive to the kinds of protection artificially supplied by organizations such as the block associations. It raises the possibility of designing buildings and neighborhoods, even in dense urban centers of population, in such a way as to encourage maximum interaction among neighbors, and constant surveillance of persons and property.

Newman,[50] an architect, has been a dominant figure in this approach. He has stressed the correlation between certain types of housing development (for example, high-rise apartments) and a high crime rate, and has argued that the best means of curbing the crime rate is to restructure the environment in which we live in such a way as to provide the sense of community, which generally characterized nonurban settlements. According to Newman,

> we are witnessing a breakdown of the social mechanism that once kept crime in check and gave direction and support to police activity. The small-town environments, rural or urban, which once framed and enforced their own moral codes, have virtually disappeared. We have become strangers sharing the largest collective habitats in human history.
>
> In our society there are few instances of shared beliefs of values among physical neighbors. Although this heterogeneity may be intellectually desirable, it has crippled our ability to agree on the action required to maintain the social framework necessary to our continued survival. . . . It is clear to almost all researchers in crime prevention that the issue hangs on the inability of communities to come together in joint action. The physical environment we have been building in our cities for the past twenty-five years actually prevents such amity and discourages the pursuit of a collective action.[51]

Newman claims that the key to reversal of these trends is to change the physical environment. He sees the need for a clearly defined area—outside of the hidden privacy of the home, but also beyond the exposed and open nature of the public domain—that will "belong" to the immediate inhabitants, where they will have security, and from which outsiders will be excluded. Any intruders into such an area will likely be asked to explain and justify their presence.

Newman suggests the concept of "defensible space" as a "model for residential environments which inhibits crime by creating the physical expression of a social fabric that defends itself."[52] He explains that defensible space is a surrogate term for the range of mechanisms—real and symbolic barriers, strongly defined areas of influence, and improved opportunities for surveillance—that combine to bring an environment under the control of its residents. A *defensible space* is a living residential environment which can be employed by inhabitants for the enhancement of their lives, while providing security for their families, neighbors and friends. . . .

The public areas of a multi-family residential environment devoid of defensible space can make the act of going from street to apartment equivalent to running the gauntlet. The fear and uncertainty generated by living in such an environment can slowly eat away and eventually destroy the security and the sanctity of the apartment unit itself. On the other hand, by grouping dwelling units to reinforce associations of mutual benefit; by delineating paths of movement; by defining areas of activity for particular users through their juxtaposition with internal living areas; and by providing for natural opportunities for visual surveillance, architects can create a clear understanding of function of a space, and who its users are and ought to be. This, in turn, can lead residents of all income levels to adopt extremely potent territorial attitudes and policing measure which act as strong deterrents to potential criminals.[53]

Newman's idea is to create a gradual transition from private into public areas through the use of what he calls semiprivate and semipublic areas allowing for maximum surveillance from the private areas into the semiprivate and semipublic areas, through judicious positioning of the various spaces, the use of large windows, and so on. Newman claims that, in buildings which approximate to these standards, there is a lower crime rate, a greater sense of security, and a greater willingness to be active as a bystander.

Newman's analysis is focused mainly on the specific housing area; other writers have adopted a broader perspective of the total neighborhood. Writing before Newman, Jacobs has described how to make the cities attractive and safe for its citizens.[54] Whereas Newman describes how the immediate housing area, semiprivate and semipublic, can be made safer by facilitating interaction among the residents and by subtle exclusion of strangers, Jacobs focuses on the public areas and shows how these too could be made safer by increasing the voluntary surveillance of people who live and work in the neighborhood. "Where city streets are being properly used they fulfil certain 'self-government functions' . . . to weave webs of public surveillance and thus to protect strangers as well as themselves: to grow networks of small-scale, everyday public life and thus of trust and social controls; and to help assimilate children into reasonably responsible and tolerant city life."[55]

She claims that the best way to ensure the security of citizens is to create conditions which will lead to as much activity as possible in the streets at all times. The prevention of crime will flow not so much from police patroling but from a vital community in which all regular users of the streets recognize that they constitute the "eyes and ears" of the community—sensitive to any nuances of change, alert to any lurking dangers, prepared to become personally involved. Like Newman she feels that the environmental structure is of prime importance, and calls for thoughtful planning in which due consideration is given to the human aspects and the way in which urban settings can best facilitate social interaction.

There is clearly a need to delve much deeper into all the ramifications of the criminal triad, and of the overall impact that knowledge of, and fear of, crime has for people. This is an aspect of crime that has been far removed from the concerns of most criminologists. Even within victimology the focus has tended to remain on the immediate interaction between criminal and victim. Yet the key factor differentiating crime from other wrongdoing is that it is presumed to cause harm to the society at large. From this perspective it behooves us to measure the nature of that harm.

The 1967 President's Commission on Crime noted the impact that a high crime rate has on people's perceptions of the community, and how it affects their daily behavior—the involvement in the life of the community; the willingness to move about freely, particularly at night; the transitory nature of people's life as they search for safer areas.

Conklin[56] is one of the few criminologists who have devoted a full study to the subject. He warns against the danger of excessive personal precautions against crime, which might become pathological. People may get trapped in houses that they have barred too effectively; guns, bought for protection, may go off suddenly, killing innocent people. Sometimes the very efforts made to secure personal protection may hinder the efforts at a community interaction of the type described by Jacobs. In setting up protective devices, barriers also become erected that hinder easy and natural contacts among neighbors.

The French sociologist Durkheim,[57] in a theoretical presentation that has had much influence on modern criminological thinking, claimed that crime, in reasonable proportions, might serve a functional purpose in helping to integrate the community as it united against criminal outsiders. This is a theme that has been used by other writers who see conflict as being an important integrative force in society.[58] Conklin, however, takes issue with Durkheim and suggests that "crime often drives people apart by creating distrust and suspicion."[59]

The consequences of crime are in fact varied. A community's resilience is often severely tested. While the desire to ensure one's own personal security is understandable, the best protection is probably vouchsafed when community bonds are strengthened, and neighbors provide mutual assurances of support.

Notes

1. See Irving M. Piliavin, Judith Rodin, and Jane Allyn Piliavin, "Good Samaritanism: An Underground Phenomenon?" *Journal of Personality and*

Social Psychology, 1972, *24*, pp. 392-400; and J.A. Piliavin and I.M. Piliavin, "Effects of Blood on Reactions to a Victim," *Journal of Personality and Social Psychology*, 1972, *23*, pp. 353-361.

2. See discussion in chapter 2 of research by Russell D. Clark and Larry E. Word, "Why Don't Bystanders Help? Because of Ambiguity?" *Journal of Personality and Social Psychology*, 1972, *24*, pp. 392-400.

3. See Bibb Latané and John Darley, *The Unresponsive Bystander: Why Doesn't He Help?* (New York: Appleton-Century-Crofts, 1970), chapter 8, "The Bystander and the Thief," pp. 69-78.

4. Ibid., p. 69.

5. R. Lance Shotland and Margaret K. Straw, "Bystander Response to an Assault: When a Man Attacks a Woman," *Journal of Personality and Social Psychology*, 1976, *34*, pp. 990-999.

6. G. Borofsky, G. Stoll, and L. Meese, "Sex Differences in Bystander Reactions to Physical Assault," *Journal of Experimental Social Psychology*, 1971, *7*, pp. 313-318.

7. John E. Stewart and Daniel A. Cannon, "Effects of Perpetrator Status and Bystander Commitment on Responses to a Simulated Crime," *Journal of Police Science and Administration*, 1977, *5*, p. 318.

8. Donna M. Gelfland, Donald P. Walder, Patrice Hartman, and Brent Page, "Who Reports Shoplifters?—A Field-Experimental Study," *Journal of Personality and Social Psychology*, 1973, *25*, pp. 276-285.

9. Leonard Bickman, "Attitude toward Authority and the Reporting of a Crime," *Sociometry*, 1976, *39*, pp. 76-82.

10. Leonard Bickman and Susan K. Green, "Is Revenge Sweet? The Effect of Attitude toward a Thief on Crime Reporting," *Criminal Justice and Behavior*, 1975, *2*, pp. 101-112.

11. Ted L. Huston, Gilbert Geis, Richard Wright, and Thomas Garrett, "Good Samaritans as Crime Victims," In E. Viano, ed., *Crimes, Victim and Society* (Leiden: Sitjhoff International, 1976).

12. See Janez Pecar, "Involved Bystanders: Examination of a Neglected Aspect of Criminology and Victimology," *International Journal of Contemporary Sociology*, 1972, *9*, p. 81. See also "Involved Bystanders—Victimological Aspects," *Rev. Kriminalist. Kriminol.*, *22*, p. 172, indexed in *Abstracts in Criminology, 12*, p. 76.

13. Marvin E. Wolfgang, *Patterns in Criminal Homicide* (Philadelphia: University of Pennsylvania Press, 1958).

14. Theodor Irwin, "A 16-Year-Old Boy Asks: Does It Pay to Be a Hero?" *Parade*, October 19, 1975, p. 28.

15. John Barbour, "To Samaritans Scars are Minor," *Los Angeles Times*, June 26, 1977, p. 1.

16. See Paul W. Tappan, *Crime, Justice and Correction* (New York: McGraw-Hill, 1960), p. 286.

17. Wolfgang, p. 209.

18. See, for instance, the editorial "Citizens Against Crime," *New York Times*, June 20, 1973, which relates three occasions within a week in which bystanders in New York took an active part in preventing street crimes. The paper notes "a gratifying re-emergence of public co-operation with police efforts to combat crime."

19. Joseph P. Treaster, "Two Young Bike Thieves Kill Youth Who Chased Them," *New York Times, 23*, July 1974.

20. Personal communication from Gilbert Geis and Ted Huston.

21. Thorsten Sellin, *Research Memorandum on Crime in the Depression* (New York: Science Research Council, 1937), pp. 69-70.

22. See Terry Eisenberg, Robert H. Fosen, and Albert S. Glickman, *Police-Community Behavior Patterns* (New York: Praeger, 1973). For a specific experimental program, involving a demilitarized uniform, more in keeping with civilian modes of dress, see James H. Tenzel and Victor Cizanckas, "The Uniform Experiment," *Journal of Police Science and Administration*, 1973, *1*, p. 421.

23. See, for example, Francis Wellman, *The Art of Cross-Examination* (Garden City: Garden City Books, 1948).

24. Michael Ash, "On Witnesses: A Radical Critique of Criminal Court Procedures," *Notre Dame Lawyer*, 1972, *48*, pp. 386-425.

25. Ibid., p. 388.

26. Ibid., p. 399.

27. Laura Banfield and C. David Anderson, "Continuances in the Cook County Criminal Court," *University of Chicago Law Review*, 1968, *35*, p. 261.

28. Kenneth L. Penegar, "Appraising the System of Criminal Law, Its Processes and Administration," *North Carolina Law Review*, 1968, *47*, pp. 69-157.

29. Neil K. Komesar, "A Theoretical Empirical Study of Victims of Crime," *Journal of Legal Studies*, 1973, *2*, pp. 301-322.

30. Frank J. Cannavale, Jr., and William Falcon, *Witness Cooperation: With a Handbook of Witness Management* (Lexington, Mass.: Lexington Books, 1976).

31. Ibid., part II, chapters 2 and 3.

32. Ash, p. 413.

33. James Marshall, *Law and Psychology in Conflict* (Indianapolis: Bobbs-Merrill, 1966).

34. Jerome Frank, *Courts on Trial* (Princeton: Princeton University Press, 1969).

35. See Ronald L. Carlson, "Jailing the Innocent: The Plight of the Material Witness," *Iowa Law Review*, 1969, *55*, p. 1; comment, "Pre-trial Detention of Witnesses," *University of Pennsylvania Law Review*, 1969, *117*, p. 700.

36. Leon S. Sheleff and David Shichor, "Victimological Aspects of Bystander Involvement," *Crime and Delinquency*, (forthcoming).

37. For a number of such instances see William L. Claiborne, "New Yorkers Fight Back: The Tilt toward Vigilantism," *New York*, 1974, pp. 49-53.

38. See Gary T. Marx and Dane Archer, "The Urban Vigilante," *Psychology Today*, January 1973, p. 45.

39. See Richard Brown, "The American Vigilante Tradition," in Hugh Graham and Ted Guss, eds., *Violence in America* (New York: Bantam, 1969). For further discussion of vigilantism and related phenomena, see next chapter.

40. Report, "Preparatory Meeting of Experts in Social Defense (African Region) for the Fourth United Nations Congress on the Prevention of Crime and the Treatment of Offenders," *International Review of Criminal Policy*, no. 27, 1969.

41. George Washnis, *Citizen Involvement in Crime Prevention* (Lexington, Mass.: Lexington Books, 1976).

42. Ibid., p. 1.

43. Ibid.

44. Ibid., p. 7.

45. Ibid., p. 9.

46. For details of various programs, see ibid., chapter 5, "Special Crime Prevention Projects," pp. 69-90.

47. For excellent concise advice on how to act in a wide range of conceivable emergencies, both in order to save oneself and to rescue others, see Anthony Greenback, *The Book of Survival* (New York: Harper and Row, 1967).

48. See C. Varah, *The Samaritans in the 70's* (London: Constable, 1973). For a critical review of their work, see Julian Bell, "The Samaritan Concept of Befriending," *British Journal of Social Work*, 1975, pp. 413-422. Bell argues that by offering to befriend strangers in need, there is a debasement of the traditional notion of friendship. For general discussion of helping programs see L.A. Hoff, *People in Crisis* (Reading, Mass.: Addison-Wesley, 1978).

49. C. Ray Jeffery, *Crime Prevention through Environmental Design* (Beverly Hills: Sage [second edition], 1977), p. 343.

50. Oscar Newman, *Defensible Space: Crime Prevention through Urban Design* (New York: Macmillan, 1972).

51. Ibid., pp. 1-2.

52. Ibid., p. 3.

53. Ibid., pp. 3-4.

54. Jane Jacobs, *The Death and Life of Great American Cities* (New York: Random House, 1961).

55. Ibid., p. 119.

56. John E. Conklin, *The Impact of Crime* (New York: Macmillan, 1975).

57. Emile Durkheim, *The Rules of Sociological Method* (New York: The Free Press, 1938).

58. See Lewis Coser, *The Functions of Social Conflict* (Glencoe, Illinois: The Free Press, 1956).

59. Conklin, p. 68.

**Part II
Law**

5 Historical Survey

There are theoretical assumptions behind, and historical precedents for, the attempt to use active community involvement to prevent crime and protect the public. The theoretical assumptions flow from a feeling that such localized controls may, in the final analysis, be the best means of preserving order and safeguarding rights, as well as an important means of withstanding the encroachments of a professionalized and organized police force, which may often be remote from the immediate concerns of the community and may even pose larger problems of total domination of the community by the centralized government.

The historical precedents are found in the continual attempts at all stages of societal development to maintain localized machinery for preserving order at the local level. It is often only when the increase in societal complexities undermines such an approach and after the deficiencies of a localized system have reached intolerable levels that the community will agree to surrender some of its authority.

Seagle[1] has argued that the protection of the population from rampant crime has traditionally been one of the key factors inducing people to accept the authority of a centralized power. He sees administration of justice as being the first major "social service" offered by governments to their people, long before accepted modern concepts of social welfare such as free subsidized education, health care, unemployment benefits, and other similar social programs. In the early stages of government, there were three major functions—the waging of war, the collecting of taxes, and the administration of justice; it was only the latter function that was directly beneficial to the public and thus conducive to public support. In fact, as Seagle might have added, part of the collection of revenue came specifically through the administration of justice in the form of fines levied. Allen, in his analysis of the Queen's Peace,[2] has noted the important part that the need to bolster up the monarch's coffers played in the development of the criminal law. He claims that much of "constitutional history could be written in terms of the struggle of the sovereign for a living wage. . . . Even in days when he was by far the wealthiest man in the country, it is probable that he could ill have spared the profits which accrued to him from the misdeeds of his errant subjects."[3]

Yet, the surrender of local control has never been complete—for a centralized police force is almost always confronted by the paradox that, however organized it may be, it is dependent on public cooperation for its success;

without victims and bystanders being prepared to report crime, and testify as to their knowledge of it, the police are unable to function at a satisfactory level.

There are various reasons why such cooperation may not be forthcoming. In some cases the public bypass the law-enforcement units, preferring to mete out their own brand of justice, ranging from self-help, restitutive measures to various forms of punitive actions, especially against outsiders; in other cases, the particular intimacies of kin and community may lead to a reluctance to take any steps against the wrongdoer.

In many respects, bystander behavior in combating crime might be seen as both reflecting and forging the character of a society. The calls issuing at present for greater community involvement are an expression of the present breakdown of the community spirit, and the sense of a need to restore it. The concern for the present incapacity of communities to ensure their own safety and security are part of a large awareness of the failings of modern society. Writers such as Jeffery, Jacobs, Newman, and Conklin[4] are claiming that the crime problem is not merely, or even mainly, a problem of the aberrant actions of the wrongdoer, but of the structure and nature of the community. Other more radical thinkers have also called for community controls in the form of neighborhood police and even parallel local courts.

The call for better community protection against crime is an echo of the larger issue of reinstituting community in the modern age. Tönnies[5] himself had envisaged a stage in the future where the most extreme forms of impersonal *Gesellschaft* life would inevitably generate a need for reintroducing aspects of the *Gemeinschaft*. In the light of the present emerging accent on reconstituting direct, constant, and activist involvement by the community in crime prevention, it would seem worthwhile to investigate how such systems have worked in the past—the advantages that accrue to the community, the demands that are made on the citizenry, the effect on the rate of crime, and the pitfalls and even dangers of such law-enforcement systems with their occasional selectivity, inefficiency, and/or cruelty.

Kin's Protection

Most early societies have relied on some form of active citizen involvement in crime control and the preservation of social order. In its earliest forms, this can take the form of self-help or the blood feud; despite this apparent anarchic practice, in reality there is a close societal scrutiny of the operations, with clear rules as to the rights of the victim, the liability of the wrongdoer, the familial relationships that are involved (for example, which relatives are obliged to help the contending parties), and the means of resolving any conflict that might ensue. Even if there is no law enforcement by any centralized organ of the society, the members act within clearly defined norms as to what is acceptable and what is not. It is not necessary to enter the debate as to whether or not the customs of preliterate and tribal societies constitute law—suffice it to note that the protection afforded by kinsmen and clansmen formed the original model for crime control; modern manifestations of this are to be seen in the blood feuds that are still part of the accepted norms of some societies.

There is little published material on the blood feud; and much popularized thinking on the subject involves gaudy accounts of almost indiscriminate and endless bloodletting. In reality, most societies that have obligatory norms of revenge for harm done also have definitive rules for mediating between the rival parties and for an amicable resolution of their conflict.[6]

In lesser offenses, compensation would be made, and in the course of time, generally at an early stage of development, there would be provisions for a 'composition' also for killing, with the culprit and his family making material compensation to the family of the victim. In some cases the compensation would be predetermined; in other cases it would be subject to bargaining between the sides, often through a recognized mediator.

For our purposes it is important to note that both wrongdoer and victim are dependent on their kinsmen for support; it is the awareness of such support that gives people a sense of security in their everyday activities despite the absence of any policing or punishing authorities; it is the threat of such support for a potential victim that serves as an effective deterrent for any potential wrong-doer. In Seagle's words, "In primitive societies which have not yet developed judicial institutions it is true to say that every man is his brother's keeper. An individual almost always has rights only as he is the member of a kinship group. . . . The legal system rests upon collective solidarity. The central reality of primitive law is the solidarity of the kinship group. . . . Peace of the kindred antedates the peace of the king or chief."[7] In such a system it is the "eyes and ears" of the kin that serve as a constant guarantee of a person's protection.

Yet it is not just in small tribal societies that such influence is felt. Often at much later stages of societal evolution its impact is noted, even when centralized law-enforcement and judicial bodies exist. Phillpotts[8] has suggested that in some countries of Europe the kindred was a relevant factor in social life for a long period of time, providing both support and surety in the case of criminal action and aid in the case of natural disasters and personal misfortunes. She has documented the existence of the kindred in parts of northern Europe in the seventeenth century in Denmark, the fifteenth century in Belgium and Friesland, and in Sweden in the fourteenth century.

Seen in its broadest conceptualization, the bystander becomes the basis of early law. The norms of the society obligate response, not only for bystanders immediately and directly present, but also for those who are subsequently informed of the commission of a wrongful act. It is up to such bystanders to apprehend the wrongdoer and to exact the penalty by which amends may be made—often without the existence of centralized organs for the administration of justice, yet clearly within the recognized norms of the society.

It is interesting to note that where such norms still prevail in the modern world, as in some Mediterranean societies, for instance, they may be of more obligatory power than the laws themselves; sometimes the modern police force has no alternative but to allow, or even encourage, the formal resolution of such a feud, according to the internal norms of a subculture, in the full knowledge that the coercive authority of police, courts, and corrections systems, in and of themselves, are inadequate to terminate the feud and to restore peace and order to the community.[9]

The King's Peace

As the power of the kin wanes, so there is a need to ensure protection from other sources. The "King's" or "Queen's Peace," with its official centralized organs of social control, emerges only as the end result of a long evolutionary process in which the dwindling role of the kindred is slowly replaced by the more meaningful community association. Even after the state's power is clearly entrenched, with an advanced system of administration of justice, the everyday operations of the system depend, to a large extent, on extensive public support—from victim, bystander, family, and the community at large.

Many of those who have written of the earlier stages of legal development have, in their emphasis on the more formalized aspects of the law, tended to ignore how the law was actually implemented. It was one thing to formally declare, for instance, that theft, assault, or murder were to be treated as a crime and as a breach of the peace, and not merely as a tort action between the aggrieved party and the wrongdoer, and their respective family groups; it was another thing to actually enforce such provisions. In effect, whatever the formal provisions of the law, the success of law enforcement remained dependent on active kin and community involvement.

Thus, Calhoun,[10] in his analysis of the Greek law in ancient times, notes that in the fourth century B.C. there was still resort to self-help, alongside the court system. He writes, "Among the Greeks of the heroic age, as in other primitive societies, the individual depended for personal security chiefly upon the compensation which would be demanded by his family, in the event of his being slain, from the family of the slayer."[11]

In Roman law the obligations of bystander were spelled out more clearly, applicable not merely to kin or community, but to any innocent bystander who by chance happened to be in the vicinity of a potentially dangerous situation. Lintott writes that "*fidem implorare* and *quiritare* are the common phrases used to describe a cry by an injured or threatened person who expects those near to use force on his behalf. . . . Thus in a state which had no police force to speak of, it was not only proper but expected to answer such an appeal. This kind of communal self-defence was the rule in many ancient and medieval societies and in some cases even required by law."[12]

Lintott notes particularly the recourse to neighbors in the case of a theft, with often drastic consequences. "It would be natural to deal with a thief by summoning the aid of neighbors. . . . If the thief came by night or used a weapon the proper course was to draw attention and to gather supporters by shouts: then, if he was not killed in the struggle to seize him, it would be possible to execute the thief after a hearing before a council of neighbors."[13]

The system of community involvement was extensively used in feudal times, receiving its most explicit expression in the frankpledge system, which was instituted in England in the period before the Norman conquest and then subsequently expanded and embellished by the Norman conquerors. In many respects this was a unique system, differing in many salient aspects from practices followed in the rest of Europe, though having certain similarities with systems of community involvement found in Asia, especially Japan and China.

The frankpledge system provides an example of the manner in which societies with much centralized power resolved the tremendous problems of ensuring social tranquility and personal security for its citizens in all parts of the realm, despite primitive means of communication, and the limited resources of personnel and matériel then available.

The frankpledge system involved the mutual responsibilities and guarantees that citizens provided for each other, such responsibility comprising not so much the need to go to the aid of a victim as the need to apprehend any wrongdoer within the network of relationships that were established.

Jeudwine gives a concise description of the manner in which the frankpledge system came to replace the kindred system, and of the key aspects of its operation:

> The kinsfolk gradually cease to be considered in the courts as responsible for the fault of the accused.
>
> Their place is taken in the township by the frankpledge, by which the hundred protects or ought to protect itself against disorderly men dwelling within its borders. . . .
>
> The theory of the frankpledge was that everyone above twelve was to be registered in a tithing, a very small body of which each would know the other, in which each would have a common responsibility for the other's acts—an admirable conception so long as conditions made it possible.[14]

In his authoritative review of the frankpledge system, Morris quotes the definition of a twelfth-century writer as "all men in every vill of the whole realm were by custom under obligation to be in the suretyship of ten (or tithing), so that if one of the ten commit an offence, the nine have him to justice."[15] Morris adds his own succinct interpretation: "Frankpledge, then, was a system of compulsory, collective bail fixed for individuals not after their arrest for crime, but as a safeguard in anticipation of it."[16]

With the kinship system breaking down and with the centralized government limited in its capacity to ensure the security—and thereby also the loyalty—of its citizens, an intricate system of community involvement was set up, whereby the citizens themselves were to bear major responsibility for preserving order within the community.

Morris notes some confusion and debate as to the actual origins of the system. He notes the first manifestations of the system in Anglo-Saxon times in London, where the citizens

> were organized into groups of ten, each with a chief man to direct the other nine in the discharge of the duties set forth in the ordinance. The tens were arranged in larger groups called . . . hundreds, the head man of each directing ten heads of tithings. These tithings were, however, far from being frankpledge groups; for their members did not act as sureties for each other. Their object was merely the capture and punishment of thieves, and the re-imbursing of their own members for stolen property.[17]

However, although tens (or tithings) and hundreds were the clear numerical basis for the early practice in London, the frankpledge system, in its full flowering, was closely tied to territorial divisions, even though the same terminology was used. Those areas of England using the frankpledge system (about two-thirds of the country) were divided into territorial units known as hundreds, which in turn were further subdivided into tithings. According to Morris, the territorial basis was "essential to the successful pursuit of a thief, not only that the tithing live in the neighborhood of the crime, but that the members live near enough together for co-operation."[18]

Morris explains the extension and the obligatory nature of the frankpledge system with mutual sureties being guaranteed, as a consequence of "governmental action of a deliberate and vigorous nature prompted by the imminent danger to which the public peace was exposed from the ordinary freemen of the realm."[19] More specifically the sophisticated and all-embracing nature of the system seems to have been also directly related to the dangers to which the Norman conquerors were exposed at the hands of their Anglo-Saxon subjects. Morris argues that William the Conqueror extended the system "in a drastic regulation for the avowed protection of his followers from assassination—a mandate by which he held the whole hundred accountable. . . ."[20] Stubbs, the great constitutional historian, also suggests that the Anglo-Saxon frankpledge system was likely used by the Norman conquerors as a "precaution taken by the new rulers against the avoidance of justice by the absconding or harboring of criminals."[21]

Whereas, before the conquest, suretyship was mainly voluntary, and perhaps of particular importance for anybody with a bad reputation, after the conquest, and in the light of ongoing resentment against the foreigners, it became obligatory for everyone. The Normans were introducing a system of collective punishment, based on collective responsibility, as a means of maintaining control over their antagonistic subject people. "Now that the government had to guard carefully against the complicity of sureties in the crime and flight of their pledges, the best way, both to prevent their running away together and to collect fines in case of flight, was to make every man in the community responsible for every other man."[22]

The development of the frankpledge system bears further testimony to the fact of the close interrelationship between political factors and the means used to enforce compliance with the law, particularly the criminal law.

Nevertheless, even though the frankpledge was expanded in an effort to impose order where resentment against the government was rife, and even though the commitment of citizens to preserve the peace was necessitated by the lack of professional policing agents, Morris emphasizes that the widespread use of the frankpledge system in England was "one of the clearest manifestations of strong central government in the England of the twelfth and thirteenth centuries."

In contrast, on the Continent, the local peace was preserved by direct mutuality between the local lord and his vassals, the former owing the latter protection in return for their loyalty and work on his behalf. The Continental system arose out of concerns and considerations similar to those of the British—of seeking a means of preserving order and social stability—but differing historical and geographical factors led to different approaches being adopted. Ganshof, in his major treatise on the feudal system, notes that "the Frankish monarchy, partly as a consequence of an immense territorial expansion which it underwent during the reign of Charlemagne, lacked an efficient administration, and the structure of the state was inadequate to the tasks which it had to fulfill. Charlemagne and his advisers had to take account of this, and they hoped to find in vassalage a means of remedying the defect."[23] The Continental system of feudalism—reaching its peak in the twelfth century at the same time that the English frankpledge system reached its zenith—was a hierarchical system with most of the common people under the vassalage of a local lord who offered them protection, defense, and warranty in return for various services and oaths of fidelity that vassals owed him. Ganshof explains that "the lord was bound to come to his vassal's aid when the latter was unjustly attacked, and that he was bound to defend him against his enemies . . . to defend [him] in a court of law . . . [and] if he had granted him a fief, he was bound to guarantee him its possession by defending it against any attempts which might be made to deprive him of it."[24]

So, whereas in England it was the common people who bore major responsibility for keeping peace by their mutual responsibilities to the king, on the Continent it was the lord who was obliged to keep the peace as part of his obligations to those under his control. Somewhat paradoxically it was the stronger centralized power of the English king that, in the long run, led to a greater activation of the populace at large in maintaining the peace; related to this was the fact that the British resisted the establishment of a professional police force long after most countries of the Continent had recognized the need for such a force.

For over 200 years the English frankpledge system seems to have worked with a fair amount of success. But complete success was never attained. The very fact of a close relationship among the members of a hundred or tithing often made the members reluctant to take action against the wrongdoer. Not only would they be remiss in apprehending one of their own people; in some cases they would readily take an oath of compurgation, testifying as to the innocence of a friend or neighbor, even when they had little or no knowledge as to the alleged event, and their oath was tantamount to perjury—although some writers claim that the oath was used to attest mainly as to the general good character of the suspected person and not specifically to the alleged crime. Allen cuts through the key weakness of the system with his remark that "a little elementary psychology might have warned that small groups with local pride were more likely to shield than to arraign their brethren, and were ready to treat an oath very lightly . . . in order to shield the malefactor."[25] By the thirteenth century there was a general awareness of a disturbingly high crime rate. According to Morris:

> The system of frankpledge had clearly lost its old effectiveness both in preventing crime and in securing the punishment of criminals. . . . The ordinary members of the tithing . . . were . . . being farther and farther separated from direct touch with the police and criminal administration. To bring home to each locality a realizing sense of its responsibility, therefore, Edward I enacted a new law making the people of each hundred and franchise responsible for robberies and damages arising from the failure to produce the offenders. The half-mark usually paid by the tithing for the escape of an offending member . . . had now come to represent a far slighter value, the payment of which was inadequate to spur the community to capture a fugitive neighbor with whom it was in sympathy. . . . By the end of the thirteenth century the clumsy plan of utilizing the frankpledge tithing as constabulary had, in short, become obscured. . . .[26]

At this stage, too, there was a growing tendency to use special peace officers, sheriffs, and constables.[27] In the future it was their work that would play an increasingly important role in preserving social order. But even so, the part-time nature of these offices with only token remuneration meant that security in the home and the community and on the highway continued to be a function of the community's willingness and capacity to cooperate.

Morris sums up the impact of the frankpledge system as having contributed to arousing an awareness of allegiance to the king through having his power directly brought to bear on the individual. As for its specific peace-keeping functions, Morris argues that, whatever its deficiencies, it seems "to have secured in an effective manner the observance of the king's peace by the peasants of England, until at the end of the thirteenth century the plan failed because of a changed standard of economic values, as well as through . . . an inefficient system of gaol delivery."[28]

The frankpledge system provided an important example of community control over harmful acts committed; of community involvement in combating and preventing crime; and of community responsibility for the welfare of all. Just as the kindred system lingered on with various residual effects on the Continent, as pointed out by Phillpotts, so the heritage of communal involvement and responsibility affected later crime control and security practices in England. Morris claims that survival of the system may be noted as late as the nineteenth century. There were even occasions when the concern for increasing crime and disorder led to calls for a renewal of the frankpledge system.

Although most of the English historians have referred to the unique nature of the frankpledge system, and clearly differentiated it from the Continental practice, there are close similarities to systems of community involvement that were set up in China and Japan. The resemblances between the systems relate not only to the use of community obligations in the preservation of order, but also to the numerical basis of ten as the foundation of the system, and the skillful manipulation of the system by powerful centralized government, originally also alien conquerors, to ensure the compliance and the loyalty of the population in the far-flung rural areas.

Parallel Systems in Asia

The Chinese system—*pao-chia*—was originally set up in the eleventh century, but it was not until the Ching dynasty in the seventeenth century that the system was given its full elaboration, as the new Manchu rulers attempted—in a manner similar to the Norman conquerors in England—to consolidate their power.

Hsiao has described in some detail how effectively the new conquerors of China utilized the *pao-chia* system. "Instead of relying solely on military power, they undertook to maintain their rule by making use of the techniques and institutions of control that had been developed by previous dynasties. As soon as the new rulers entered Peking, they adopted the entire administrative and subadministrative structure left behind by the Ming dynasty. . . . The *pao-chia* was one of the most important subadministrative apparatuses which constituted that structure."[29]

At an early stage of the dynasty an edict was issued which included in its sixteen principles the exhortation to strengthen the *pao-chia* system, to prevent robbery and thievery, as well as the warning not to protect lawless elements in order to avoid involvement in conspiracies.[30]

Ch'u gives a succinct summary of the system:

> It was a magistrate's duty to organize the households in his district into
> units of *pai* (10 households), *chia* (100 households) and *pao* (1,000
> households) and to appoint heads for each unit. . . . The magistrate
> issued annually to each household a door placard listing the name, age,
> and occupation of the family head and the names of other persons in
> the household, including relatives and servants. . . .
>   . . . The fundamental function of *pao-chia* was to set up a police
> network to detect lawbreakers, particularly robbers and bandits. Under
> some officials it also incorporated such functions as encouraging good
> conduct and thus improving local custom. The main idea behind the
> *pao-chia* system was that one's activities could hardly escape the eyes
> and ears of one's neighbors, and if the neighbors were organized and a
> register of their households kept, it would be difficult for strangers and
> lawbreakers to hide among the law-abiding residents.[31]

A headman would be appointed over each *pao*, whose task it was to report
unlawful activities, to keep an eye on suspicious strangers, to submit regular
reviews of activity, and to record the comings and goings of people into the area;
failure to carry out these functions would lead to punitive sanctions.

Ch'u argues that the system was not completely effective, and criticizes the
many writers who have exaggerated its effectiveness and have overemphasized
the supposedly heavy punishments meted out to those who failed to report
crimes. According to him the system was only of limited value, and it was only
in rare instances that the magistrate would successfully utilize it.[32] Hsiao
concurs partly in noting that the "efficacy of the system did not measure up to
its theoretical usefulness. The government often found it difficult to enforce its
operation; it was unable even to establish uniformity in its structure."[33]
Nevertheless, he does concede that the system did make some contribution in
strengthening the centralized government. Indeed, its major impact might have
been not so much in stamping out crime at the individual level against the local
inhabitants, but in deterring group actions, conspiracy, the instigation of riots,
and so on, because of the mutual fear and suspicion that were instilled. In fact,
whatever defects the system might have had at the local level, the centralized
government related to it favorably, more concerned about the control of
potential subversion than about the actual crime rate in the local communities,
and sufficiently content in the capacity of the system to control the subversive
activities. Hsiao notes various emperors in the eighteenth and nineteenth
centuries who emphasized the importance of the system, tried to strengthen and
expand it, and used it effectively to suppress uprisings and insurrections. He
quotes an edict from 1799 that stated that "the method of *pao-chia* . . . as a
means of detecting wicked and criminal persons and suppressing banditry at its
source, is truly an excellent way to maintain local order."[34]

An 1815 edict exemplifies the manner in which the system was used not merely for maintaining peace and order in the community, but also, and particularly, for forestalling any potentially subversive activities against the government.

> If there are suspicious persons in the neighborhood, they should be reported immediately to the government. If seditious criminals are apprehended, not only will the person who makes the initial report be rewarded with money and official appointment, but the ten households in his *pai* will also be suitably rewarded. If, however, seditious criminals are harbored and no report is made . . . the households that harbor them will be held jointly responsible.[35]

However, these attempts to utilize the *pao-chia* system not only for peace and order in the local community but for control of subversive elements were successful only under certain conditions.

> It appears that the *pao-chia* proved an effective deterrent only in times of relative tranquility . . . but in a period of general unrest the *pao-chia* was no more able than any other instrument of imperial control to operate with its peacetime efficiency (or more accurately, semi-efficiency). It was, in fact, outmoded by the changed circumstances.[36]

In fact, the system was used less and less in the nineteenth century, and then mainly in attempts to exploit the system for the purpose of coping with the group problem of 'banditry," as the Ching dynasty entered its years of decline. On the whole, it was falling into disuse because the social order itself was crumbling. As Hsiao notes, "The dynasty as a whole was in a process of disintegration; inevitably, the institutions of the imperial system—including the *pao-chia*—also rapidly deteriorated."[37] Given the weakness and the distance of the central government, and the violence and the proximity of the bandits, the average person "found it more prudent not to incur the wrath of desperados than to fulfil a legal obligation which the government often failed to exact."[38] It would thus appear that, just as was the experience in the West, a system of localized control on behalf of a centralized government must be predicated on the strength of the latter.

In Japan, a similar system was used, originally adopted from the Chinese. Clifford, in his analysis of crime in Japan, claims that much of the willingness of the public to help cope with crime may be traced to the tradition of mutual concern and mutual aid, as developed in the *gonin-kumi* system, whereby "groupings of five families under a leader, kept law and order among themselves and were held responsible to deliver up an offender."[39] In rural Japan, a similar system was set up known as *burakukai*, based on household units.[40] It fulfilled a wide range of collective functions.

Although the *gonin-kumi* system was formally abolished at the time of the

Meijii Restoration, these family groupings were replaced by neighborhood groups, first informally, and later, in the early 1940s on a more formalized basis, known as *tonari-kumi*, whereby groups of ten families each were set up for purposes of mutual assistance and strengthening national morale during the war, a further example of exploitation of a community's desire for security by imposing also forms of allegiance to the central government.

After the war the system was abolished, but Clifford claims that "the system still survived informally and still provides a powerful incentive for individuals to meet group or neighborhood expectations. Involving such informal groups in community action can then be a powerful control."[41] Clifford stresses that public participation in helping activities is deeply embedded in Japanese culture and firmly established in practice. These features are expressed also in the realm of crime control, aimed not necessarily at actually interfering to stop a crime and apprehend a criminal, but mainly in a wide range of voluntary responses to the treatment and rehabilitation of offenders, with individuals, organizations, and businesses devoting time and effort to these tasks.

Clifford is arguing basically that, because of values central to the Japanese culture, there is a greater propensity for the public to show concern for the plight of a fellow human being, and this is a significant factor in making for a low crime rate in Japan, whether expressed through a formal control system as in the *gonin-kumi* or the *tonari-kumi*, or through informal voluntary associations that sprung up after they were abolished. He stresses that these values lead not so much to a willingness to intervene in the typical bystander situation where a citizen is suddenly confronted by the plight of a stranger, but rather in overall ongoing concern for the welfare of the community and in participation in activities calculated to reduce crimogenic situations. Clifford notes "a vast reserve of community counseling and community potential that can be brought to bear on any individual to help him (or coerce him) to avoid crime-creating situations. This is a source of community control and support that is extensively used by the Japanese authorities at all levels."[42]

In England also, with the disappearance of the frankpledge system, alternative means of activating public participation were sought. As already noted, residual aspects of the frankpledge system persisted; but the most significant institutional arrangement conducive to public participation now became the hue and cry, which had existed contemporaneously with the frankpledge as a separate system, but gained an added significance after the abolition of the frankpledge system.

Hue and Cry

The concept of hue and cry has a long history in the development of English law, yet it is rarely given any more than a passing reference in most histories of

English constitutional and criminal law. There is as yet no overall treatment of the subject, as has been done for the frankpledge and other parts of English legal history. Yet it seems clear from the evidence that the hue and cry was an integral and important aspect of community involvement in law enforcement at all stages of English history. Holdsworth, in his major analysis of the history of English law, deals with the origins of the hue and cry in the context of a discussion of self-help in Anglo-Saxon times. He notes that ". . . where an owner of property was allowed to retake property which had been stolen or lost . . . the owner must at once raise the hue and cry. All were liable if they did not assist when the hue and cry was raised. . . . So stringent was the duty of assisting the injured man that a person who allowed a thief to escape, or concealed in any way the theft, was liable to pay the thief's wergild."[43]

Holdworth also quotes one of the earliest direct references to the hue and cry in Anglo-Saxon times. Where cattle had been stolen, and the hue and cry had been raised, then it was necessary "that every man of them who has heard the orders should be aidful to others, as well in tracing as in pursuit, so long as the track is known; . . . either to ride or to go . . . thither where most need is," and "that no search be abandoned either to the north of the march or to the south before every man who has a horse has ridden one riding."[44]

References to the hue and cry are to be found in legislation and documents throughout the centuries. In the thirteenth century, both the liabilities of the hundreds and the obligations of hue and cry were given legislative basis by the Statute of Winchester of 1285. From the context it seems clear that the systems of frankpledge and of hue and cry were parallel and complementary. Cam writes that "anyone who considered that the king's peace was being broken could raise the hue and cry, and then everyone within earshot was bound to help. . . . The frankpledge groups were penalized if any member of a tithing escaped scot-free after committing a crime."[45] After the abolition of the frankpledge system, collective punishments were still imposed on local communities for their failure to respond to the hue and cry, although the actual responsibility for raising the hue and cry would generally now devolve upon the official constabulary.

In general, it is difficult to know to what extent the hue and cry was effective and enforced. There is a paucity of material, and there is a danger of generalizing on the basis of isolated reported instances. Bellamy maintains that already in the fifteenth century "there was a definite reluctance on the part of the local inhabitants to participate" and adds that "by the sixteenth century men were wont to say 'God restore your losses, I have other business at this time.' "[46]

Radzinowicz notes that although in the eighteenth century there was still some reliance on the hue and cry, there is clear evidence of problems in activating it. An act of 1735 set out to remedy the position where neglect and delay often led to felons escaping, without any responsibility being attached to anyone; in addition, since the police worked only part-time for nominal remuneration, they could not always be relied on. Thus provision was now made for punishing any constable who was remiss in raising the hue and cry or who failed to take part in it.[47] The position of the police was unenviable. As Pringle[48] has noted, the police would often be in an awkward dilemma when trying to raise the hue and cry; the populace could not always be relied upon to respond, while the consequence of raising the hue and cry might well evoke a response from friends of the wrongdoer, who would try to free him.

Finally, the system gradually fell into disuse as experience taught that there might be other means of activating citizens, such as by offering rewards to those who contributed to crime control. In Radzinowicz's words, "The ancient institution of Hue and Cry, of hot and instantaneous pursuit, had almost died out and its place was taken by a new device with private interest as its motive power."[49] Radzinowicz devotes much of one of his four volumes on the history of the criminal law to a detailed recounting of the reward system as a major factor of peace-keeping at a stage when community control, in the hundreds and through the hue and cry, was disappearing, but before a full-scale constabulary had been set up.

Aware of the limited powers of the sheriff, the justices of the peace, and other officials, many of whom were unpaid, part-time, and temporary workers, and aware of the increasing reluctance of the public to cooperate in crime control, particularly in London and the other large cities, the legislature passed a law in 1692 "for encouraging the apprehending of Highwaymen"[50] which offered rewards to anyone for helping to capture criminals. Accomplices were expressly included in the category of those entitled to a reward, and enticements to accomplices became an accepted and important means of fighting crime, thereby laying the basis for the use of informers and agents provocateurs in modern times.

Radzinowicz writes that "the incentives were many. Offenders were promised impunity; honest citizens, exemption from performing certain public services."[51] In addition there were monetary rewards, which could be considerable; in the sixteenth century the capture of a highwayman entitled the citizen to a reward of forty pounds. "As the years went by it became part of the policy of the Legislature to enact an increasing number of such provisions, until the whole body of the criminal law became permeated with statutory rewards."[52]

In addition to the official rewards offered by governmental authorities, often private rewards would also be offered, this being particularly noted in times of ongoing disorder and in the wake of particularly vicious crimes. Insurance companies played a leading role in these private offers of reward, particularly in the case of arson; also active in the announcement of rewards were voluntary associations formed for the purpose of prosecuting felons, there being no official prosecution office at the time.[53]

In addition the role of typical prosocial community behavior may be noted. "Friendly neighbors and other inhabitants, prompted by fear, by sympathy with the victim or by professional or economic ties, joined together to raise money by subscription in order to make the bait more tempting."[54]

Legislation also made provision for compensating any citizen harmed in the attempt to apprehend a criminal; the police also were entitled to rewards, this being an acceptable supplement to their meager earnings.

In the early nineteenth century, these practices came under attack, being seen as blood money, and often evoking abhorrence in the public. At the same time, those who attacked the system of rewards agreed to the need to at least compensate for expenses incurred by those willing to undertake the often onerous and expensive task of helping to prosecute a criminal. Given the primitive, almost nonexistent state of the public prosecution, in many instances it was only the willingness of private prosecutors to take the suspected wrongdoer to court that would ensure conviction.

A proposal for a change in the automatic system of rewards occasioned much debate as opposing viewpoints were presented on the utility and the morality of the reward system. Finally a compromise was agreed upon whereby the fixed and automatic system of payment, as laid down by Parliament for the more serious offenses, was replaced by a discretionary system in which the court was empowered to determine, in each particular case, whether a payment should be made to anyone involved in apprehending the convicted wrongdoer, and the sum to be paid.

While the system of predetermined "statutory rewards" was greatly minimized, the parallel approach of advertised rewards continued—both by private groupings and by public authorities, more particularly at the local level. Sometimes the local officials themselves would take the lead in raising money to advertise a reward. Radzinowicz concludes that "public rewards by advertisement had thus become an important part of the machinery of police. At that time it was as natural to announce a reward as it would be today to report a crime to the police."[55]

Running as an undercurrent through much of the debate on, and the development of, these rules and practices of the reward system was an ambivalence as to the degree to which the state could commit itself to a total onslaught on the scourge of crime, without making serious inroads into the freedom of the common people. A reluctance to set up official full-time police and prosecution units was obligating the state to make alternative provisions for ensuring effective procedures for combating crime. Thus, while continually concerned about the dangers to life, body, property, and honor, the society was no less apprehensive of the dangers to its liberty that would possibly be entailed in a professional police. Long after most other countries in Europe had set up a full-fledged professional police, the English were still wary as to the dangers to their personal rights that might arise out of such a force.

Pringle[56] has shown how the struggle in the eighteenth century by the Fielding brothers—Henry and John, who were magistrates in London—for a recognized police force was hindered by their own hesitancy in presenting outright the case for a professional police, and their constant resort to devious tactics in attaining the money and resources necessary to equip and maintain such a force; as magistrates they effectively developed the Bow Street Runners into a unit that became renowned throughout the country, and was to become the basis for the establishment of the police force in the nineteenth century.

Yet whatever success they had in setting up the force was limited; they continued to be dependent on public support and aid. They made particularly effective use of London newspapers, including the specizalized *Police Gazette*, in order to make appeals to the public to cooperate and in order to publish announcements of specific crimes that had been committed.

However, during this period, it was not the Bow Street Runners or the efforts of casual bystanders and witnesses that was the key to law enforcement, but the activities of a group of people known as thief-takers, who, for commission, would attempt to trace stolen goods and return them to their rightful owners, acting as go-betweens between victim and thief, generally without the intervention of the police at all.[57] Victims would often prefer to avail themselves of the good offices of such thief-takers rather than reporting the crime to the authorities, as the former course was often the more efficient, giving them better prospects of recovering their goods, without the cumbersome procedure of prosecuting the criminal in a court of law, especially since in most instances the prosecution would be a private one, at the victims' expense.

Unfortunately, perhaps inevitably, the system led to abuses. Many of the thief-takers were criminals themselves, their knowledge of the criminal under-world being a useful quality in their new job. In many cases they would actually be in collusion with the thieves, arranging for the theft in order that the victim would request aid, the commission later to be shared between thief and thief-taker, both secure in the knowledge that, with the return of the property, there was almost no chance that the crime would be reported to the police, or if reported, that the police would take any further steps. In other cases, the thief-taker might need or desire a pardon for past crimes; here, in order to gain a pardon, he would actually have to apprehend the criminal, and Pringle reports instances where the thief-taker would instigate the crime, and then hand over the unsuspecting accomplice, often a young boy, to the police.[58]

Finally, as the dimensions of the practice became known, together with its abuses and the occasional exploitation of innocent people, there was an outcry, and the system was gradually abandoned. In these cases may be seen the operation of a system where feigned concern for the welfare of a victim was being used for further exploitation. Bystander behavior in these cases was devoid of any concern for the plight of the victim, and stemmed solely from the greedy desire to exploit.

While the hue and cry, the rewards, and the thief-takers were all oriented to remedying the consequences of a crime after its commission, the principle of watch and ward was set up to use citizens in preventive functions. This institution also had a long history. Pike notes the existence of rules relating to watch and ward in the thirteenth century.[59] Citizens would be called upon to patrol the streets and guard the gates and entrances to the cities and villages at night. Special emphasis was placed on close surveillance of strangers. Similar arrangements and rules remained in force until the nineteenth century, although here again Radzinowicz makes several references to the incompetence and corruption of those in the watch and ward.[60] Allen dismisses the watch and ward as a "farce" and suggests that for the most part they were "less of a safeguard than a nuisance, with their perpetual banging of staves and bawling the hour throughout the night."[61] Often the inefficiency of the official watch and ward led many people and companies who could afford it to employ their own private watchmen.

In the final analysis, though, all the procedures adopted and the rules laid down—the frankpledge, the watch and ward, the hue and cry, the rewards, on the one hand, and the sheriffs, the justices of the peace, the Bow Street runners, on the other—were dependent on the capacity to act vigorously against wrongdoers, specifically to arrest them and bring them to trial. It was here that the systems often broke down. Lacking a police and prosecution, because of the commitment to liberalism and individualistic values—it often became extremely difficult to arrest, indict, convict, and punish wrongdoers.

Citizen's Arrest

Pringle[62] notes that the weakness of the policing and prosecution systems, and the many safeguards provided the suspect, made it inordinately difficult to convict a criminal; he argues that the obverse aspect of this difficulty was to impose excessive punishments when anybody was convicted. The severity of punishment was linked to the liberality of the procedure. Since there was little fear of being caught and punished, deterrence was sought mainly by a severe sentencing policy. Unfortunately most writers gloss over the issue of arrest, yet much of the actual operation of the criminal law was dependent on the manner in which this aspect of the law was carried out.

The citizen encountering a crime and wanting to arrest was faced by a difficult situation. As Bellamy writes: "The powers of arrest possessed by the ordinary citizen were, like today, ill-defined."[63] Bassiouni[64] notes the significant role of private persons in criminal law, and shows that the right to arrest inhered in all citizens—but there would often be complicated and ambiguous situations in which the exact extent of the right would be in doubt. Often the issue would be whether the citizen was obligated to arrest, or only authorized to do so; in the former case, he could be punished for default, as where he failed to take part in the hue and cry. Similarly, direct knowledge of a felony would also necessitate making all efforts to arrest the felon; however, mere suspicion as to the commission of a crime would often place the citizen in a quandary. Generally he would be entitled to arrest in such instances, but not obliged—while an error in judgment could lead to dire consequences, where he could be sued for wrongful imprisonment. Pollock and Maitland succinctly describe the dilemma of the citizen. "The ordinary man seems to have been expected to be very active in the pursuit of malefactors and yet to 'act at his peril.' This may be one of the reasons why . . . arrests were rarely made, except when there was hot pursuit."[65]

After the arrest by a citizen had been effected the problems might multiply with the obligation of watching over the arrested suspect until he could be transferred to a justice of the peace, a sheriff, or other law officer. Further, since there was no official prosecution, the final fate of the arrested person could depend on whether a private prosecution was instituted against him; these possibilities would only deepen the dilemma of the concerned citizen—whether victim or bystander—as to whether the effort, the risks, and the expenditure were worthwhile.

Those involved in watch and ward had additional powers of arrest, including the right to arrest merely on suspicion for what would now be considered "status offenses"—for instance, where a stranger found in the streets after dark, or a person acting in a strange manner, could be arrested. Bellamy refers to a 1332 statute which "ordered the arrest at any time of armed men or others suspected of evil-doing who should pass through the township. A moderate degree of suspicion now sufficed instead of the virtual certainty required before."[66]

The rules for outlaws were even more extreme and explicit. In the twelfth and thirteenth centuries anyone could arrest them at any time, ". . . and if he resisted he could be slain."[67] Later, even after restrictions were imposed on the right to kill, the court might adopt a tolerant attitude to a citizen using such extreme violence.

In cases where the outlaw sought sanctuary in a church but was not entitled to the rights of sanctuary, because of the nature of his crime, groups of citizens might come together in order to carry out a watch on the place of the sanctuary. In some cases this vigil would be considered a duty, and if the fugitive escaped they were liable to punishment. Sometimes a deal would be made where the outlaw, after admitting his guilt, would be allowed to take an oath that he would abjure the realm forever; under such circumstances he would be allowed to leave the sanctuary, make for the nearest port, and depart on the first ship for foreign climes.

Where the fugitive outlaw refused to cooperate, the citizens might prolong their watch over the sanctuary in the hope of bringing psychological pressure to bear, or to starve him out. Bellamy[68] reports also instances where the sanctity of the church would be violated and the citizens would invade the place of sanctuary and forcibly remove the wanted suspect.

The various procedures discussed—from the frankpledge to the right of arrest—show a fluctuating approach to the vexing question of reconciling the conflicting claims of peace and order in the community, and the rights of the individual, free of the restraints an official police force would impose. Related to this is the capacity of the centralized government to maintain control at the farthest ends of the kingdom.

These are problems that do not permit facile solutions. Certainly the historical evidence provides no simple model as to how to minimize police control while maximizing the citizen's security. The English example is of particular import because of its rather unique conjunction of circumstances: on the one hand, of a strong centralized government using the local community to ensure order, and on the other hand of a libertarian ethos and a population unwilling to accept a proper and professional police force, despite the rising crime rate. As a result various stopgap measures were tried, for example, of rewards, to partly rectify the faltering system.

Vigilantism

In direct contrast to the English experience there are also certain historical situations in which localized community enforcement is established, not because of the strength of the centralized government, and on the basis of a formalized system such as the frankpledge, but because of its weakness, and on the basis of extralegal arrangements, such as vigilantism. The classic example of such arrangements is in the case of frontier societies, geographically and politically far removed from the centers of power, and unable to rely on normal, or even minimal, peace-keeping frameworks being set up, and peace-keeping functions performed. In addition to the practical considerations, impetus for such arrangements derives from the existence of norms which sanction and encourage such extralegal punitive measures.

Such was the situation in many of the border areas of North America as the move westward got under way. In lieu of sufficient protection by recognized government authorities, vigilante groups were set up to maintain peace. Brown, in his survey article of vigilante movements in the United States,[69] writes that from the first such movement in 1767 until about 1900 "vigilante activity was an almost constant factor in American life,"[70] and he documents the existence of 326 movements. While there have been isolated vigilante groups set up on many occasions in Europe, Brown argues that, in its dimensions and nature, American vigilantism was indigenous and unique.

Those responsible for establishing and organizing the vigilante movements were often the leading members of the community, seeing themselves as guardians of the values of civilization, and more specifically protectors of the lives and property of their fellow citizens. For many, vigilantism became more than a mere pragmatic technique for resolving the community's problems with those who tried to exploit the lack of organization in the new settlements; it was buttressed by an ideology that, in the course of time, "suffused America. . . . To be vigilant in regard to all manner of things was an ideal that increasingly commanded Americans as the decades passed. The doctrine of vigilance provided a powerful intellectual foundation for the burgeoning of vigilante movements. . . ."[71] The fundamental and inviolate rights of the people were seen to be a legitimate basis for acting where the law was inadequate, and in some cases, to be even superior to the law. Vigilante action was seen to be not just a protective device or a deterrent warning to those who threatened the well-being of the new frontier society, but took on the aura of a symbolic statement of societal values and of commitment to those values.

Brown points out that there were two basic models for vigilante action—the socially constructive groups, and the socially destructive ones. Of the first he notes that these were responses to a genuine problem of disorder, that grew out of a community consensus on the need to take concerted action, and were directed solely against criminals and outlaws. The outcome of their efforts was a significant contribution to the welfare and stability of the community. A contemporary writer, Bancroft, referred to the acts of the vigilantes as popular tribunals and justified those acts because of the complete ineptness of officialdom to cope with the problem of crime and lawlessness.[72]

On the other hand, in the socially destructive forms of vigilante action there would be little community consensus; often the members would consist of those prone to violent tendencies. In some cases opposing groups would compete with each other, and private vendettas might be carried out under the cloak of vigilante activity. These vigilante groups sought not merely to keep the peace, but also to give expression to the basest emotion through extreme penalties meted out after the rough procedures of summary justice. In the course of time lynching became a common aspect of vigilante activity, later to take on clear political and ideological overtones.

Summing up the overall impact of the vigilantes in American life, Brown suggests that, in short practical terms, the movement might have been a "positive facet of the American experience. Many a new frontier community gained order and stability as the result of vigilantism which reconstructed the community structure and values of the old settled areas while dealing effectively with a problem of crime and disorder."[73] In the larger perspective, however, vigilantism had its negative aspects, often being "extended into areas where it was wholly inappropriate."[74] Brown notes the development of what he terms neo-vigilantism in the latter half of the nineteenth century in the wake of the Civil War as "large a response to the problems of an emerging urban industrial, racially and ethnically diverse America." From a largely rural phenomenon, it became largely urban, and now "found its chief victims among Catholics, Jews, immigrants, Negroes, laboring men and labor leaders, political radicals, and proponents of civil liberties."[75]

Cutler, in his analysis of lynching,[76] has shown how closely intertwined vigilantism was with lynching, and how easily actions taken originally for protective reasons deteriorated subsequently into self-righteous violations of civil rights, reaching its peak in the widespread lynching practiced against blacks, where such vigilante activity was prompted not by a lack of official law-enforcement machinery but by racist attitudes.

Brown has noted that in the 1960s there was a resurgence of vigilante sentiment and activity. Most of these new movements worked within the law, and often with the cooperation of the law-enforcement officials; but he warns against the danger of such groups taking the law into their own hands, using the precedents provided by earlier American vigilantism.[77]

While most writers see the vigilantism in American as a unique phenomenon, similar situations may be noted in other parts of the world, and in other periods of history. Cutler draws attention to the Vehmic courts[78] that were set up in some parts of Europe in the fourteenth and fifteenth centuries as a response to widespread lawlessness and the disregard of authority.

In Africa, too, Clinard and Abbott[79] have noted the special conditions of weak law enforcement in modern times, which have led to extreme reactions, mostly not of organized groups but of spontaneous bystander reaction, within the accepted norms of the society. They write that "the traditional custom of publicly beating and sometimes murdering an apprehended thief complicates the role of the police in the control of crime . . . in a large part of Africa. Thieves who fall into the hands of a mob are often seriously injured with fists, clubs, or stones and many have been killed. . . . A large proportion of all property offenders are apprehended by the public and not the police."[80] They attribute such behavior to the lack of sufficient police manpower, often aggravated by the fact that there is a fear that the legal organs will not deal with sufficient severity with the culprit, and to the value that even minor possessions may have in a poor country.

Their view receives some official confirmation in United Nations symposia on crime prevention which drew attention to the overzealous responses of some bystanders, noting that in "some parts of Africa, there was evidence of people taking the law into their own hands, sometimes punishing thieves [and] . . . lynching offenders."[81] It was awareness of such a situation that tempered the approach of some of the United Nations experts and prevented them from coming out with too strong a statement on the desirability of active citizen involvement.

However, the closest parallel to the American situation is probably in the activities of some vigilante groups on the island of Sicily, some of which formed the basis for later Mafia-oriented activities. In an interesting analysis, Hobsbawm[82] has described how the isolated conditions of Sicily and its neglect by the central government led, in the course of time, to the community recognizing and supporting the need for extralegal crime control. Hobsbawm notes that alongside the weak official machinery of law enforcement there grew up a parallel machine of law and power. "In a society such as Sicily, in which the official government could not or would not exercise effective sway, the appearance of such a system was as inevitable as the appearance of gang-rule, or its alternative, private posses and vigilantes in certain parts of laissez-faire America. What distinguishes Sicily is the territorial extent and cohesion of this private and parallel system of power."[83]

This system, being more efficient, became more important than the official law-enforcement organizations. Leading citizens accepted it, not merely through fear, but through positive acceptance of its vital role in safeguarding the welfare of the community. While some of the groups were part of the Mafia, others retained their original aim of ensuring the welfare of the community. Hobsbawm mentions the Onarate Societá (Honored Society), which functioned as a "parallel system of law, capable of returning stolen property or solving other problems (for a consideration) much more efficiently than the . . . State apparatus."[84]

Hobsbawm discusses these groups not as examples of community crime control but as little-recognized incipient social movements, struggling within the special social conditions of time and place, for political power.

We have thus seen that strong centralized governments may use local communities for law-enforcement purposes in order to ensure and enhance their control over these communities, or, in contradistinction, weak governments may abdicate their control and thereby allow local extralegal community groups to fill the social vacuum and to become key factors in crime control, with important repercussions for political and social developments.

These efforts may bring clear benefits to the community, or lead to abuses—from nepotic protection of friends, relatives, and neighbors to unfair and extreme disposition of justice.

It is thus seen how closely considerations of bystander involvement impinge on larger considerations of centralized power or localized control. It also points out the tenuous connection between responsible volunteer involvement in crime prevention and unbridled campaigns of revenge.

A prime need therefore is for serious consideration to be given to the creation of an approach that will allow effective citizen participation as a rational and meaningful expression of empathy and concern, thereby avoiding both the apathy of the bystanders as shown, for instance, in the Genovese incident, and the excesses of indiscriminate punitive actions sanctioned by the summary justice of angry, organized vigilantes or casual bystanders acting within the framework of distorted community norms.

Notes

1. William Seagle, *The Quest for Law* (New York: Knopf, 1941), p. 65.

2. Sir Carleton K. Allen, *The Queen's Peace* (London: Stevens and Sons, 1953), p. 2.

3. Ibid., p. 20.

4. As discussed in the previous chapter.

5. Friederich Tönnies, *Gemeinschaft and Gesellschaft* (Berlin, 1887).

6. See, for example, Margaret Masluck, "The Albanian Blood Feud," in Paul Bohannan, ed., *Law and Warfare* (New York: The Natural History Press, 1967).

7. Seagle, p. 43.

8. Bertha Surtees Phillpotts, *Kindred and Clan in the Middle Ages and After: A Study in the Sociology of the Teutonic Races* (Cambridge: Cambridge University Press, 1913).

9. For further references to these possibilities see Leon S. Sheleff, "A Critique of the Criminal Law," *Tel Aviv Studies in Law*, vol. 3, 1978 (forthcoming).

10. George M. Calhoun, *The Growth of Criminal Law in Ancient Greece* (Berkeley: University of California Press, 1927).

11. Ibid., p. 67.

12. Andrew W. Lintott, *Violence in Republican Rome* (Oxford: Oxford University Press, 1968), p. 11.

13. Ibid., p. 13.

14. J.W. Jeudwine, *Tort, Crime, and Police in Medieval Britain: A Review of Some Early Law and Customs* (London: Williams and Norgate, 1971), pp. 91-92.

15. William A. Morris, *The Frankpledge System* (London: Longmans, Green and Co., 1910), p. 1. The quotation is from *Leges Edwardis Confessoris*, xx.

16. Ibid., p. 2.

17. Ibid., p. 10.

18. Ibid., p. 13.

19. Ibid., p. 30.

20. Ibid.

21. William Stubbs, *Constitutional History of England, in Its Origin and Development* (Oxford, 1897), vol. 1, p. 299.

22. Morris, p. 37.

23. F.L. Ganshof, *Feudalism* (New York: Harper Torchbooks, 1964), p. 51.

24. Ibid., pp. 94-95.

25. Allen, p. 81.

26. Morris, pp. 152-153.

27. For a fuller discussion of the manner in which various law officers gradually took over the functions of the frankpledge see Irene Gladwin, *The Sheriff: The Man and His Office* (London: Victor Gollancz, 1974); R. Stewart-Brown, *The Serjeants of the Peace in Medieval England and Wales* (Manchester: Manchester University Press, 1936); Helen M. Cam, *The Hundred and the Hundred Rolls: An Outline of Local Government in Medieval England* (London: Methuen, 1930).

28. Morris, p. 165.

29. Kung-Chuan Hsiao, *Rural China: Imperial Control in the Nineteenth Century* (Seattle: University of Washington Press, 1967), p. 43.

30. See Dun J. Li, *The Ageless Chinese: A History* (New York: Charles Scribner & Sons, 1965), p. 323.

31. T'ung-Tsu Ch'u, *Local Government in China Under the Ch'ing* (Stanford: Stanford University Press, 1969), p. 150.

32. Ibid., p. 151.

33. Hsiao, p. 46.

34. Ibid., pp. 49-50.

35. Ibid., pp. 53-54.

36. Ibid., p. 55.

37. Ibid., p. 74.

38. Ibid., p. 78.

39. William Clifford, *Crime Control in Japan* (Lexington, Mass.: Lexington Books, 1976), pp. 98-99.

40. Richard K. Beardsley, John W. Hall, and Robert E. Ward, *Village Japan* (Chicago: University of Chicago Press, 1959).

41. Clifford, p. 99.

42. Ibid., pp. 97-98.

43. Sir William Holdsworth, *A History of English Law* (London: Methuen, Sweet and Maxwell, 1903), vol. 2, p. 101.

44. Ibid., p. 80; the quotation is from Athelstan v, pp. 4-5.

45. Cam, p. 68. See G.J. Salisbury-Jones, *Street Life in Medieval England* (Oxford, 1918), p. 138, for a positive appraisal of the system; see also G.G. Coulton, *Social Life in Britain from the Conquest to the Reformation* (Cambridge, 1918), p. 50.

46. John Bellamy, *Crime and Public Order in England in the Later Middle Ages* (London: Routledge and Kegan Paul, 1973), p. 93 (see footnote 5).

47. Leon Radzinowicz, *A History of English Criminal Law and Its Administration*, vol. 2: "The Clash Between Private Initiative and Public Interest in the Enforcement of the Law" (London: Stevens and Sons, 1956), p. 27.

48. Patrick Pringle, *Hue and Cry: The Story of Henry and John Fielding and Their Bow Street Runners* (New York: William Morrow and Co., 1955), p. 52.

49. Radzinowicz, p. 37.

50. Ibid., p. 29.

51. Ibid., p. 35.

52. Ibid.

53. Ibid. for extensive treatment of these various aspects of community participation in crime control.

54. Ibid., p. 36.

55. Ibid., p. 111.

56. Pringle, chapter 6.

57. Ibid., chapter 2, "Thief-Taker General," in particular for his discussion of Jonathan Wild, an ex-criminal who developed the work of thief-taker into a sophisticated profession. On p. 35 Pringle notes that "thief-takers were eighteenth-century England's substitutes for policemen." See also Pringle, *The Thief-Takers* (London: Museum Press, 1958).

58. Ibid., p. 36. Pringle writes that on the whole the thief-taker system "created more crime than it suppressed, and judged by results it was an expensive form of police."

59. Luke O. Pike, *A History of Crime in England: Illustrating the Changes of the Laws in the Progress of Civilization*, 1873-1876, reprinted by Patterson Smith, 1968, vol. 1, pp. 218-220.

60. Radzinowicz, pp. 193-196.

61. Allen, pp. 96-97.

62. Pringle, pp. 50-53. See also the detailed explanation of the position in Essex in the sixteenth century in Joel Samaha, *Law and Order in Historical Perspective: The Case of Elizabethan Essex* (New York: Academic Press, 1974), pp. 45-48.

63. Bellamy, p. 102.

64. M. Cherif Bassiouni, *Citizen's Arrest: The Law of Arrest, Search and Seizure for Private Citizens and Private Police* (Springfield, Ill.: Charles C. Thomas, 1977), pp. 9-14.

65. Sir Frederick Pollock and Frederick W. Maitland, *The History of English Law Before the Time of Edward I* (Cambridge: Cambridge University Press, 1968), p. 583.

66. Bellamy, p. 102.

67. Ibid., p. 105.

68. Ibid., p. 109.

69. Richard Maxwell Brown, "The American Vigilante Tradition," chapter 5, in Hugh D. Graham and Ted R. Gurr, eds., *The History of Violence in America* (New York: Bantam, 1969), pp. 154-225.

70. Ibid., p. 154.

71. Ibid., p. 179.

72. Hubert H. Bancroft, *Popular Tribunals* (San Francisco, 1887).

73. Brown, p. 196.

74. Ibid., p. 197.

75. Ibid.

76. James E. Cutler, *Lynch-Law: An Investigation into the History of Lynching in the United States* (New York: Longmans, Green and Co., 1905). See also James H. Chadborn, *Lynching and the Law* (Chapel Hill: University of North Carolina Press, 1933).

77. Brown, p. 201.

78. Cutler, p. 5.

79. Marshall B. Clinard and Daniel J. Abbott, *Crime in Developing Countries: A Comparative Perspective* (New York: John Wiley and Sons, 1973).

80. Ibid., p. 226.

81. Report, "Preparatory Meeting of Experts in Social Defense (African Region) for the Fourth United Nations Congress on the Prevention of Crime and the Treatment of Offenders," *International Review of Criminal Policy,* no. 27, 1969, p. 66.

82. E.J. Hobsbawm, *Primitive Rebels: Studies in Archaic Forms of Social Movements in the 19th and 20th Centuries* (New York: Praeger, 1963).

83. Ibid., p. 35.

84. Ibid., p. 51.

6 The Duty to Rescue

Modern society, with its recognized central governing authority, and its special-ized law-enforcement agencies and other rescue organizations, has a greatly diminished need for citizen involvement; and the modern law reflects, to a large degree, these changed social conditions, with bystander involvement relegated to a peripheral aspect of the law. Yet, because there are still situations where bystander aid may be crucial, because there are still situations where bystanders actually do help, and because certain consequences flow from such situations, a legal framework is necessary within which bystander response, or lack of response, to distress circumstances, are regulated and adjudicated.

In analyzing the necessity and desirability for bystander action, and the legal implications, there are four key issues which have to be examined:

1. whether the law should impose a *duty to rescue*;
2. whether the law should allow *compensation* for injury suffered in the course of helping;
3. whether the law should grant *immunity* from claims where the intervention inadvertently causes harm to the victim or others;
4. whether bystanders should be given *rewards* for prosocial behavior on behalf of others.

Traditionally there has been a clear-cut distinction drawn between the common-law countries—most of the English-speaking world—and the Continen-tal systems of law. The former generally place no duty on a citizen in distress, while the latter generally do impose such a duty to rescue.

As a corollary to these differences, the two legal systems also differ in the extent to which they provide protection for the active bystander. The Anglo-American systems occasionally display a reluctance to compensate the bystander injured in his attempt to help, and more often refuse to justify the intervention when the bystander inadvertently causes harm. In fact the pronouncements of judges often indicate clear disapproval of such acts, and bystanders have, on occasion, been admonished for offering such help. On the other hand, the Continental system, in recognizing the duty to help, also generally recognizes the need to offer judicial backing to the bystander in the form of compensation for harm suffered, and/or immunity from claims for harm caused.

The common-law approach has, however, been subjected to increasingly critical review in the past few years, and there has been a slow, yet clearly discernible, shift in legislative enactments and judicial pronouncements. Some of the criticisms of the standard common-law approach arose directly out of the Genovese case; in its wake the University of Chicago Law School organized in 1965 a conference on the "Good Samaritan and the Bad—The Law and Morality of Volunteering in Situations of Peril or of Failing to do so."[1] The common-law jurists have given increasing attention and approval to the Continental approach, and while the two systems of law still remain apart on the issue of the bystander, there has recently been a gradual acceptance of new concepts and ways of thought that are similar to the Continental approach.

In a survey article Linden sums up the situation, and the nature of the change: "Everyone admires a rescuer and a good samaritan." But the common-law denial of recovery to injured rescuers, and the imposition of damages for inadvertent harm caused, "could hardly have encouraged altruism. . . . Happily, in the last few years tort law has begun to cast off these harsh ways, [and] in some situations, a duty to render aid is being established, where no such duty existed before.[2]

The clearest distinction between the two systems of law lies in the issue of the duty to rescue. This is an aspect of bystander behavior that has undergone the least change; the common law, with minor exceptions to be noted later, still absolves the bystander from any responsibility in either criminal or civil law for harm caused to a victim which could have been avoided had the bystander rendered aid.[3]

The Anglo-American Approach

The essential thrust of the common-law approach is clear: there is no duty to go to the aid of a stranger in distress, even when there is, on the one hand, a perceivable real danger to the victim, and on the other hand, when the rendering of aid would entail no danger, or even inconvenience to the bystander.

A whole series of legal pronouncements has bound this approach into the woof and warp of the law and has created an edifice of legal pronouncement providing unequivocal legal justification for refusing to proffer assistance to strangers in peril.

This trend is exemplified in the Restatement of American Law based on the accumulated wisdom of legislative and judicial work. Expounding on the nature of the civil obligation that one individual owes another, the Restatement declares: "The fact that the actor realizes or should realize that action on his part is necessary for another's aid or protection does not of itself impose upon him a duty to take such action." Lest there be any doubt as to the meaning of this statement the full implications of this approach are then spelled out in an illustration which clarifies the stark nature of the abstract rule: "A sees B, a blind man, about to step into the street in front of an approaching automobile.

A could prevent B from doing so by a word or touch without delaying his own progress. A does not do so and B is run over and hurt. A is under no duty to prevent B from stepping into the street, and is not liable to B."[4] The Restatement refers only to the blind man being hurt, but it is clear that no liability would apply even if he were to be killed. Although intent on providing as extreme an example as possible, the authors of the Restatement refrained from specifying what would be the ultimate implication of their example—the death of the blind man. But other jurists have not been so circumspect.

In actual law cases, even when confronted with the most extreme instances of maximum danger to potential victim and minor inconvenience to the bystander, the courts have often been reluctant to deviate from their position that no duty to rescue be imposed. According to this approach people cannot be held liable for omissions, however despicable and callous the bystander's indifference, however dire the victim's plight, and however dear the ultimate consequences.

In an 1897 case[5] the Chief Justice of New Hampshire argued that "there is a wide difference—a broad gulf—both in reason and in law, between causing and preventing an injury. . . ." He argued that whereas there is a clear legal duty to *refrain* from causing a wrong, no such legal duty exists to *actively prevent* a wrong. "The duty to protect against wrong is, generally speaking and excepting certain intimate relations in the nature of a trust, a moral obligation only, not recognized or enforced by law." In order to give vivid expression to the abstract principle the judge also chose an extreme example, perhaps even more so than that of the Restatement: "I see my neighbor's two-year-old baby in dangerous proximity to the machinery of his windmill in the yard, and easily might, but do not, rescue him. I am not liable in damage to the child for his injuries . . . because the child and I are strangers, and I am under no legal duty to protect him."[6]

However, there seems to be a subtle error of logic and/or nomenclature. The neighbor's baby is *not a stranger*; the neighbor's baby is a *neighbor*. Even if one owes no obligation to a stranger, it may still be theoretically possible to have a rule imposing obligations at least on behalf of a neighbor, especially one as helpless and as vulnerable as a two-year-old. In fact, if no such obligation exists, then, in order to clarify the extreme nature of the law, the judge should have spelled out specifically that the lack of duty related to the baby *as a neighbor*. However, while the judge's choice of language is clearly faulty, his interpretation of the law may be valid. In a later case[7] it was held specifically that there was no duty to prevent a neighbor's child from hammering on a dangerous explosive. Prosser, in a leading volume on the law of torts, has strongly criticized this decision, and others of a similar nature. He writes that

> the law has persistently refused to recognize the moral obligation of
> common decency and common humanity, to come to the aid of
> another human being who is in danger, even though the outcome is to

cost him his life. Some of the decisions have been shocking in the
extreme. The expert swimmer who sees another drowning before his
eyes is not required to do anything at all about it, but may sit on a
rock, smoke his cigarette and watch the man drown . . . [one is not]
required to play the part of Florence Nightingale and bind up the
wounds of a stranger bleeding to death, or to prevent a neighbor's child
from hammering on a dangerous explosive . . . or even to cry a warning
to one who is walking into the jaws of a dangerous machine.[8]

While it is recognized that there are exceptions to the general rule these have
usually been interpreted as narrowly as possible. The duty within the family
obviously exists, though the degree of relationship is not always precisely
delineated. For instance, while one would be obliged to rescue one's own child
from proximity to a dangerous machine, it is not clear whether this duty would
apply to a nephew or a niece not of that moment in one's custody.

Some of the most surprising decisions have been those where judges have
refused to recognize a duty of rescue even when the victim and defendant had
some obvious prior relationship, generally contractual, and often on an employer-employee basis.

In a leading case[9] an employee of a company was held to have no action
against the company where other employees had failed to render the necessary
aid, when he had been stricken with frostbite in the course of his work in an
outlying area. It was held that however reprehensible, immoral, and inhuman the
conduct of the defendant's employees in failing to help their fellow worker, the
company could not be considered to have a legal duty to transport him to a
point of safety where he could be cared for.

In another earlier case[10] there was affirmation of this lack of responsibility
of an employer for his employees, where an employee had caught her hand in a
mangle and been unable to release it for about half an hour, all this time
receiving no help from other workers. The judge explained that the only duty of
the employer "is one of humanity, for a breach thereof the law does not, as far
as we are informed, impose any liability."[11]

Some later cases, however, have rejected this narrow concept of an
employer's responsibilities, although it is possible that the earlier cases quoted
would still be considered in many jurisdictions as representing the law at present.

In the 1921 case of *Carey* v. *Davis* the court held that "where in the course
of his employment, a servant suffers serious injury or is suddenly struck down in
a manner indicating the immediate and urgent need of aid to save him from
death or serious harm, the master, if present, is in duty bound to take such
reasonable measures or make such reasonable effort as may be practicable to
relieve him."[12] In a 1957 case[13] an employer, also a railway company, was held
responsible where an employee who had suffered a sunstroke was left unattended.

Some of the most important cases where the courts have approved the rule of no duty to rescue were those in which there actually was a response to another's plight. However, in discharging this moral duty to help, the defendants had been negligent to one degree or another. In measuring the nature of the legal responsibility that flowed from their negligence in aiding, the courts have sometimes taken the opportunity to reiterate that there was no need for intervention in the first place, even where there might have been a presumption that some kind of relationship had come into being, as, for instance, between the owners or operators of business premises and their customers. While tolerating no negligence in the actual care of the victim, the courts approvingly contemplate the possibility of total neglect. In the 1935 case of *Zelenko* v. *Gimbel*, the judge indicated that the defendants, the owners of a shop on whose premises the decedent had collapsed, and later died, had no obligation to render aid to the customer. "The general proposition of law is that if a defendant owes a plaintiff no duty, the refusal to act is not negligence . . . we will assume that defendant owes her no duty at all; that defendant could have let her be and die."[14] The defendants were found liable for negligence; had they done nothing, they might have been absolved.

Similarly in the case of *Osterlind* v. *Hill*,[15] referred to earlier, the court had not attached any responsibility to the owner of a boat lent for hire, when one of the customers had drowned after it had capsized. In the latter case the victim had specifically called out for help, yet the judges had not found these appeals for help as constituting any additional responsibility. A later 1966 case[16] also held that there was no responsibility to a customer, even though it was a child who was in danger.

In the case of *Yania* v. *Bigan*[17] the defendant was held not liable to the decedent where the latter, an invitee on a business visit on the defendant's land, had accepted a challenge to jump into a ditch that was filled with about ten feet of water, and, on experiencing difficulties, had been ignored by the defendant, despite his pleas for help.

The irrelevance of a direct appeal for help is borne out in a case[18] where a railroad was held not to be responsible when a train had stopped on the line in such a way as to interfere with the efforts of fire-fighters to put out a fire. The railroad employees had been requested to move the train in order not to hinder the fire-fighting activities, but had refused to do so even though no hazards were involved in complying with the request. "The law imposes no duty on one man to aid another in the preservation of the latter's property but only the duty not to injure another's property in the use of his own." The court went on to explain that while passive inaction, as exemplified by the refusal to move the train, did not give rise to any liability, the active use of the property might have led to action, for example, where the train had deliberately gone over the firemen's hose. In fact a case of this nature has actually been decided where a railway company was held responsible when one of its trains went over a fire hose, tearing it and reducing the water pressure.[19]

Often, though, this approach, absolving from all obligations to help, applies even in cases where the defendant is actually involved in causing the harm, provided only that the harm is caused inadvertently, and without any fault on the part of the defendant. A number of these cases deal with injuries caused in train accidents. If the court has been satisfied that the driver and the other railroad employees were not at fault in causing the accident it has held that there was no obligation to help the injured person.

In one of the leading cases of this type, *Union Pacific Railway Company* v. *Cappier*, the court was at pains to draw a clear distinction between moral and legal obligations.

> With the humane side of the question courts are not concerned. It is the omission or negligent discharge of legal duties only which come within the sphere of judicial cognizance. For withholding relief from the suffering, for failure to respond to the calls of worthy charity, or for faltering in the bestowment of brotherly love on the unfortunate, penalties are found not in the laws of men, but in that higher law, the violation of which is condemned by the voice of conscience, whose sentence of punishment for the recreant is swift and sure.[20]

On the basis of this reasoning the company was held not to be liable where a person had been knocked down by a train, and had died a few hours later. In this case the court went beyond the dicta in some of the other cases quoted, finding that even the lax manner in which some of the employees had offered aid to the decedent would not constitute negligence; since there was no duty to act in the first place the defendant could not be held liable if their help was not performed satisfactorily.

Of course, some of the problems arising out of the train accidents could have been resolved had legislative rules been laid down specifically to cover the special nature of a transport carrier; for instance, the greater likelihood of being involved in an accident with a stranger, the possibility that the accident would take place far removed from the victim's home, and/or far removed from places of ready treatment as has been done in situations on the road, at sea, or in the air, as will be discussed later.[21]

But even without special rules there are both British and American cases which indicate that, under special circumstances where one person might be placed in a dependent situation to another—such as being hit, and then indisposed—a duty to aid might come into force. In the British case of *Heaven* v. *Pender*, the court explained that "whenever one person is by circumstances placed in such a position with regard to another that every one of ordinary sense who did think would at once recognize that if he did not use ordinary care and skill in his own conduct with regard to those circumstances he would cause danger of injury to the person or property of the other, a duty arises to use ordinary care and skill to avoid such danger."[22] This is a majority opinion—

there were strong dissenting judgments, as well as subsequent judicial criticisms of, and reservations about, the decision,[23] as it seems to recognize indirectly the very duty to help, which the courts had been so studiously avoiding.

Nevertheless the case itself has been quoted approvingly by an American court, in *Depue* v. *Flateau*, in order to substantiate the court's reasoning that there may be situations where even though "defendants were under no contract obligation to minister to plaintiff in his distress . . . humanity demanded that they do so, if they understood and appreciated his condition." The court went on to clarify that "though those acts which humanity demands are not always legal obligations,"[24] they could, as in the case being adjudicated, become such, where the plaintiff, having taken sick in the home of the defendant, had been refused permission to stay overnight and had been helped on his way into the cold night; then while traveling home he had apparently fainted and fallen, and spent the night unconscious in the snow, suffering injury as a result of his experience.

This case, however, does not really clarify the issue of the duty to rescue, or the responsibility of bystanders. It revolved far more around the question as to whether the defendant could have foreseen that the plaintiff, having taken ill, would on his way home encounter the difficulties that he did.

Nearly all of the cases dealing with the duty to rescue have arisen out of civil law claims, where the victim has sought redress from a bystander whose behavior was seemingly so reprehensible that, prima facie at least, it seemed to hold out the possibility of proving liability. On the other hand, in the absence of any clear criminal provisions, there is almost no chance of discussing such questions within the framework of a criminal trial. However, the legal issue of being an accessory to the crime sometimes touches on questions of this nature, as may be seen in a case decided by a British court-martial[25] in Germany dealing with British troops stationed there, subject to the overall principles of the British criminal law.

A number of soldiers were charged with aiding and abetting the crime of rape. The soldiers on hearing a girl screaming while being raped had entered the room where the rape was being committed and remained passive bystanders of the act. On the one hand, they had not tried to help her; on the other hand (which was crucial for the charge against them), "there was no evidence that they had touched the victim or prevented others from helping her or had hindered her escape or her attempts to ward off her attackers; nor had they done or said anything to encourage the principal offenders or discourage the victim." Originally convicted, they were all found not guilty on appeal since they had been completely passive.

Yet, had they been brought before a German court instead of a British court-martial they would probably have been convicted for having failed to come to the rescue since Article 330 of the German Criminal Code reads:

Anybody who does not tender aid in an accident or common danger or in an emergency situation, although aid is needed and under the circumstances can be expected of him, especially if he would not subject himself thereby to any considerable danger, or if he would not thereby violate other important duties, shall be punished by imprisonment not to exceed one year or a fine.[26]

This case highlights the stark contrast between the traditional common law and the Continental approaches; in fact the incongruity of the present common-law position is clearly manifested. By the reasoning of the judges, verbal exhortation to the offender, or discouraging comments to the victim, would have been sufficient to have convicted the accused of being accomplices in one of the most heinous crimes on the statute book. Yet conversely, standing idly by and watching the act being committed, after having deliberately entered the room for that specific purpose, evokes no legal sanction at all, not even of the mildest type.

The Law in European Countries

In contrast, the duty to rescue has been firmly embedded into the legal systems of most Continental countries, with criminal sanctions, of varying degrees of severity, for those who fail to respond to the plight of a fellow being in distress. A concise comparative analysis has been given in a number of articles[27] in the American law journals, providing good examples of the importance of comparative law, where the experience of other legal systems may be used in order to test the value of existing law and to indicate possibilities of changes in the future.

Rudzinski in his article surveyed the salient aspects of the law in thirteen countries in Europe that have adopted a duty to rescue, since the first enactment of such laws in the Netherlands in 1866 and in Portugal in 1867. The duty is applicable to all sorts of distress situations, irrespective of whether the causal antecedents were criminal, accidental, or negligent.

In some instances the duty is applicable only if the victim is in danger of his life; in other jurisdictions the danger is a broader one. On occasion the duty is linked directly to the need to prevent crime, either as a sole duty, or as part of a larger principle of the law. Article 63 of the *Code Penal* in France reads: "Whoever is able to prevent by his immediate action, without risk to himself or others, the commission of a serious crime or offense against the person, and voluntarily neglects to do so shall be liable."[28]

In France the duty to rescue was originally imposed in 1941 during the period of the German occupation, as part of the attempts by the occupation forces to maintain control over the local population.[29] The law was passed after a German officer had been killed and fifty French hostages had been put to death as a reprisal. Fearful of further acts of violence against German soldiers, and of lack of voluntary cooperation from the French citizens in preventing crimes, in saving the victim and in divulging any information that they might have, the Germans imposed on the French a legal and binding duty to act. After the war the rule itself was retained, though the wording was changed to make it more acceptable in a democratic society. The genesis of the law in France then bears close resemblances to the origins of the frankpledge system in Britain, and the *pao-chia* in China. Both these systems had been set up to help a conquering group to consolidate their social control, and also to prevent acts of vengeance against their own supporters.[30]

In many societies the duty to rescue is closely linked to the overall ideology, the duty being seen as part of the basic expressions of service to the state and its well-being. In the Soviet Union, for instance, in addition to specific rules there is also a general provision obligating active intervention by bystanders. Hughes[31] contends that intervention by a bystander can be expected in terms of Article 130 of the constitution of the USSR, which states that it is the "duty of every citizen . . . to respect the rules of socialist intercourse."[32] Hazard argues too that "it would violate Article 130 of the Constitution of the USSR if a healthy person who knew how to swim failed to render aid in the summer time to another person who was drowning in a river not far from the bank."[33]

Most rules imposing a duty to rescue are incorporated into the criminal code, with provision being made for both prison sentences and fines. In one year in France, in 1962, fifty-two people were sentenced to prison terms for the failure to comply with the provisions of the law.[34] Once the criminal sanction has been clearly laid down it may give rise to a civil claim as well.

Dawson[35] notes that, in his examination of the German case-law, he was unable to find any cases where the criminal sanction had been used as the basis for a civil claim, although he argues that in principle this extrapolation should be possible. Dawson adds that, in France, it is possible for the victim to appear as a third party during the criminal trial and make a claim for damages in the form of a civil action. He quotes one case where a refusal to help led to the accused being sentenced to three years in jail and a compensation payment of 25,000 francs to the victim. The facts in this case[36] were rather unique, and, in fact, even in the Anglo-American law might have given rise to a civil action.

A father-in-law had failed to help his son-in-law after the latter had fallen through ice into a deep canal, specifically refusing to join with another person in handing a nearby iron bar to the drowning man, which he could have held on to. Since the two were obviously not strangers, this case poses an interesting hypothetical problem for the Anglo-American law—whether a familial relationship of this type would give rise to any action at law or, if not as between in-laws, whether liability would apply where the victim was an adult child, or an elderly parent. I have been unable to trace cases in which the nature of the responsibility within a family—as between independent adults—has been examined. I would suggest that the logic of decision as to the independence of adults, the importance of individualism as an ideological concept, and the lack of responsibility to neighbors and to employees might well lead to decisions that even within the family—at least where the parties involved are adults and do not constitute one household—no responsibility would lie.[37]

While generally it seems that a criminal law duty to rescue could provide sufficient basis for a civil law claim, in some cases, the duty in civil law is specifically spelled out.

The original Portuguese law of 1867[38] provided for a civil action against a bystander, present during a crime of violence, who was able to help but failed to do so. While the Portuguese law limits the action to damage caused by crimes of violence a recent Czechoslovakian law is more broadly based, covering not only the duty to crimes of violence, or cases where the victim's life is in danger, but all instances where there is danger of serious damage. Failure to act or to report to the authorities without just cause leads to liability as laid down in section 425 of the Civil Code, which provides that "any individual who failed to fulfill his duty . . . , although its fulfillment would have prevented imminent damage may be ordered by a court to contribute to the compensation of the damage to an extent appropriate to the circumstances of the case, unless the damage may be compensated otherwise. The court shall take into consideration in particular what had obstructed the fulfillment of such duty and the social importance of the damage as well as the personal and material situation of the individual who had failed to do his duty."[39]

The experience of the Continental legal systems shows that a duty to rescue can be implemented. The Genovese case, and many other instances of bystander indifference, raise inescapable questions which the Anglo-American systems are unable to avoid. Underlying the present Anglo-American approach is an overall framework comprising legal factors which make for a reluctance to punish for mere omission, ideological factors which make for a reluctance to coerce free individuals to perform positive acts, and philosophical factors which make for reluctance to use the law in order to further the prospects of moral behavior.[40]

The Rationale of Nonintervention

Discussing the legal aspects Bohlen has noted that "there is no distinction more deeply rooted in the common law and more fundamental than that between misfeasance and non-feasance, between active misconduct working positive injury to others and passive inaction, a failure to take positive steps to benefit others, or to protect them from harm not created by any wrongful act of the defendant."[41]

A legal note has claimed that, historically, the distinction between misfeasance and nonfeasance arose out of the difficulty of incorporating inaction into the traditional writs of the English law—thus, the "law could find no duty from which a promise to perform could be implied."[42]

Beyond these historical and procedural factors, the legal problems of nonfeasance are closely bound up with ongoing modern concepts of the law. In the civil law there are very real issues of the proof of causation; where there is no action on the part of a bystander, serious problems of proof arise as to the capacity to attribute causative responsibility for harm subsequently ensuing. It is not just the lack of duty, which is stressed by most of the court decisions, but also the sometimes more complicated problem of showing an irrefutable connection between the final harm caused and the acts leading up to that harm. Inaction itself generally lacks, in legal thought, causative powers.

In the criminal law, too, problems arise out of the basic principle that criminality must involve a junction of criminal intent (*mens rea*) and the criminal act (*actus reus*). In many cases it becomes difficult to conceive of indifference to another as justifying the attribution of *mens rea*; in other cases the passive inaction can hardly be considered to supply the requirements of the *actus reus.* However, modern developments in the law have provided many exceptions to these rules—for instance, crimes of strict liability no longer require *mens rea* in its traditional meaning.[43]

Referring specifically to the question of attributing legal responsibility on the basis of omissions two writers have suggested possible solutions for perceiving an omission within the acceptable norms of liable behavior. Gregory suggests using an extended definition of negligence. He argues that "negligence occurs not only by doing things in substandard fashion. It also occurs by failing to do certain things under circumstances indicating that such failure is likely to prove harmful to others."[44]

Frankel,[45] after a discussion of the meaning of *mens rea*, and the problems of omission as causation in the law, suggests legal rules could be laid down based upon social norms which give rise to certain expectations of behavior. A failure to act in a situation of peril for another could be seen as "disregard for . . . the expectations arising from a system of limiting freedom of choice by legitimately communicated rules for the common good.[46]

Other articles critical of the present legal approach have focused less on the specific legal principles and more on the underlying ideological concepts that influence legal thought. Hale, who is critical of the lack of any obligations, suggests that there are two main assumptions for "judicial reluctance to recognize affirmative duties. . . . One of these is that a rugged, independent individual needs no help from others except such as they may be inspired to render him out of kindness or such as he can induce them to render by the ordinary process of bargaining, without having the government step in to make them help. . . . The other assumption is that when a government *requires* a person to act, it is necessarily interfering more seriously with his freedom to act . . . Yet neither of these assumptions is universally true."[47]

Hale feels these assumptions are of only dubious value in society as at present constituted. The idea of fair bargaining certainly seems to have no place in a perilous situation.

In fact, Justice Frankfurter once provided an example to show the circumstances in which fair bargaining between presumably equal parties would clearly break down. He noted the "familiar example of the drowning man who agrees to pay an exorbitant sum to a rescuer who would otherwise permit him to drown. No court would enforce a contract under such circumstances."[48] Further, to make the victim dependent solely on the kindness of bystanders may in many instances be a misplaced hope, as is indicated in some of the cases already noted.

The second assumption with its emphasis on the individual's right to be free of government coercion is a more serious issue, and requires deeper analysis. Several articles on the American law as to criminal omissions have stressed the strong individualistic ethos of American society and its reflection in the law as a fundamental reason for the lack of coercive rules for bystander intervention. There is an unmistakable reluctance to impose penalties for mere omissions. In Kirchheimer's words, "A narrow conception of the duty to assist others has been regarded as the expression of an individualistic order of society."[49]

However, Kirchheimer argues that the stress on unbridled individualism might be an anachronistic conception of modern societal reality:

> Conception of an isolated individual whose legal obligations are few compared to his range of possible activity deviates from the facts of present-day society. A greater amount of group dependency on the part of each individual as well as a steady increase in the number of affirmative duties established by statute is discernible everywhere. The problem of finding sufficient legal basis for affirmative duties has become less acute than it was under a more individualistic form of society. The emphasis shifts to the necessity of providing for adequate methods to enforce such affirmative duties by the means of criminal as well as administrative law.[50]

If this analysis by Kirchheimer had any validity when written in 1942 it takes on added significance now, given the increasing limitations that have been placed on individualism by modern states with their welfare orientation. However strongly individualist the countries of the common law have traditionally been, they have not been averse to setting up an extensive network of social welfare agencies, of increasing taxation, of conscription for military service. Inasmuch as the Anglo-American countries have cultivated an individualistic ethos they have done so as part of a larger philosophy which holds that, by pursuing greater freedom for the individual, society itself will reap the benefits, and that the individual will be inspired by this liberty to nobler endeavors which will enrich the social fabric. But what if the hopes are misplaced, what if the desired actions are not forthcoming? Can a society afford to so sanctify the concept of individualism that its consequences may be an inability to react authoritatively and positively even when faced with omissions bordering on sheer cruelty, such as in the case of a neighbor failing to save a neighbor's two-year-old child, or failing to respond to the cry for help of a customer in one's boat or on one's land, or failing to contact the police when witnessing a murder?

Frankel has posed the basic problem facing modern society: "In a society strongly motivated by an attitude of individualism, how far should one go in legislating humanitarian obligations?"[51] An answer to this pivotal question had already been given a century before in one of the most persuasive and cogent arguments for individual liberty ever written. John Stuart Mill,[52] even while presenting an extreme thesis for the rights of the individual to live free of governmental restraints, with almost no limitations on human freedom, as an essential prerequisite for the very well-being and progress of the society, nevertheless unequivocally placed one reservation on the individual's unqualified liberty: "There are," he wrote, "many positive acts for the benefit of others which ... [a person] may rightfully be compelled to perform such as ... to perform certain acts of individual beneficence, such as saving a fellow creature's life.... A person may cause evil to others not only by his action—but by his inaction, and in either case he is justly accountable to them for the injury."[53]

Although Mill does not elaborate on the theme, this should not be seen as an idle remark casually thrown in. Mill's short work is a masterpiece of tightly organized arguments, carefully delineating the logical consequences of individualism in society, favoring even circumstances when total freedom might have detrimental effects, since, in the long run, society would benefit from the totality of freedom. But even this extreme libertarian stance recognized the possible untenable implications of allowing bystanders the freedom to refuse to act when confronted by a situation of maximum danger to a victim and minimum inconvenience to themselves.

Bentham,[54] writing from a similar perspective to that of Mill, but far more steeped in the intricacies of the legal system, and searching for a just, rational, and utilitarian criminal law, also justified placing limitations on the range of pure individualism inasmuch as there was a need to ensure rescue actions on behalf of those in distress. "In cases where the person is in danger, why," he asks, "should it not be made the duty of every man to save another from mischief, when it can be done without prejudicing himself ...?"[55]

Another British jurist, Stephen,[56] had felt that minimum obligations could be demanded of a bystander to the plight of another person. He asserted that "a man who caused another to be drowned by refusing to hold out his hand would in common language be said to have killed him...."[57]

More recently Hughes[58] has argued that, in the absence of general legal principles which might have allowed for judicial extension of liability, the possibilities should be explored of legislative imposition of liability for a failure to aid those in peril.

A very useful attempt at formulating legislation has been made by Miller and Zimmerman, who present their suggestions for a Model Good Samaritan Act,[59] with appended explanations of the rationale for, and possible operations of, such a law. Rudzinski, in an appendix to his survey article,[60] also gives examples of the specific legislation adopted in a number of countries.

Rudolph,[61] on the other hand, is of the opinion that no legislative change is required but that the judges could themselves carve out the necessary framework by laying down a suitable judicial rule. He proposes the following rule:

A person has a duty to act whenever:
1. The harm or loss is imminent and there is apparently no other practical alternative to avoid the threatened harm or loss except his own action.
2. Failure to act would result in substantial harm or damage to another person or his property and the effort, risk or cost of acting is disproportionately less than the harm or damage avoided.
3. The circumstances placing the person in a position to act are purely fortuitous.[62]

In the case of *Jones* v. *United States*[63] the court noted that there were four situations in the American law where the failure to rescue might constitute a breach of legal duty. Apart from the situations already dealt with—through status relationship between victim and bystander (for example, in the family), through assumed contractual duty to care (as in the doctor-patient relationship), and where a bystander had assumed the care of a victim, and was then obliged to perform that aid satisfactorily—there were also situations where legal duties had been specifically imposed.

Some of these rules have been the result of the British and American legislatures incorporating rules of international law into the domestic legal system, particularly regulations as to obligatory assistance in international waters or air space.

The 1948 Convention for the Safety of Life at Sea lays down that: "the master of a ship at sea, on receiving a signal from any source that a ship or aircraft or survival aircraft thereof is in distress, is bound to proceed with all speed to the assistance of the persons in distress, informing them if possible that he is doing so."[64]

An interesting development has applied similar principles of obligatory rescue to the potential problems of outer space. The 1968 Agreement on the Rescue and Return of Astronauts, and the Return of Space Objects Launched into Outer Space, calls upon all signatory states to cooperate in rendering assistance to space explorers in order to save their lives and safeguard their health.[65]

Changes in the Law

Within the national law of the Anglo-American states there have also been slow changes in the law providing for obligatory actions, generally on specific classes of people. The laws generally do not involve the necessity to assume any risk behavior by the bystander, but are oriented to enhancing the prospects of maintaining satisfactory standards of social order. One of the major examples is the obligation to assist in the case of traffic accidents as found in nearly all states. It should be noted that this is a general provision aimed not so much at helping the victim, but at ensuring control of the traffic situation. The duty is bound up with the fact of the accident and not the plight of the victim—thus, the duty sometimes is only imposed on the driver of the car actually involved in the accident, and not on other drivers, or on passengers or pedestrians.

People in certain professions are also naturally assumed to have accepted an irrevocable duty to rescue; fire-fighters, the police, lifesavers, ambulance drivers, mountain-climbing guides have all, by the terms of their employment, committed themselves to endanger their own lives in order to save others, no matter how culpably negligent these others are in having endangered themselves.[66]

In recent years attempts have been made to enforce intervention behavior for other professional categories. Thus, as a result of a heightened consciousness as to the problem of child abuse,[67] a series of laws has been passed obligating doctors, nurses, teachers, social workers, and other similar groups to report any suspicion of child abuse toward a child.[68]

These laws are based on the fact of acute peril to helpless, innocent victims in circumstances generally of privacy where the prospects of discovering the crime are minimal, and where only the practiced discernment of experts liable to have independent contact with the victim offers any hope of alleviating the victim's burden, and of beginning to cope effectively with a problem whose total dimensions can only be guessed at, precisely because of the intimate and private circumstances in which it is practiced.

Finally there is an old legal provision, rarely used today, which does actually obligate some form of action in the event of knowledge of the commission of a crime. The crime of misprision of felony lay disused for a long time, but, as Waller[69] points out, has been revived in law cases in Australia and Britain. It provides for criminal sanctions where a person has knowledge of a crime but fails to inform authorities. This crime is in a sense paradoxical, for while there may be no duty to prevent a crime while it is actually being committed, one may be legally obliged to report it afterwards.

This crime was resuscitated in a 1959 Australian case[70] where the victim of an assault was convicted of misprision of felony for refusing to divulge the name of his assailant, his refusal being based on a fear of further attacks, in which he might even be killed. The Australian precedent was picked up a few years later in Britain.[71] However, here the prosecution had sought to get conviction against a person whom they believed to have committed a far more serious offense (receiver of stolen property, the property being guns) for which they had insufficient evidence; misprision of felony became a means of ensuring a conviction at least on a lesser charge. In this case the court conceded that there might be situations where the old law of misprision could not be enforced, such as the case of a privileged communication: but the court stressed that such exceptions to the law would not apply to where the information had been supplied by a member of a family. Quoting ancient precedent for this view the court referred to the rule of the hue and cry: "In 1315 it was held that it was the duty of a brother to raise hue and cry against his own brother."[72]

In his discussion of these recent cases Waller questions whether the rule could be applied in the United States. He notes that some states have specifically rejected it, as in Michigan where it was held that it was "wholly unsuited to American criminal law and procedure."[73] Waller claims that the law might still be applicable in certain jurisdictions, including the federal, provided that the nondisclosure was through willful refusal and not mere neglect.

Parenthetically it is interesting to note that none of the known bystanders in the Genovese case would have been liable for misprision of felony as all of them cooperated subsequently in giving evidence to the police; it was in fact through this witness cooperation that the facts of their passivity became known.[74] It is doubtful if any of them were motivated to their frankness which was socially so detrimental to themselves, because of the rule as to misprision of offense, which probably none of them knew of, just as it is not obvious that the existence of a legal duty to rescue would have prodded them to action.

In the final analysis, however, the legal issue goes beyond the existence of specific laws to cover limited and special cases, or even whether the courts are able or willing to be flexible in their decisions so as to accept a duty in certain particularly acute cases, as has occasionally been done. The key question is whether there is room for overall legislation in favor of a duty to rescue. The question of principle is delicate and multi-faceted; the details of any such principle are potentially intricate.

The issues of principle have been pithily stated in the musings of Lord Macaulay. In his work as the head of a commission charged with the task of devising a penal code for India in the nineteenth century he poses the nuances of responsibility that exist:

> It is true that none but a very depraved man might suffer another to be drowned when he might prevent it by a word. But if we punish such a man, where are we to stop? How much exertion are we to require? Is a person to be a murderer if he does not go fifty yards through the sun of Bengal at noon in May in order to caution a traveler against a swollen river? Is he to be a murderer if he does not go a hundred yards?—if he does not go a mile?—if he does not go ten? What is the precise amount of trouble and inconvenience which he is to endure? The distinction

between a guide who is bound to conduct a traveler as safely as he can, and a mere stranger is a clear distinction. But the distinction between a stranger who will not give a halloo to save a man's life, and a stranger who will not run a mile to save a man's life, is very far from being clear.[75]

Macaulay's conclusion is that, in the vast majority of cases, it would not be possible to utilize the criminal law as a means of ensuring bystander response unless "they are distinguished . . . by some circumstances which mark them out as particularly fit objects of penal legislation."[76]

Macaulay has of course slightly prejudged the issue by presenting the proposed criminal liability in terms of murder. What is actually suggested is not such an extreme definition of the inaction, even where the victim were to die, but a law which would have larger implications for prosocial behavior in general, not just for a victim in danger of life.

If legislation is to be considered then there are a series of facts that have to be examined. In one way or another the Continental countries have dealt with these issues; any attempt to probe the need for a duty to rescue must deal with the following issues:[77]

1. The degree of danger or damage confronting the victim: must there be a threat to life or will the duty apply to lesser threats to a person's body and/or property?

2. The nature of the demands made on the bystander: the degree of risk and/or inconvenience which the bystander can be obliged to assume; must they be prepared to endanger their lives, or merely be prepared to undergo minor inconvenience, such as wasted time, or making a telephone call?

3. The degree of effectiveness required: is a futile heroic gesture to be considered fulfilling the norm, when a lesser act, such as calling the police or a doctor, would have been clearly more relevant?

4. The nature of the bystander's knowledge of the victim's plight: what degree of proximity to the scene is required, and what degree of perception as to the fact and seriousness of the victim's plight may be presumed?

5. The nature of any limitations on the duty: how is legal responsibility to be apportioned where there are many bystanders, and only some of them can be presumed to be able to act effectively?

6. The nature of the causal antecedents of the victim's situation: is it to be applicable in all situations or only where a crime is involved, or alternatively, where there is danger to the whole community, as in a natural disaster?

7. The attitude of the victim: how relevant is an appeal for help by the victim, or alternatively, a specific demand that no help be given as in the case of a suicide attempt, or as in the case of a family quarrel, where neighbors are requested to refrain from intervening?

8. The nature of the sanction: should it specify the criminal sanction only (of imprisonment and fines), or a civil liability only (of compensation), or both?

The issue of coercion to virtuous acts is by no means an easy one. Nevertheless, however complicated the details, the challenge of bystander behavior is a relatively straightforward one—can society afford to ignore the social implications and the harmful consequences of the indifference of an unresponsive bystander? Is it desirable that it is legally perfectly permissible to stand idly by while a baby drowns in a few inches of water, a blind man walks toward a dangerous situation where a word of warning would save him, a neighbor, customer, or business acquaintance asks in vain for help in a moment of danger?

Gordon contends vigorously that recognition of a duty to rescue would not negate a healthy individualism; such a duty would be no more than a recognition that "our modern society is interdependent and that the days of unrestricted individualism are behind us. The argument for the new doctrine is rooted in the conviction that a truly civilized society cannot abide a situation where one man turns his back and lets another die when by a safe and simple act he could have saved his life."[78] In fact, the strongest argument in favor of a duty to rescue may very well be the results and implications of those cases in which the duty to act was nonexistent despite the moral reprehensibility and the harmful results of the bystander's lack of response.

Notes

1. The proceedings of this conference, together with some additional articles, were published in book form. See James M. Ratcliffe, ed., *The Good Samaritan and the Law* (New York: Anchor Books, 1966).

2. Allen M. Linden, "Rescuers and Good Samaritans," *Modern Law Review*, 1971, *34*, pp. 241-259.

3. In this chapter, I shall deal only with the problem of the duty to rescue. The other issues of immunity, compensation, and rewards are dealt with in the next chapter. For a general discussion of the duty to act as it devolves on employers, family members, and particularly public bodies, see Marshall S. Shapo, *The Duty to Act: Tort Law, Power, and Public Policy* (Austin: University of Texas Press, 1977). There is a brief discussion of the "unrelated" bystander, pp. 64-68.

4. American Law Institute, *Restatement of American Law: Torts*, 2nd Topic, 7, in "General Principles of Tort: Duties of Affirmative Action," para. 314.

5. *Bush* v. *Armory Mfg. Co.*, 69 N.H. 257; 44 Atl. 809 (1897) at 213.

6. Ibid.

7. *Sidwell* v. *McVay*, Okl. 1955, 282 p. 2d 756.

8. William L. Prosser, *Handbook of the Law of Torts*, 4th ed. (St. Paul: West, 1971), p. 340. The examples given are all taken from real cases, namely: *Osterland* v. *Hill*, 1928, 263 Mass. 73, 160 N.E. 301, 56 *ALR* 1123; *Hurley* v. *Eddingfield*, 1901, 156 Ind. 416, 59 N.E. 1058; *Sidwell* v. *McVay*, 1955, Okl. 282 p. 2d. 756; *Gautret* v. *Egerton*, 1887, L.R. 2 C.P. 381.

9. *King* v. *Interstate Consolidated St. Rwy. Co.*, 23 R.I. 583, 51A 301 (1902).

10. *Allen* v. *Hixson*, 1900, 460 Ga. 36 S.E. 810.

11. Ibid.

12. *Carey* v. *Davis*, 190 Iowa 720, 180 N.W. 889 (1921).

13. *Rival* v. *Atchison, T. & S.F. Ry.*, 62 N.M. 159, 306 p. 2d 648 (1957). For further discussion of the employer-employee relationship, see Shapo, *The Duty to Act*, pp. 7-13.

14. *Zelenko* v. *Gimbel Bros.*, 158 Misc. 904, 287 N.Y. Supp. 134 (1935) at 135.

15. *Osterlind* v. *Hill*, above.

16. *Handiboe* v. *McCarthy*, 1966, 114 Ga. App. 541, 151 S.E. 2d 905.

17. *Yania* v. *Bigan*, 397 Pa. 316, 155 A.2d 343 (1959).

18. *L. & N.R.R.* v. *Scruggs and Echols*, 161 Ala. 97, 49 So. 399 (1909).

19. *Metallic Compression and Casting Co.* v. *Fitchburg Ry. Co.*, 109 Mass., 277 (1872).

20. *Union Pacific Ry. Co.*, v. *Cappier*, 72 P. 281, Kan (1930), 66 Kan 649, 69 C.R.P. 513.

21. The obligations on the road, at sea, and in the air will be discussed later. It might be noted that a book on the law of railways, published at the beginning of the century (Elliot on *Railroads*, 2nd ed. 1907), specifically stated that the railroad was absolved of all responsibility. For critical analyses of the law see Warner, "Duty of a Railroad to Care for a Person Rendered Helpless," *California Law Review*, 1919, 7, p. 312. For analysis of later developments recognizing a minimum humanitarian doctrine to render assistance, even when there is no negligence, see Becker, 'The Humanitarian Doctrine," *Modern Law Review*, 1947, *12*, p. 395, and 1948, *13*, p. 374.

22. *Heaven* v. *Pender*, 11 Q.B.D. 496 (1883).

23. See comment in P.A. London, *Pollock's Law of Torts*, 15th ed. (London: Stevens and Sons, 1951), p. 326.

24. *Depue* v. *Flateau*, 100 Minn, 299, 111 N.W. 1, 8 L.R.A. (N.S.) 485.

25. *R.* v. *Clarkson*, 3 All E.R. 344 (1971); see report of case in *Journal of Criminal Law*, No. 141 (1971), p. 43.

26. As quoted in F.J.M. Feldbrugge, "Good and Bad Samaritans: A Comparative Survey of Criminal Law Provisions Concerning Failure to Rescue," *American Journal of Comparative Law*, 1966 *14*, p. 655.

27. In addition to the article by Feldbrugge, see Aleksander W. Rudzinski, "The Duty to Rescue: A Comparative Analysis," in Ratcliffe, *The Good Samaritan and the Law*, pp. 91-134; Joseph Hofstetter and Wolfgang V. Marshall, "Amendment of the Belgian *Code Penal*: The Duty to Rescue Persons in Serious Danger," *American Journal of Comparative Law*, 1963, *11*, p. 66; note, "The Failure to Rescue: A Comparative Study," *Columbia Law Review*, 1952, *52*, p. 631.

28. As quoted by Graham Hughes, "Criminal Omissions," *Yale Law Review*, 1958, *67*, p. 632.

29. See Andre Tunc, "The Volunteer and the Good Samaritan," in Ratcliffe, p. 46.

30. See William A. Morris, *The Frankpledge System* (London: Longmans, Green, 1910), and T'ung-Tsu Ch'u, *Local Government in China under the Ch'ing* (Stanford: Stanford University Press, 1969), and the discussion in the previous chapter.

31. Graham Hughes, ' Criminal Omissions."

32. Ibid., p. 633.

33. John N. Hazard, *Material on Soviet Law*, Columbia University Mimeo, p. 51.

34. See Tunc, "The Volunteer and the Good Samaritan," p. 58.

35. John P. Dawson, "Rewards for the Rescue of Human Life?" in Ratcliffe, p. 71. See also his article "*Negotiorum Gestio*: The Altruistic Intermeddler," *Harvard Law Review*, 1961, *74* pp. 817, 1073.

36. Dawson, "Rewards . . . ," p. 72.

37. The suggestion that there may be a difference depending on whether the family members share a household is based on victim compensation schemes where compensation is allowed even if the victim and the criminal are of the same nuclear family, provided only that they are not living in the same household.

38. See Rudzinski, "The Duty to Rescue."

39. As quoted in ibid.

40. For a discussion of the implications of law and morality for the bystander issue, see Leon Shaskolsky Sheleff, "Morality, Criminal Law and Politics," *Tel Aviv University Studies in Law*, 1976, *2*, pp. 213-222. See also Antony M. Honoré, "Law, Morals and Rescue," in Ratcliffe, pp. 225-242.

41. Francis H. Bohlen, "The Moral Duty to Aid Others as a Basis of Tort Liability," *University of Pennsylvania Law Review*, 1908, *56*, p. 219.

42. Note, "The Bad Samaritan: Rescue Re-Examined," *Georgetown Law Journal*, 1966, *54*, pp. 631-632.

43. See Peter Brett, *An Inquiry into Criminal Guilt* (Sydney: The Law Book Co., 1963). For a discussion of the impact of the rules of strict liability on the Good Samaritan, see Richard Epstein, "A Theory of Strict Liability," *Journal of Legal Studies*, 1973, *2*, pp. 151-204.

44. Charles O. Gregory, "Gratuitous Undertakings and the Duty of Care," *De Paul Law Review*, 1951, *1*, p. 31.

45. Lionel H. Frankel, "Criminal Omissions: A Legal Microcosm," *Wayne State University Law Review*, 1965, *11*, pp. 387-393.

46. Ibid., p. 393.

47. Robert L. Hale, "Prima Facie Torts, Combination and Nonfeasance," *Columbia Law Review*, 1946, *46*, p. 214.

48. *U.S.* v. *Bethlehem Steel Corp.*, 315 U.S. 289, 330 (1942).

49. Otto Kirchheimer, "Criminal Omissions," *Harvard Law Review*, 1942, *55*, p. 641. Copyright 1942 by the Harvard Law Review Association.

50. Ibid., pp. 641-642.

51. Frankel, "Criminal Omissions," p. 386.

52. John Stuart Mill, *On Liberty* (New York: Appleton-Century-Crofts, 1947).

53. Ibid., p. 11.

54. Jeremy Bentham, *An Introduction to the Principles of Morals and Legislation* (London: Athlone Press, 1970).

55. Ibid.

56. J.F. Stephen, *History of the Criminal Law of England*, vol. 3, 1883. The writings of Mill, Bentham, and Stephen touch also on the vexed issue of law and morality which will be discussed in more detail in chapter 9.

57. Ibid., p. 10.

58. Hughes, "Criminal Omissions."

59. Warren P. Miller and Michael A. Zimmerman, "The Good Samaritan Act of 1966: A Proposal," in Ratcliffe, p. 279.

60. Rudzinski, "The Duty to Rescue," appendix, in Ratcliffe, pp. 125-134. The countries for which Rudzinski provides examples of the laws are Portugal, Switzerland, the Netherlands, Italy, Norway, Russia, Turkey, Denmark, Poland, Germany, Rumania, France, Hungary, Czechoslovakia, and Belgium. Rudzinski also includes one Asian country, China. For a discussion of the duty to rescue in South Korean law, see the introduction to Gerhard O. Mueller, ed., *The Korean Criminal Code* (London: Sweet and Maxwell, 1960).

61. Wallace M. Rudolph, "The Duty to Act: A Proposed Rule," in Ratcliffe, p. 243, and *Nebraska Law Journal*, 1965, *44*, p. 499.

62. Ratcliffe, p. 243.

63. *Jones* v. *United States*, 308 F. 2d 307, 310 (D.C. Circ. 1962).

64. 46 U.S.C. Ann. para. 728; U.S. Statutes at Large, Vol. 37, Part 1, Chp. 268, Sec. 2.

65. See G.P. Zhukov, "Space Law: The New Extra-Terrestrial Jurisprudence," *Impact of Science on Society*, 1971, *21*, p. 237.

66. In certain cases there may be a presumption that the professional person offering the aid will be entitled to normal rates of remuneration for his professional services, especially if self-employed, as in the case of an ambulance

driver or a doctor. An interesting possibility would be where a person endangered himself by specifically disobeying an order of an expert, whose job it was to protect the public—for example, a swimmer drowning after having been warned by a lifeguard about dangerous undertow, and who would be unable to rescue that person should he get into difficulty. Under such circumstances would the expert be entitled to refuse to attempt a rescue? If the expert were injured while making such an attempt, would he be entitled to sue for damages?

67. Much work is now being done in this area. For some of the pioneering studies see R.E. Helfer and C.H. Kempe, eds., *The Battered Child* (Chicago: University of Chicago Press, 1968); David Gil, *Violence Against Children* (Cambridge: Harvard University Press, 1970). See also my discussion of parental and adult hostility, "Beyond the Oedipus Complex: A Perspective on the Myth and Reality of Generational Conflict," *Theory and Society*, 1976, *3*, pp. 1-44.

68. See Monroe Paulsen, Graham Parker, and Lynn Adelman, "Child Abuse Reporting Laws—Some Legislative History," *George Washington Law Review*, 1966, *36*, p. 482. See also Henry H. Foster and Doris Jonas Freed, "The Battered Child: Whose Responsibility . . . Lawyer or Physician?" *Trial*, vol. 3 (Dec./Jan. 1966/67), 33. They note that, prior to 1960, there was only one such law in the United States, but by 1966 all but three states had enacted them. These laws were passed at about the time that Helfer and Kempe and their coworkers began publishing articles on the subject. See, for example, C.H. Kempe et al., "The Battered Child Syndrome," *Journal of American Medical Association*, 1962, *181*, p. 17.

69. Louis Waller, "Rescue and the Common Law: England and Australia," in Ratcliffe, pp. 148-152.

70. *R. v. Crimmins* (1959) V.R. 270.

71. *Sykes* v. *Director of Public Prosecutions* (1962) A.C. 528.

72. Ibid., p. 564.

73. *People* v. *Lefkowitz*, 294 Mich. 263 (1940).

74. See A. Rosenthal, *Thirty-Eight Witnesses* (New York: McGraw-Hill, 1964).

75. Lord Macaulay, "Introductory Report: Notes on an Indian Penal Code," in Macaulay, *Complete Writings* (London: Sedgewick, 1900), *18*, p. 309.

76. Ibid.

77. See Leon S. Sheleff, "The Criminal Triad: Bystander, Victim, Criminal," *International Journal of Criminology and Penology*, 1974, *2*, pp. 159-172: also in I. Drapkin and E. Viano, eds., *Victimology* (Lexington, Mass.: Lexington Books, 1974), *1*, pp. 111-126.

78. Gerald L. Gordon, "Moral Challenge to the Legal Doctrine of Rescue," *Cleveland-Marshall Law Review*, 1965, *14*, p. 334.

7

The Rights and
Rewards of Bystanders

Although the key legal issue of bystander involvement relates to the duty to rescue, differences exist also between the Anglo-American and Continental approaches to two other important issues, that of compensation to the bystander who is injured or incurs loss while trying to aid the victim, and that of immunity from civil claims or from criminal sanctions as a result of injury or damage caused inadvertently while in the process of attempting to rescue or help someone in distress.

Since the Continental approach generally imposes a duty to rescue, it is only natural that bystanders are also protected should there be any adverse consequences to their action. Sometimes this protection is implied, arising axiomatically out of the prior duty to rescue; sometimes it is specifically spelled out. In some instances the rights of the bystander are derived from general principles of law such as *negotiorum gestio*, which refers to the implied mandate to manage the affairs of others in the event of an emergency, without their express permission in order to safeguard their interests.

In the British and American systems of law the lack of duty to rescue has also on occasion served as the basis for narrowly interpreting the rights of the intervening bystander to claim compensation and/or immunity. In the absence of a duty to help, the courts have not always been prepared to recognize the right to legal protection when well-meaning efforts to help a fellow being fail.

A further factor causing reticence on the part of the courts in Britain and the United States is that the principle of *negotiorum gestio* has never been incorporated into the British and American legal systems, and so cannot be used as a fundamental principle, going beyond the question of a duty to rescue and justifying legal support for bystander activity. Instead the courts have sometimes resorted to other concepts such as agency by necessity, unjust enrichment, or implied contract to grant aid to bystanders. These provide, however, far less flexibility than the rule of *negotiorum gestio*, as will be shown.

Further, it would seem that the courts have never fully resolved the ambivalence between their desire to support and encourage the virtues of helpful and altruistic behavior and their reluctance to be bound by all the consequences of such behavior, where it is not entirely successful, or where it involves certain costs. If there is ab initio no duty to rescue, then the rescuer's activities, however necessary, heroic, or desirable, are seen as risks voluntarily undertaken, in the full realization of the consequences, and with a willingness to accept them, without the right to demand of the victim, the wrongdoer, or society at large that they share in the costs of these risks. The attitude that is sometimes adopted by the courts is best summed up in the label "officious intermeddler"[1] that the courts have assigned to the intervening bystander, in order to indicate their disapproval of intervention which is not directly the concern of bystanders, for which in many cases they lack the necessary expertise, and for which the law itself makes no demands. Caveat intervenor—let the intervenor beware—has been the thrust of much legal reasoning; help offered, being at the risk of those who intervene, it is their responsibility to ensure that the aid rendered is faultless in its execution, or else suffer the consequences.

Yet, as Linden[2] notes, there has been a slow transformation in this position, as the Anglo-American systems move, partly through legislation, partly through creative judicial decisions, to a position more compatible with support for bystander rescue activity.

Fleming, in his study of tort law in Britain, also notes that support for the rescuer is a fairly recent phenomenon: "Legal doctrines reflected perhaps overlong the values of a rugged individualism that, if not actually deprecating anyone's aspiration to be his brother's keeper, thought it at least extravagant of him to expect someone else to pay the bill of his indulgence if Samaritan virtue went awry."[3] Yet he goes on to argue that the "least the law can do, even if unwilling . . . to *compel* one citizen to help another, is to encourage him to do so. An important contribution towards that end is to assure him of compensation for an injury he may sustain in the venture."[4]

In general there is a greater willingness to allow claims for compensation, especially where the victim has substantially benefited by the intervention, than to allow immunity from claims, where, by the very nature of the claim, it appears that the well-meaning intervenor was not entirely successful in his prosocial behavior. In this latter instance courts have the wisdom of hindsight to upbraid the bystander for action that was at least partially unavailing, may have been foolhardy, and was done voluntarily without any legal coercion.

Since for the most part there is no clear-cut legislation on these two issues, there are often subtle nuances in the judgments which distinguish approval for the action and concomitant legal rights from disapproval and the denial of legal rights.

Court Decisions on Compensation

Inasmuch as there has been a development in the law toward recognizing the rights of the intervening bystander, Fleming acknowledges the important role played in both the United States and in Britain by a leading American case from 1921, *Wagner* v. *International Railroad*, where Justice Cardozo, in two short, telling sentences, described the essential basis for allowing legal redress: "Danger invites rescue. The cry of distress is the summons to relief."[5]

In a leading American textbook the writers also remark that "prior to this case the courts had difficulty in finding a basis for the defendant's duty to the rescuer but subsequent to *Wagner* this difficulty vanished."[6] While the Wagner case is of extreme importance it should be noted that it was preceded by a similar case, *Eckert* v. *L.I.R.R. Co.,*[7] in which a bystander was allowed compensation for injury sustained when going to the rescue of a stranger on the rails in front of an oncoming train. In fact this case was approvingly quoted in the Wagner case, as well as in British cases. However, it is probably true that it was the persuasive opinion and the full authority of the Supreme Court in *Wagner* which created a climate conducive to judicial cognizance of the rights of rescuers.

The difficulties encountered by the courts in recognizing these rights arise from a number of factors. Firstly, since these are civil actions directed against the defendant—who might be the victim, or more commonly a third party—the rescuer has been obliged to show both some measure of wrongdoing or negligence on the part of the defendant, and some degree of foreseeability that any such wrongdoing or negligence would evoke an effort at rescue from a bystander. Secondly, since the bystander has no legal duty to act, he has often to overcome the available alternative defenses of the defendant, namely that there was contributory negligence on the part of the rescuer, or that the rescue action was an independent act breaking the chain of causation (*actus novus interveniens*), or that the rule of *volenti non fit iniuria* applied, namely that a voluntary assumption of risk was a bar to claiming compensation for damage that ensued from that risk. To overcome these defenses, the court generally requires that the rescuer act intuitively and spontaneously without having the time to fully conceive the nature of the risk he was undertaking, or the time to realize its full implication—so that the risk could not be said to have been voluntarily undertaken.

Over the years the courts have gradually whittled away at these reservations, painstakingly carving out a legal framework more generous in its recognition of the rights of a rescuer. In many instances it has been the specific facts of the case, or the specific attributes of the rescuer, that have facilitated the process of providing protections which were not originally available. This may be seen in the Wagner case, where, although the court acknowledged the need to compensate a rescuer and laid down a general rule recognizing this need even for strangers, in their reasoning they took account of the fact that there was a familial relationship between the rescuer and the victim, and it was this fact that enabled them to understand the conduct of the rescuer, which possibly might not have been acceptable had the relationship been that of total strangers.

Wagner had been traveling in the night on a crowded train with his cousin when the latter was thrown from the train as it lurched while going over a bridge. The emergency cord was pulled, and passengers got out of the train to look, in the dark, for the missing person. Whereas most people went to look under the bridge, the plaintiff had gone back along the bridge, where he had missed his footing and fallen off the bridge and been injured. At the original trial the plaintiff's case had been dismissed, as the jury was unable to find that the defendant, the railway company, was responsible for the manner in which the plaintiff had conducted the search for his cousin.

On appeal the court held that it was not possible to differentiate between the original negligence toward the victim, and the legal responsibility of the defendant toward any person who attempted to remedy the results of their original negligence.

> The wrong that imperils life is a wrong to the imperiled victim; it is a wrong also to his rescuer. The state that leaves an opening in a bridge is liable to the child that falls into the stream, but liable to the parent also that plunges to its aid. . . . The risk of rescue, if only it be not wanton, is born of the occasion. The emergency begets the man. The wrongdoer may not have foreseen the coming of a deliverer. He is accountable as if he had.[8]

The argument of the defense had been that whatever the responsibility for the original negligent act that had caused harm to the cousin, the subsequent actions of the plaintiff were a separate sequence of acts—a *novus actus interveniens*. The plaintiff, according to this contention, had not acted instinctively and spontaneously, but had had sufficient time to consider the most advisable course of action, and had thus voluntarily assumed the risk, and thereby accepted legal liability.

Although such a doctrine had a sound basis in the law as interpreted at that time, the court held that it was not prepared to differentiate between impulsive behavior oblivious to the peril, and deliberate behavior allowing time to measure the cost. However, in analyzing the actual behavior of the plaintiff, the court *did* indeed pay attention to the impulsive and spontaneous nature of the plaintiff's actions, in particular when his behavior was compared to that of the other passengers who had behaved more prudently in searching below the bridge, where the cousin had actually been found. The court stressed that time was of the essence, and that there was a danger that another train might come on the track. Then, trying to restructure the thought processes of the plaintiff, the court stressed specifically the fact of a familial relationship. "The plaintiff had to choose at once, in agitation and with imperfect knowledge. He had seen his *kinsman and companion* thrown out into the darkness"[9] (my italics). This reference to the victim's having been a kinsman and a companion raises the question as to whether any of the other passengers would have received the same degree of understanding from the court if they had been injured acting as the plaintiff/cousin had—in their case the voluntary assumption of risk might well have led to a denial of their claim.

Interestingly, one of the leading British cases, *Videan* v. *British Transport*

Commission,[10] also involves a rescue attempt carried out by a family relation, with an additional element being the fact that the rescuer was also an employee of the railway company being sued.

The decedent, a stationmaster, had gone to the rescue of his two-year-old son, who, while visiting his father, had wandered onto the railway tracks in front of an oncoming train. The father had been killed and the son injured. The court held that the railway company had no liability to the son who was a trespasser in going on to the railroad, and therefore his sudden presence on the railway line could not reasonably have been foreseen, but that there was a liability to the father, since they could have anticipated that the father, *in his capacity as a stationmaster*, might suddenly dash onto the track to effect a rescue. It is difficult to understand the reasoning of the court. If a nonemployee or a stranger or the mother had gone to the son's rescue, it would seem that there may have been no action against the railroad company.

In fact, on one occasion, in a U.S. case, the court had clearly indicated that the standards of behavior applicable to a parent would be different from that of a stranger. The parent might be allowed to show less prudence in attempting a rescue, and still be entitled to claim compensation for harm suffered.

In the 1898 case, *Walters* v. *Denver Consolidated Electric Light Co.*, the court had allowed an action by a rescuer, a mother, even where the action was clearly futile.

> The instincts of a mother, when she sees her child in distress, will lead her to rush headlong to its rescue, without stopping to count the cost or measure the risk she is incurring; and to say that an act to which her affection irresistibly impelled her should be charged against her as something imprudent and unnecessary would be to shock a sentiment as universal as mankind. The law is not the creature of cold-blooded merciless logic, and its inherent justice and humanity will never for a moment permit the act of a mother in saving her offspring, no matter how desperate it might have been, to be imputed to her as negligence, or at any time or in any manner used to her detriment.[11]

(Of course, for the plaintiff to succeed there was still the need to prove negligence on the part of the defendant.)

The nature of the person's employ might also be a factor in the court's decision. It seemed to have had much relevance in the Videan case in Britain, and was again a factor in another leading British case, *Haynes* v. *Harwood,*[12] though once again there is some confusion; for, while the courts present the rights of the rescuer in general terms as applicable to all strangers, the judgment itself takes note of the fact that, in this particular case, the rescuer was a policeman, and therefore it was more reasonable to presume that his rescue efforts could have been foreseen by the defendants.

Two horses, holstered to a van, had been left unattended in the street; they had run away and were approaching a group of pedestrians, who were in danger of being run over, when a policeman, at great risk to himself, seized hold of the horses and managed to bring them to a standstill, injuring himself in the process.

The court held that the defendants, owners of the horses and van, were liable for the harm caused to the policeman. Although the court indicated that the behavior could have been justified by any stranger intent on preventing harm to potential victims, the court referred to the fact that "the man injured was a policeman who might readily be anticipated to do the very thing which he did, whereas the intervention of a 'mere passer-by' was not so probable."[13] Again, despite the broad rule laid down in this case, the question remains as to whether the court would have been as understanding of a "mere passer-by" who might have been injured in a rescue attempt. This judgment also tried to eliminate the distinction between rescuers acting on an impulse (for whom the courts normally had consideration) and others who acted after giving the matter due thought (for whom the courts were much stricter). "It would be absurd to say that if a man deliberately incurs a risk he is entitled to less protection than if he acts on a sudden impulse without thinking whether he should do so or not."[14]

In one exceptional case—predating most of the cases which slowly began to acknowledge the rights of a rescuer—a court in Georgia, in a case decided in 1885,[15] found for the plaintiff, whose husband had been killed in a vain effort to prevent a train accident. The deceased had been in the employ of the defendant, working as an engineer on a train which was headed for a collision as a result of negligence on the part of other servants of the defendant. Instead of jumping from the train to save his life as he might have done, the engineer stayed at his post in an unavailing attempt to prevent the accident. It is not clear again how much the court was swayed by the fact of his having been in a position of responsibility on the train, similar perhaps to the traditional role of the captain of a ship sinking at sea. In any event, the rule laid down by the court, apparently little noticed in the succeeding years, was a firm commitment of understanding support for those prepared to risk their lives in order to save the lives of others. The court felt that "to remain at his post in the hope of saving other lives would be an act of heroism so exalted as to constrain approval from all hearts," and went on to argue that the court "should not scan closely the grounds of hope he might have had to save others, though risking himself in the effort."[16]

Whatever the precise standards that the courts are prepared to adopt there can be no doubt that extreme actions such as in the latter case will only be sanctioned when there is a risk to a person; lesser standards apply where it is property that is endangered. Thus, an employee killed while going into a burning building in order to make a telephone call to give the alarm was not considered to have acted within acceptable standards, and his estate was not entitled to claim.[17] The rule is clear, then, that risks that might be justified to save life or even limb, will not be justified to save only property. In *Henjun* v. *Bok*[18] the court referring to the "so-called rescue doctrine" specifically declared that the rescuer would not be entitled to special consideration except when attempting to save a life; yet even here the Restatement of Law has attempted to suggest limits on rescuer activity: "The risk of rescue may be so great or the chance of its success so slight as to make it unreasonable even when human life is at stake."[19]

Sometimes, however, even when these conditions are met the court may be reluctant to grant a remedy to the plaintiff. In *French* v. *Trace*[20] a truckdriver had gone to the aid of a driver trapped in an overturned car, who was screaming for help. The plaintiff, together with others, had lifted the car to extricate the trapped driver. Later the plaintiff had suffered from a bursitis condition in the shoulder, and had sued for compensation. In the trial court the decision had gone in favor of the plaintiff, but on appeal the judges had found that the plaintiff had unnecessarily overexerted himself.

Even so, in a leading British textbook on restitution,[21] Goff and Jones state that it is the American approach which shows a greater tendency to assist the bystander acting on behalf of a stranger. "In England," according to them, "the courts have adopted a more austere attitude, and the stranger is generally denied restitution, no matter how grave was the emergency which prompted his intervention."[22]

Tiley, in an article[23] written shortly afterwards, takes strong issue with this approach. While not denying that reluctance of the courts to recognize the rights of the rescuer, Tiley argues forcefully for the acceptance of a "rescue principle."

In his extensive survey of the subject Tiley claims "that there is a rescue principle and that it is capable of precise formulation."[24] The principle is that "where the defendant has created a situation of peril for another, the victim, the defendant will be held in law to have caused not only the peril to the victim, but also his rescue, and so to have caused any injury suffered by the rescuer in his rescue attempt. The rescue principle is a causation principle. . . . The rescuer recovers despite his voluntary act."[25] Tiley argues convincingly for the need for such a rescue principle in order to avoid forcing the plaintiff to disprove the existence of the major defenses available to the defendant. He writes that "most cases have been concerned to show that neither *volenti non fit iniuria* nor *novus actus interveniens* is a defense to a rescue claim."[26] Tiley sees this approach as being negative; since "rescue is an exception to two well-recognized defenses [this approach] leads naturally to a reluctance to extend the principle lest the exception should shake the rule."[27]

Shortly after this article was published a case[28] was decided in Britain which applied the concept of a rescue principle in its most extensive form, granting compensation to the family of a rescuer acting on behalf of complete strangers, where the response exceeded that which might have been expected of a reasonable person, where the rescue operations went on for a considerable period of time, and where the harm in the form of delayed psychological damage leading to the rescuer's death seemed both remote and difficult to foresee.

In the words of the court:

> The accident happened some two hundred yards from the Chadwicks'
> house. Mr. Chadwick was told of the accident by his wife and he
> immediately ran out of the house to help. Mrs. Chadwick did not see
> him again until 3 o'clock in the morning when he came in, covered with
> mud, with blood on his hands and clutching a small golliwog brooch
> which he gave to Mrs. Chadwick to look after. He went out again and
> did not return until 6 o'clock in the morning. He was a mess with blood
> and the like. He would not go to bed and he was upset and shaking. The
> golliwog brooch belonged to a small boy, three years of age, who had
> been killed in the accident.[29]

Evidence was given of the stark change that came about in Mr. Chadwick's
condition after the accident. He "had been running a successful window cleaning
business. ... He took an interest in social and charitable activities ... had a
happy disposition and got on extremely well with people. After the accident, he
started sleeping badly, waking up in the night and talking of the little boy whom
he had seen ... four or five weeks after the accident he stopped working. His
condition was diagnosed as 'catastrophic neurosis,' an illness which is known to
result from major catastrophes such as earthquakes, fires, floods and major
accidents or disasters."[30]

The unforeseen and unfortunate consequences of an innocent bystander's
responding to the plight of an unknown stranger are clearly brought out in this
case, as is the degree of understanding and help that a court may provide to
mitigate at least some of the adverse results.

Theoretical Approaches to Compensation

A special situation applies where prosocial conduct is aimed not at saving a life
but at protecting or enhancing property. Generally there are no particular risks
involved. Under such circumstances, the question becomes: what specific
conditions do the bystanders have to fulfill in order to qualify for the right to
compensation, should they incur any costs? There are a number of legal
concepts which cover such a situation, the most notable and comprehensive
being that of *negotiorum gestio*, the unauthorized administration of the affairs
of another for the latter's presumed benefit.

This rule is well established in most Continental legal systems, having its
origins in the Roman law; but it has not been incorporated into the British or
American systems. The Continental systems thus generally find it easier to grant
compensation to unsolicited altruistic actions than the Anglo-American systems.
In fact *negotiorum gestio* can, and has, been used to claim compensation also for
emergency rescue operations, even though its more regular use is in the case of
benefits conferred on property.

Discussing the original development of the law in Roman times, Schulz notes that "the underlying idea was that a man should help his fellow man in case of emergency. The Romans carried through this idea with their usual common sense without confusing morality and law. Nobody is bound to care for the affairs of another . . . but the law should favor and facilitate such altruistic action by granting to the *gestor* the right to claim reimbursement of his expenses."[31]

In its broadest form the doctrine of *negotiorum gestio* gave rise to rights, generally connected with property rights. An absentee owner might find, on his return, that his property had been looked after by a gestor, a person acting to protect the property from damage, as in the case of a fire breaking out, which the gestor might extinguish; or even enhance the property, by watering the trees, pruning the branches, or picking the fruit. The two parties would afterwards work out the details of the mutual benefits accrued (for instance, where the gestor had eaten the fruit), and the expenses incurred, and then make a total accounting of profit and loss. In many cases, of course, the gestor would be somebody who was actually acquainted with the owner of the property (such as a neighbor) but the principle is also applicable as between total strangers. In any event, the principle must always be applied with caution to prevent exploitation of another's property during his absence, for example, unemployed laborers working on another's property during the owner's absence, and subsequently claiming restitution for their expenses.

Rubin, in his historical survey of the concept,[32] shows that the original aim was the encouragement of altruistic actions, and that it was this factor that was dominant as the doctrine was borrowed by later legal systems. The gestor must have acted with the welfare of the beneficiary uppermost in mind.

Dawson notes that, from its inception in Roman times through to the modern period, "the rule of *negotiorum gestio* was justified essentially by a moral ideal that placed a high value on disinterested service to others."[33] While initially it had been used mainly for the protection of economic interests, Dawson shows how easily the doctrine can be applied in instances where the implied mandate to do acts on behalf of another involves also the rescue of human life or limb.

The British legal system has never accepted the doctrine and as a result lacks an easy capacity to grant aid in certain circumstances. Because of the rejection of the doctrine of *negotiorum gestio*, other more limited concepts, but aimed at the same results, have been developed—of unjust enrichment, implied contract, quasi-contract, restitution, or agency by necessity. On one occasion the doctrine of *negotiorum gestio* was specifically denied by the court: " . . work done by one man to preserve or benefit the property of another does not create any obligation to repay the expenditure incurred."[34] On the other hand, the acceptance of some of these other doctrines has enabled the British courts to reach decisions similar to those which flow from *negotiorum gestio*. In a 1943 case the court held that "it is clear that any civilized system of law is bound to provide remedies for cases of what has been called unjust enrichment or unjust benefit, that is, to prevent a man from retaining the money of, or some benefit derived from, another which it is against conscience that he should keep."[35]

The doctrine of necessity is, in some cases, similar to that of *negotiorum gestio*, although limited to cases of emergency, such as the work of a salvage crew rescuing property from likely loss, or a doctor performing an emergency operation, or a mountain guide searching for lost persons or rescuing injured persons.

However attractive the doctrine of *negotiorum gestio*, and other similar rules, Dawson has posed some difficult questions as to the desirability of using it too broadly, particularly since he feels that, in many cases, the beneficiary could be adversely affected by too liberal an application of the rule. In fact he raises serious questions for the whole issue of compensation for help given. "How can one," he asks, "place a money value on the time, energy, and risk in carrying a body from a burning building or in extracting a drowning person from deep water?"[36] He extends his probing: "Should the life-salvor . . . have a civil remedy to reimburse him for his losses against the person whom he attempted by appropriate means to save from imminent peril, whether or not the attempt succeeded?"[37] Finally, he suggests that the beneficiary alone should not bear the responsibility for restitution. ". . . Are there other ways in which the work of reimbursing rescuers can be more widely distributed or cast on others who are better able to pay than the imperilled persons themselves?"[38]

Dawson argues that every effort should be made to avoid a private law solution in cases where an intervenor has aided someone else in an emergency. To him "private law remedies are misapplied when they create liability without fault in the person whose life or health is saved."[39] He comes to the conclusion that while the Continental approach may be correct in punishing for the failure to rescue, when no risk is involved, it seems "a different question whether the one who conforms to or exceeds his duty should receive from another in desperate need either reward or indemnity for the aid he gives."[40]

Inasmuch as society is interested in encouraging such acts, Dawson suggests that it would be advisable "to spread the cost over the widest possible group of contributors,"[41] using the full resources of the society.

This approach is being given increasing consideration, particularly as part of the ongoing battle to allow maximum protection and insurance against the many hazards of modern living, given the great risk of being victimized without any fault on one's part, and with little hopes of recovery from the agent of one's misfortune. Why should the victim then have to bear responsibility for making restitution to the rescuer?

Within the field of criminology and victimology regular calls have gone out to provide protection for those injured in crime. This was an issue that agitated the participants of the first international conferences on crime held in the nineteenth century, received renewed impetus with Fry's major work[42] in the

1950s on the need to compensate victims of crime, and, ever since the acceptance of victimology as a recognized discipline, has become the focus for academic and general articles pointing out the advantages of public compensation schemes.

In some of the legislation that has been enacted recently, state compensation is recognized not only for the victim but also for the intervening bystander,[43] that is, the bystander claims not from the victim, who has benefited from the intervention, nor from the criminal who was the prime cause of the action, but from the state, on whose behalf theoretically the bystander is considered to have acted.

This legislation deals only with crimes of violence, but provides a basis for the kind of assistance that can be made available through activating total societal resources. One of the early examples of such a law is that passed in New York City in 1965.[44] This law was passed the year after the Genovese incident; yet the more specific catalytic reason for the legislation was an incident, referred to in chapter 1,[45] where a passenger on the New York subway system, Arthur Collins, was killed while attempting to thwart another person from molesting some of the other passengers. The New York City Transit Authority decided to make ex gratia payments to his family at the rate due to a policeman of the Authority killed while on duty. It was at the later request of the Transit Authority that the administrative code of the city of New York was amended to provide relief for the Good Samaritan.

Sec 67-3.2. now provides for:

Awards for death or injuries received by persons other than peace officers while attempting to prevent the commission of crime, preserve the peace or prevent public disturbances. Direct action on the part of private citizens in preventing crimes against the person or property of others, preserving the peace or preventing public disturbances, benefits the entire public. . . . The board of estimate is hereby authorized and empowered to make an award for the death of or injury to any person or persons other than peace officers, which has been . . . caused while such person is engaged . . . in attempting to prevent the commission of a crime against the person or property of another, preserve the peace or prevent public disturbances. Such award shall be fixed in the discretion of the board of estimate as a matter of grace and not as a matter of right and shall in the case of personal injuries be based upon the medical expenses and loss of earnings incurred by such person injured while attempting to prevent the commission of a crime, preserve the peace or prevent public disturbances. In the case of the death of such person, such award shall be made to the widow, child, or other dependent of such person and the award may be in a single payment, or may be made in periodic payments.[46]

New Zealand, which was one of the first countries to set up a victim compensation scheme, has now expanded its program to include compensation for a broad range of victimization, including not only the victims of crime but also of traffic accidents, work accidents, and so on, to the extent that the traditional rights of the law of tort are being supplanted by these government compensation plans.[47] In most modern societies there are extensive social security systems which serve to minimize the harm caused to those who, for whatever reason, are adversely affected by the fortuitous vicissitudes of modern living. In the case of natural disasters, for instance, large sums of money and resources are made available to the victims in order to rehabilitate themselves.

It seems then that the losses suffered by a bystander displaying prosocial behavior could also be incorporated within such a system, as has been done in some instances.[48] There is no reason why payments should be limited only to the victims of crimes of violence. If the overall aim is to reduce the losses of any particular party, and to spread these losses as much as possible so as to minimize the inevitable injustices of the random blows inflicted by fate, then there seems no reason to deny societal support from those who go to the aid of someone in distress; there seems to be no reason why the victim and the bystander should be subsequently locked in combat in an attempt to determine the degree of culpability of the victim or the degree of caution displayed by the rescuer in his efforts. If the total interests of society dictate that victimization should be minimized, and that bystanders should be encouraged (even if not coerced) to help those in distress, then surely adequate resources must be set aside to ensure that recompense will be readily available for losses incurred.

While it is true that in most cases there is the possibility of the bystander suing in a civil court, this avenue is almost never pursued. Victims of crime are also entitled to sue the criminal, yet rarely do so. It is the awareness in recent years of the neglect of the interest of the victim of crime that has led to the move to have victim compensation schemes. But there is still little concern for the bystander. It is not known how many people are harmed in rescue attempts, not necessarily involving crime, but who never receive recompense for the harm they suffer.

The Carnegie Hero Fund, for instance, provides not only for medals of merit, but also for monetary compensation to the rescuer, where injury occurs, or to the family in the case of death. Yet, the scope of this program is obviously limited. There are rescuers, whose risks do not perhaps qualify them for recognition as heroes, but who nevertheless suffer injury. From an overall point of view, is it sufficient to leave them to the vagaries of civil suits which, in turn, may impose unjustifiable demands on an innocent victim, or even sometimes on a wrongdoer; or to the prospects of obtaining an ex gratia award from an understanding public authority? Of course, any such scheme would have to ensure that there was no exploitation—whether crass, in the form of fabricated incidents, or subtle, in the form of double or multiple payments—where rescuers could claim from more than one source. But, of course, these are not unique problems; they are an ongoing part of the legal complications of tort and insurance law, and there are ample legal and technical precedents for coping with them.

If a compensation scheme were to be set up, it might avoid the nagging dilemmas often confronting those who are perfectly willing to help, but wish to be assured that any harm suffered will be adequately recompensed. Honoré describes the kind of considerations that occur frequently. "A mountain guide with a hungry family is called to rescue a foolish climber trapped on the north face of the Eiger. Does anyone imagine him to be indifferent to the questions of how his family will be kept if he is killed?"[49]

At the international level in dealing with the problems of rescue operations at sea, such compensation is assured. Not only is there a duty to rescue, but there is accepted practice of adequate recompense for the effort. Encountering a situation where the potential rescuers of a stricken ship preceded their rescue attempt by buying the ship at a low price the court refused to sanction the sale and held that "the general interests of commerce will be much better promoted by requiring the salvor to trust for compensation to the liberal recompense usually awarded by courts for such services."[50]

This principle could easily be adapted for all rescue operations, with a special board to determine the amount. An official overall compensation scheme would not only provide deserved aid for the rescuer, and avoid some of the more intricate legal issues that have arisen, as shown in some of the cases discussed; it would also be a statement of intent, indicating societal appreciation of altruistic and helping behavior.

Protection for Bystanders

However difficult the position of those bystanders who claim compensation for a rescue attempt (which in most cases has the distinct virtue of at least having helped to alleviate the plight of the victim), far more complex is the position of bystanders who not only fail to alleviate the plight, but actually aggravate it, or cause harm to others, or misinterpret the situation. Since they have no duty to act in the first place, and since their intervention has actually had detrimental results, they thereby expose themselves to possible criminal indictment and civil claims, which may be entered by the very victim they were intending to help, by the very wrongdoer whose initial action was the cause of the intervention, or by innocent bystanders totally unconnected with the incident.

Even where there is a *right* to intervene but for as long as there is *no actual duty* to do so, the courts tend to adopt the most stringent standards in determining whether there was negligence or not. In Gregory's language, "The very act of charity puts a noose around the neck of the kind-hearted person, from which he can escape only by persuading a court and jury that he proceeded without reproach."[51]

The high standards of judicious and cautious behavior demanded of intervenors are well borne out in the case of *People* v. *Young*, discussed in the introductory chapter,[52] where a citizen of New York, only a short time before the Genovese incident, which was to shock the conscience of so many, had been declared by a New York court to be an "officious intermeddler," who was liable for all negative consequences, arising out of the fact that his concern for the presumed plight of a young teenager, and his altruistic actions on his behalf, were the result of an incorrect perception of what had occurred.

The problematical nature of the legal position is also well exemplified in this case, as judges at different stages of the proceedings came to differing decisions, including vigorous dissenting judgments at every stage. For an attack on two policemen whom the accused had mistakenly presumed to be beating a young teenager, Young was found guilty at the trial level, and then had the verdict overturned in the appellate decision, and was finally convicted by the higher court of appeals.

In the judgment itself the court referred to the fact that there was no uniformity in the different jurisdictions throughout the country; however, the judges maintained that "the weight of authority holds . . . that one who goes to the aid of a third person does so at his own peril."

In a strong dissenting judgment Judge Froessel claimed that the majority judgment was denying the defendant the widely accepted defense of a reasonable mistake of fact, a defense which could even be used in a homicide charge. The majority judgment had stated that the mental intent of the bystander was irrelevant—he was only entitled to the same rights that the "victim" himself had. Since in this case there was no victim, as the youth was being legally arrested by the policemen, and was illegally resisting his arrest, there could be no defense for the intervenor, regardless of the fact that he had no mental intent to commit a crime, and regardless of the fact that had the circumstances been as he had presumed, his action would have been perfectly legitimate, and even laudable. In the court's words, "The right of a person to defend another ordinarily should not be greater than such person's right to defend himself."

Waller's comment on this case is unequivocal. He ponders as to what the accused, a citizen in New York, "thought if and when he read the fate which overtook Kitty Genovese" and then goes on to denounce decisions of this type as *"perverse* judgments which do nothing more than raise barriers before those who would come to the rescue of their fellows in distress"[53] (italics in original).

In insisting on equating the legal position of the bystander with that of the supposed victim the courts are denying a major factor—namely that, precisely because of the willingness to take risks on behalf of a stranger in distress, the rescuer is entitled to special consideration.

While the mere fact of rescue, in and of itself, obviously cannot justify blanket endorsement of any action, no matter how reckless or harmful, the key issue to be determined is whether special considerations are to be applied to the intervening bystander, as are, for instance, routinely applied to policemen using force in the course of their arrest procedures. A refusal to apply such special considerations may, in the long run, erode any desire to help, and justify any tendency to ignore the plight of a stranger. This need for special considerations, and rights of indemnity, may well be at the heart of the bystander issue. Thus ordinary citizens may be reluctant to intervene in a crime situation unless they have clear guidelines as to their authority—for instance, the right to arrest and the conditions under which it may be executed. Doctors may well be reluctant to provide their specialized services unless there are assurances that they will not be exposing themselves to subsequent civil claims for undertaking treatment in an emergency without obtaining the prior permission of the person whom they are trying to help.

Both of these areas are crucial for an understanding of bystander behavior—in both of them there was a spate of legislation in the early 1960s which was actually aimed at broadening the rights of citizens to arrest, and of doctors to aid and treat.

Reference has been made in chapter 5 to the problem of citizens who not only go the rescue of someone who appears to be the victim of a crime, but also attempt to effect an arrest of the presumed culprit. Today many jurisdictions provide for such citizen's arrest, and some even provide for reasonable error as to the facts of the situation.

Bassiouni, in his book on citizen's arrest,[54] has traced the historical development of the law through different periods according to the importance attached to citizen involvement in each period, from the early hue and cry through to the common-law position today, and the impact of recent legislation. As to the modern period he shows that with the perceived increase in the crime rate in the 1960s, a trend of legislation emerged that "a private person can perform an arrest on reasonable grounds to believe that a felony has been committed, even though not in his or her view or presence, and for a misdemeanor committed in his or her view or presence, excluding a municipal ordinance."[55] Even so, not all states have passed such laws, while where they do exist they often create dilemmas for the bystander of knowing how to differentiate between a felony and a misdemeanor.[56] Can one arrest a pick-pocket on a bus? Is pickpocketing a crime or a misdemeanor? In the research of Darley and Latané, as described, of stealing from a grocery store, would other shoppers have been entitled actually to arrest the thieves, if they had wished to intervene? In fact the issue of business premises is often so complex, with large business establishments employing private detective forces, that in many cases special laws have been passed, laying down the procedures for businesses to follow in accosting, searching, and detaining a suspect.[57]

Once given the power to intervene and to arrest, further problems arise as to the degree of force that may be used to effect the arrest, when there is resistance. In some instances legislation specifically spells out this right, as in the

New York Penal Code, which states that "a person may use physical force upon another person in defending himself or a third person, in defending property, in making an arrest or in preventing an escape. . . ."[58] It is of interest to note that a further section, passed subsequently to the Young case, might well have provided a legitimate defense for him. It provides that "a person is justified in using physical force upon another person in order to defend himself or a third person from what he reasonably believes to be the use or the imminent use of unlawful physical force by such other person, and he may use a degree of force which he reasonably believes to be necessary for such purpose. . . ."[59]

However, whatever authority is given to citizens, it has to be used with a great deal of caution. As Bassiouni writes, the legal authority of citizens "is by way of a privilege and not by reason of a legal duty. . . . A citizen . . . acts at his or her own peril and only under a limited legal authority which, if exceeded, subjects him or her to legal consequences."[60] In two 1974 cases, the actions of citizens in arresting were held to have been not justified. In a case in Indiana,[61] a citizen attempting an arrest was held liable to a third party, not the suspect, for injury caused during a high-speed chase to apprehend a car thief, the injured person being a passenger in the stolen car.

In a California case,[62] a citizen was held criminally liable for the death of a burglar, since, though he was entitled to arrest the burglar, he was not entitled, on the facts of the case (a burglary committed in daylight with many other people in the vicinity, and with no threat of violence from the burglar), to use deadly force. It might be noted that, in the first case, a police officer would probably have been acquitted, whereas in the second case, there is a high likelihood that even a police officer would not have been considered justified in using deadly force. It should, however, be noted that a citizen acting at the behest of a police officer might be entitled to the rights of an officer, since in such circumstances the citizen is under a duty to act.

Further problems arise where an arrest is made on the basis of an incorrect perception of the nature of an incident—the problem of incorrect perception which had faced Young in New York. As long ago as 1906 in the case of *Pandijiris* v. *Hartman*, the court had ruled that "if it should turn out that the man who had been arrested was not guilty of the crime, the citizen causing the arrest is liable in a civil action for whatever damage the arrested man sustained in consequence of his arrest and imprisonment."[63] The arrestor is exposed not only to claims for unlawful imprisonment, but also to other civil wrongs. In a 1970 case,[64] a claim for defamation was upheld where the circumstances of the arrest were such as to harm the suspect—the arrestor loudly accused the suspect of being a thief, and publicly frisked him without discovering any proof of the charges.

Similarly where the citizen is charged with the criminal violation of wrongful arrest, the defenses available to a police officer will not be applicable. The police officer has a right to arrest, the citizen only a privilege. Thus, in sharp contrast to the police officer who has a valid defense of reasonable belief that a crime had been committed, a private citizen "is privileged to make an arrest only when he has reasonable grounds for believing in the guilt of the person arrested and a felony has *in fact* been committed."[65]

Almost simultaneously to the increase in laws slightly extending the right of citizens to arrest, there was in the United States a tremendous extension of protection to doctors and other medical personnel going to the aid of strangers in emergency situations. It had been felt that many doctors were refusing to go to the aid of strangers in need of emergency on-the-spot medical treatment because of their fear that they might subsequently be sued for malpractice. In many instances they lack the necessary time, instruments, and facilities to perform at their optimum level of proficiency, and fear that any treatment short of the accepted standards will make them vulnerable to subsequent litigation by the victim.

In order to encourage doctors to provide medical assistance without fear of incurring later legal liability most of the states in the United States have enacted legislation providing varying degrees of indemnity for doctors and members of allied professions from subsequent civil claims for harm inadvertently caused because of the emergency situation.[66]

Yet as the spate of legislation drew to an end two articles raised serious questions as to the need for, and efficacy of, these laws. Plant, in a legal journal,[67] argued that the fears of doctors being sued were totally misplaced. He was unable to find any case at the appellate level in which a physician had been successfully sued for negligence while rendering voluntary medical aid to the victim of an emergency situation. In a poll of doctors it appeared that, even at the lower court levels, none of the doctors had personal information about any such cases, though some did know of claims settled out of court.

Of course, such out-of-court settlements could also be considered to be detrimental to the willingness of doctors to help, but Plant goes on to argue that the risks involved are infinitesimal compared to the other routine risks of the average medical practice. He concluded that there was no special need for these Good Samaritan laws, and that they were mainly the result of unnecessary pressures by doctors and lawyers.

In fact such special groups as doctors were in many respects less in need of protection than other citizens. Doctors may be presumed to have foreseen the possibility of being called to an emergency situation, and to have taken the necessary prior insurance precautions along with other precautions that are routine in medical practice today. It is rather the well-meaning layperson, acting within the limits of a reasonable person, who is most in need of help. In fact, in Illinois, a law protecting doctors was vetoed by the governor on the grounds that laws of this type were discriminatory since "any private citizen untrained in first aid, who volunteers in an emergency may be held legally accountable for his actions ... but the doctor, who is the only one fully trained to render emergency care, would be the very one rendered immune by this bill from the consequences of his negligent acts."[68]

As to the impact of these laws, an editorial in the *New England Journal of Medicine* in 1965[69] stated that a survey of doctors showed that 50 percent of those polled indicated that they would still not stop to help, even after the passage of a Good Samaritan act.

So the real issue of indemnity is yet to be resolved; and relates to the question as to whether the ordinary citizen is to be granted the protection of the law in undertaking rescue or helpful actions on behalf of others. Whether or not such protection does exist, there is still a legal question as to the stage at which intervention by a bystander can be considered to have been undertaken. Gregory[70] discusses a number of situations where casual indications of a willingness to help may raise difficult issues subsequently. He poses a situation where a passerby has told the victim of a car accident on a deserted road that he will call a doctor as soon as he gets to the nearest town. What would happen if no doctor were available? How is the bystander to discharge his promise? Is it a binding promise? What if further delay would undermine other priorities of the bystander? Gregory conceives of a gratuitous promise which might be held not to be binding: "As far as gratuitous promises are concerned . . . there is no duty to carry them through unless he has compromised himself by some act closely associated with the other's interest . . . in such a way as to induce reliance of the other in the nature of an estoppel himself."[71] Epstein, raising a similar issue, goes even further, and suggests that even if the bystander had made a commitment to help by taking action (picked up a phone and then done nothing, or actually moved the victim and then desisted) there should be no liability unless the bystander had actually caused direct harm.[72]

The rights of indemnity to those causing harm in the act of saving or helping others actually have a long history, going back to early cases when the captain of a ship was held to be entitled to jettison some of the cargo in order to save the ship from sinking. The principle of granting such indemnity seems to have made its impact on much of the modern world; what is now required is a more precise formulation—in legislation and judicial decisions—of the kind of support a bystander can anticipate receiving in the event of a less-than-perfect consummation of the moral and/or practical imperative to help.

If such legal guidelines are not forthcoming then Minor's comment as to the erosion in the humane quality of the law contains much validity. He writes that while the "refusal to help the injured man might be regarded as more or less inhuman . . . it loses some of its inhumanity in view of the rule . . . that if he undertook to relieve the [imperiled] man he would become liable for damage if he failed to use proper care to carry out the undertaking with effect and, in any event, runs the risk of having to undergo an expensive trial."[73]

In effect, the issue of allowing the bystander compensation for harm suffered and indemnity for harm caused, is a means of recognizing and rewarding the bystander, not merely to resolve particular problems that might arise in the normal course of events, but also to encourage other bystanders to become active on behalf of strangers in distress.

The Reward System

Whatever reluctance there might be to allow these indirect rewards of compensation and immunity, there is a far greater reluctance to grant active bystanders direct rewards. Honoré notes that for many "virtue should be its own reward" but adds that for those who wish to keep this pristine approach to helping behavior there is no need to claim such reward, and the rescuer always retains the liberty to "preserve immaculate his moral idealism if he wishes."[74]

What, however, of those who lack the necessary altruistic qualities? Could they not perhaps be persuaded of the value of altruistic conduct by some tangible rewards? Conversely, though, would such rewards not constitute a temptation for imprudent, overzealous rescue attempts? Would a legal situation of rewards not lead to abuses (perhaps fabricated crimes) or reckless actions only causing more harm?

Any system of rewards should obviously be oriented to being no more than a judicious statement of society's gratitude for the action, where the reward itself would not entice the bystander to undertake risks that he would not have been prepared to do, or competent to handle, without a reward system.

As it is, indirectly a reward system does, in fact, already exist, partly voluntary and capricious, partly improvised in ex post facto situations, partly ongoing sub rosa. These haphazard approaches to rewards pose the need to work out a reasoned philosophy of rewards as a basis for formulating an integrated policy.

Thus, most police and fire departments do, on occasion, make rewards for citizens who have displayed courage in preventing a crime, in rescuing a victim, or in apprehending a criminal. To what extent such occasional official response may induce later similar actions is not clear. Yet, in making such rewards, society through its designated organs, is, at least, availing itself of the opportunity to express its gratitude, and of indirectly making a statement as to the kind of behavior it considers commendable. As will be seen in a later chapter it is quite likely that young people at an impressionable age are liable to be affected positively as they go through the process of learning, noticing, evaluating, and applying societal norms.[75]

Other official bodies (for example, city officials) or other groups (for example, the Carnegie Hero Fund Commission and the Red Cross) provide additional opportunities for official and public recognition for altruistic actions. In many instances a medal, together with a nominal gift, seems appropriate as a reward.

Yet there are rewards which are often far more substantial and subtle; generally they have little to do with heroic actions as such; rather they are involved with inducements to ferret out the criminals in devious ways, and so preserve public order.

In an earlier chapter, reference was made to the extensive use made of the reward system in Britain particularly at a stage when there was no official police or prosecutorial bodies. Radzinowicz devotes much of one of the four volumes on the history of the criminal law to a discussion of the reward system.[76] Despite its faults, for example, of deliberate thefts to gain the reward, or of collusion between the thief-takers and the thieves, the system of rewards did achieve a certain measure of success.

In fact, even today, there are still many instances where resort is made to such means—often in a desperate situation, where the police are unable to resolve a series of serious crimes, apparently similar in nature, and there is a perceived likelihood of continued crimes of this type; or where some particularly precious loss has been sustained, for example, the theft of a work of art or of a valuable or special object (an heirloom or pet animal) or where a single crime has caused a particularly strong public reaction.

In Los Angeles, for instance, the scare caused by the rapes and killings of some dozen young women in late 1977 by the "Hillside Strangler" led to the announcement by several groups and people, official and private, of a total reward of $140,000—put up by the City Council, by the County Board of Supervisors, by a local radio station, and by a private citizen.[77] The police noted that tips from the public increased tenfold as a result. Unfortunately, much of the increase was of irrelevant calls, and even vindictive suspicions made about personal enemies. Yet, in cases where so many small clues all add up to a total picture, and where any idle information may supply an essential clue, these large responses may well pay off.

Often rewards are offered by groups that have a high degree of risk. Thus, the California Bankers Association publishes pictures of suspected bank robbers, often from pictures taken by hidden cameras at the time of the robbery, offering rewards in return for information. Every precaution is taken to preserve the anonoymity of the caller to prevent reprisals.

Many reward attempts are based on the hope that someone close to the criminal, perhaps an accomplice who has later quarreled, will be tempted to supply confidential information. Much police work, in general, is based on tip-offs, not in return for a publicly announced monetary reward, but as part of ongoing contacts between the police and certain members of the criminal underworld in return for money or favors—such as immunity from prosecution for other criminal activities, or as part of a special deal in a particular instance, where one of a group might become a state witness in return for a promise not to prosecute. Although this is obviously not the normal example of reward, the fact is that a certain degree of law enforcement is based on these practices, and they should be considered in any discussion of the reward system.

Two former police officers have dealt in detail with the legal, moral, and practical aspects of this little-discussed but important aspect of police work.[78] They note a series of motives that might induce a criminal to cooperate with the police and incriminate their own friends—fear, revenge, egotism, money. The police, according to them, must know how to utilize these factors, always preserving a delicate balance, offering them justifiable rewards for information, while not allowing them to exploit this cooperation for continuing in illicit activities.

Without wishing to draw too close a parallel between the reward system in such cases and a potential reward system for all bystanders, there is a need for much deeper thought as to the degree of helpful behavior that might be elicited if society knew how to indicate its appreciation and acknowledgment of such behavior. In an earlier chapter the problems of bystanders/witnesses in the courts system was noted.[79] The concern here is relatively recent. For too long, those responsible for the efficient, rational, and just operation of the criminal justice system have ignored this aspect of their work. At a larger level, it may be argued that almost no thought has been given as to the need to provide even the most minimum responses of gratitude for needed and/or heroic bystander reaction. The problem is a complex one, and even the most basic work still remains to be done.

Some aspects of antisocial and criminal behavior cannot be dealt with adequately unless people are prepared to become involved in the concerns of their society. Such willingness on their part must, however, be matched by sufficient consideration for their action. In the past the question of informing revolved mainly around the criminal underworld. As awareness of far more subtle problems emerges, and as the criminal law evolves to deal with such problems, there may be a need to reconsider the role of active citizen involvement in protecting the society.

The new concerns for the environment and consumerism point out the need for a reward system to cope with problems of this nature. In the late 1960s, as awareness of environmental problems increased, a long-forgotten law, enacted at the end of the nineteenth century, in desuetude ever since, was resuscitated.[80] Its aims was to preserve the purity of the waters in the rivers and harbors. It provided that any citizen providing information as to acts of pollution of waters would be entitled, on the conviction of the wrongdoer, to an amount up to half of the fine imposed, at the discretion of the judge.

Recently, Nader[81] has suggested that there is an urgent need to provide protection for "whistle-blowers," people working within large government and private organizations, who inform on violations of the law committed within these organizations, information which can generally only be known to insiders. Nader's concern is not only to seek a means of inducing people to provide the information but also to protect those who already do so, motivated not by any desire for personal aggrandisement or advance, but out of a concern for the public good. He stresses that, at present, such people often suffer for their actions—being ostracized, losing jobs, being denied promotions, encountering difficulties in finding other employment, and so on. He stresses the need to conceive legal means of providing them with the help that their actions entitle them to receive. In some respects their action is more heroic than that of a bystander to a murder calling the police.

Thus, while rewards for positive bystander activity might seem, at first glance, to be unnecessary, and undesirable, a larger view of the problem suggests the need for creative thinking and planning in this area, in particular to cope with some of the newer problems confronting society.[82]

In truth little is known of why people wish to act in an altruistic manner, and what motivates them to prosocial conduct. Little is known of how to inculcate such values; of the impact that a reward system would have; of how to entice, encourage, or coerce to virtuous behavior. In the past these have been questions mainly for abstract philosophical discussion, left to theologians, and moral philosophers. In recent years, though, a number of researchers in the social sciences have been devoting their activities to research in this area. Both the abstract and the practical aspects of altruism in society will be discussed in the final section of this book.

Notes

1. See John P. Dawson, *"Negotiorum Gestio:* The Altruistic Intermeddler," *Harvard Law Review*, 1961, *74*, p. 817.

2. As quoted in previous chapter, Allen Linden, "Rescuers and Good Samaritans," *The Modern Law Review*, 1971, *34*, p. 241.

3. John G. Fleming, *An Introduction to the Law of Torts* (Oxford: Oxford University Press, 1967), p. 57.

4. Ibid., p. 59.

5. *Wagner* v. *International Ry Co.*, 232 N.Y. 176, 19 A.L.R. 1, 133 N.E. 437. (1921).

6. L. Green, W.H. Pedrick, J.A. Rahl, E.W. Thode, C.S. Hawkins, and A.E. Smith, *Cases on the Law of Torts* (St. Paul, Minn.: West Publishing Co., 1968), p. 629.

7. *Eckert* v. *Long Island R.R. Co.*, 43 N.Y. 502, 3 Am. Rep. 721.

8. *Wagner* v. *International Ry. Co.*, above.

9. Ibid.

10. *Videan* v. *British Transport Commission* (1963) 2 Q.B. 650; (1963) 2 W L R 374; (1963) 2 ALL E.R. 860.

11. *Walters* v. *Denver Consolidated Electric Light Co.*, 12 Colo App 145, 54. (1898).

12. *Haynes* v. *Harwood* (1935) 1 K.B. 146.

13. Ibid.

14. Ibid.

15. *Central Railways* v. *Crosby*, 74, Ga. 737 (1885).

16. Ibid.

17. *Chattanooga Light and Power Co.* v. *Hodges*, 109 Tenn 331, 70 S.W. 616 (1902). At the trial court level, the family of the employee won the case, but this decision was overruled on appeal.

18. *Henjun* v. *Bok*, 261 Minn. 74, 110 N.W. 2d 461 (1961) at 463.

19. Restatement of Law, Torts: neg., para. 472.

20. *French* v. *Trace*, 48 Wash. 2d. 235, 297 P 2d. 236 (1956).

21. Robert Goff and Gareth Jones, *The Law of Restitution* (London: Sweet and Maxwell, 1966).

22. Ibid., p. 231.

23. J. Tiley, "The Rescue Principle," *Modern Law Review*, 1967, *30*, pp. 34-45.

24. Ibid., p. 25.

25. Ibid.

26. Ibid.

27. Ibid.

28. *Chadwick* v. *British Transport Commission* (1967), 2 All E.R. 945 (1967) 1 W.L.R. 912.

29. Ibid.

30. Ibid.

31. Fritz Schultz, *Classical Roman Law* (Oxford: Clarendon Press, 1951), p. 624.

32. Leslie Rubin, *Unauthorized Administration (Negotiorum Gestio) in South Africa* (Cape Town: Juta and Co., 1958).

33. John P. Dawson, "Rewards for the Rescue of Human Life?" in James M. Ratcliffe, ed., *The Good Samaritan and the Law* (New York: Anchor Books, 1966), p. 64.

34. *Flacke* v. *Scottish Imperial Insurance Co.* 34 Ch.D. 349.

35. *Fibrosa* v. *Fairbairn*, (1943) A.C. 32 at 61. The judgment goes on to note that "such remedies are different from remedies in contract or tort, and are now recognized to fall within a third category of the common law, which has been called quasi-contract or restitution." See also Robert Goff and Gareth Jones, *The Law of Restitution.*

36. Dawson, p. 83.

37. Ibid., p. 85.

38. Ibid., p. 87.

39. Ibid., p. 88.

40. Ibid., p. 89.

41. Ibid., p. 88.

42. Margery Fry, *Arms of the Law* (London: Gollancz, 1951).

43. See Herbert Edelhertz and Gilbert Geis, *Public Compensation to Victims of Crime* (New York: Praeger, 1974).

44. City of New York, Local Law No. 1008, 1965.

45. See discussion on page 3.

46. Sec. 67-3.2 of Local Law No. 1008, 1965.

47. See Geoffrey W.R. Palmer, "Compensation for Personal Injury: A Requiem for the Common Law in New Zealand," *American Journal of Comparative Law*, 1973, *21*, p. 1.

48. See the references in Dawson, "Reward for the Rescue," p. 88, where he notes that provisions have been made in Germany in the social security system.

49. Antony Honoré, "Law, Morals and Rescue," in Ratcliffe, pp. 232-233.

50. *Post* v. *Jones*, 60 U.S. 150 (1856).

51. Charles O. Gregory, "Gratuitous Undertakings and the Duty of Care," *De Paul Law Review*, 1951, *1*, p. 44.

52. *People* v. *Young*, 210 N.Y.S. 2d 358, App. Div. (1962), rev. New York, 2d 274, C.T. App. (1962).

53. Louis Waller, "Rescue and the Common Law: England and Australia," in Ratcliffe, p. 144.

54. M. Cherif Bassiouni, *Citizen's Arrest: The Law of Arrest, Search, and Seizure for Private Citizens and Private Police* (Springfield, Ill: Charles C. Thomas, 1977).

55. Ibid., p. 24.

56. It is interesting to note that in Nigeria arrests for misdemeanors may only be made at night; see Cyprian O. Okonkwo and Michael E. Naish, *Criminal Law in Nigeria* (London: Sweet and Maxwell, 1964), pp. 223-226.

57. See Bassiouni, chapter 9, "Shoplifting Detention Authority," pp. 80-86 and appendix D, "Index to Shoplifting Statues," pp. 96-118.

58. Sec. 35.19 of Revised Penal Code, 1967.

59. Ibid., Sec. 35.15.

60. Bassiouni, p. 57.

61. *Surratt* v. *Petrol, Inc.*, 312 N.E. 2d 487 Sup. Ct. Ind. (1974).

62. 41 Cal. App. 3d, 115 Cal Rptr. 830 (1974).

63. *Pandijiris* v. *Hartman*, 196 Mo. 539, 94 S.W. 270 (1906) at 272.

64. *Great Atlantic and Pacific Tea Company* v. *Paul*, 261 A. 2d 731 Ct. App. (1970).

65. *United States* v. *Hillsman*, 522 F. 2d 454 (1975).

66. For the first such act see the California Legislation—Cal. Bus. Prod. Code No. 2144 (1959) (Physicians). For an analysis of these laws see note, "Good Samaritans and Liability for Medical Malpractice," *Columbia Law Review*, 1964, *64*, p. 301.

67. Marcus L. Plant, " 'Good Samaritan' Laws," *Trial*, vol. 2, Oct/Nov. 1966, p. 34.

68. As quoted in Wallace M. Rudolph, "The Duty to Act: A Proposed Rule," *Nebraska Law Review*, 1965, *44*, p. 502.

69. Editorial, "The Good Samaritan and the Law," *New England Journal of Medicine*, 1965, *273*, p. 934.

70. Gregory, pp. 44-45.

71. Ibid., p. 67.

72. Richard Epstein, "A Theory of Strict Liability," *Journal of Legal Studies*, 1973, *2*, p. 189.

73. H.D. Minor, "The Moral Obligation as a Basis of Liability," *Virginia Law Review*, 1923, *9*, p. 423.

74. Honoré, p. 234.

75. See discussion in chapter 9 of the positive influence of prosocial behavior.

76. See Leon Radzinowicz, *A History of English Criminal Law and its Administration, Vol. 2: The Clash Between Private Initiative and Public Interest in Enforcement of the Law* (London: Stevens and Sons, 1956).

77. See Al Martinez, "Rewards Pose Issues of Greed and Morality," *Los Angeles Times*, 25 Dec., 1977, p. 1.

78. Malachi L. Harney and John C. Cross, *The Informer in Law Enforcement* (Springfield, Ill.: Charles C. Thomas, 1960).

79. See chapter 4.

80. Sec. 13 of Rivers and Harbors Act, 1899, 33 U.S.C., S 401-415 (1964), known as the Refuse Act. See Rodgers, "Industrial Water Pollution and the Refuse Act: A Second Chance for Water Quality," *University of Pennsylvania Law Review*, 1971, *119*, p. 761.

81. Ralph Nader, Peter J. Petakas, and Kate Blackwell, eds., *Whistle Blowing: The Report of the Conference on Professional Responsibility* (New York: Grossman Publishers, 1972).

82. For a good discussion of the advantages of using a concerned outsider, who is not directly involved, see Thomas Crumplar, "An Alternative to Public and Victim Enforcement of the Federal Securities and Antitrust Laws: Citizen Enforcement," *Harvard Journal on Legislation*, 13 (1975): 76-124. The author points out the clear advantages of using outsiders over victims (with the problems of proving damage or the complications of class suits) or the state (with the dangers of excessive power which might be abused). He suggests that citizens trying to enforce these laws should be given some compensation for their efforts.

Part III
Ethics

8 Altruism in Social Life

A secondary theme of much of this study of the bystander is the concept of altruism—the empathetic feelings that people sense and the helpful actions that they perform for fellow beings in distress, involving both the motivations for action, and the consequences of action. Not all the activities discussed have flown from altruistic motivations, and the meaning of bystander activity is certainly not encompassed purely within the concept of altruism. As shown on several occasions, helpful behavior can be displayed for a wide range of motives, such as for reward or from antagonism to a wrongdoer. Yet, conversely, no study of bystander activity would be complete without trying to understand the role that altruism plays in social life as a motivating force in responding to the needs and the plight of others.

Much speculative writing exists; this is a theme which bears a great fascination for writers of all backgrounds as it touches, in many respects, on the very nature of the bond that holds people together. What feelings of empathy do strangers, living in the same society, sense for each other? What are the motivations for risk-behavior on behalf of a stranger? Can social intercourse take place only when both parties to the transaction contribute, or can it be uni-directional? Is social life predicated on an overall network of exchange relationships, or must there be some minimal amount of social activity which flows purely from considerations of the welfare of others without any quid pro quo? Is the desire for altruistic action innately imprinted in our makeup, or must it be inculcated through cultural means in order to conquer selfish impulses? Is altruism a marginal luxury which societies may welcome where it exists, but do not necessarily need; or is it an essential prerequisite of a healthy society, which may be ignored only at society's peril?

The answers to these and similar questions depend to a large extent on the perceptions that people have of human nature. The models of mankind vary from those that see human beings as prisoners of their basic drives to those that see inborn tendencies to sociable behavior and mutuality.

Some of these models do not lend themselves easily to explanations of altruism in human behavior, either because they stress self-interest as a guiding force in behavior, or else because they see social interaction as flowing only from reciprocal benefits conferred on each other by the parties. Other models, on the other hand, see altruism as a basic, binding force making society possible.

While some writers opt for emphasis on either egoistic or altruistic tendencies, others seek a blending between the two, as in the discussion by

Campbell, a social psychologist, wherein he claims that behavior often represents a mixture of "altruistic, self-sacrificial . . . motives as ambivalently balanced with own-skin-saving, self-centered ones" and goes on to state that the "normal peacetime exigencies of life are such that the altruistic . . . components are rarely tapped, and the self-centered ones predominate."[1]

For the most, however, debate rages as to where the emphasis should be placed. Three key areas have emerged as the focus of debate—in philosophy, in the natural sciences, and in the social sciences.

1. Traditionally, the discussion of altruism has revolved around the speculative discussions of philosophers, and their varying approaches to the qualities of people, ranging from egoistic and selfish orientations to magnanimous considerations of other people's needs.

2. From the time that Darwin's ideas have been accepted, attempts have been made to apply some of his key ideas about nature, such as survival of the fittest in a struggle for existence, to society. This has touched off an ongoing debate as to whether any such evolutionary struggle—in nature or in society—is resolved by individualistic efforts or by cooperative group responses. Parallel to the debate on Darwinian theory is the work of natural scientists on the apparently instinctive altruistic behavior of some animals and the question as to whether instinctive traits may be used as the basis for understanding human behavior.

3. Within the social sciences, the bulk of the work on altruism has been in the field of social psychology, as already dealt with in earlier chapters, but in the key discipline of sociology only minimal efforts have been devoted to analyzing the role of altruism in society.

Philosophical Approaches

The contrasting approaches of speculative philosophy are neatly caught in the manner in which the Chinese philosopher Mencius and the German philosopher Nietzsche relate to the specific problem of the human emotions that are aroused when witnessing a stranger in distress. Using similar examples they come to totally opposite conclusions, Mencius claiming that "all men have a mind which cannot bear [to see the suffering] of others,"[2] Nietzsche suggesting that "to behold suffering gives pleasure."[3]

Within this spectrum other philosophers have taken their stance, not always dealing directly with altruism per se, but hinting at the possibilities of altruism through the overall description of human nature. There is a constant effort to search for a viable means of reconciling the interests of the individual with those of the group.

Philosophers working from conflict approaches, such as Hobbes,[4] tend to see people as essentially driven by egoistic considerations, and, in fact, agreeing to set up social bonds as a result of an awareness that only by making such concessions to larger social groupings can their own personal interests be assured. Mandeville[5] tried to show that by allowing people to seek satisfaction for their own interests and even indulge their vices, the final outcome would accrue to the benefit of society as a whole. Mill, Bentham, and other utilitarian philosophers[6] adopted a similar approach in their search for a balance between the individual's needs and that of the society at large. On the one hand they saw individuals as rationally measuring their actions in terms of attraction to pleasure and aversion to pain; on the other hand, they saw all these actions as adding up to the greatest good for the greatest number.

Adam Smith's approach was also based on calculated reasoning; he suggests that benefits will generally accrue to those who display benevolent behavior. "No benevolent man," he wrote, "ever lost altogether the fruits of his benevolence. If he does not always gather them from the persons from whom he ought to have gathered them, he seldom fails to gather them, and with a tenfold increase, from other people. Kindness is the parent of kindness."[7]

For those thinkers who resolutely claim that all actions flow from self-interest, several possibilities have been canvassed as explanations for action that seems to be, prima facie, other-oriented with no gain to the actor—including the possibility that the actor has simply miscalculated, or, in slightly more involved form, that the beneficial act on behalf of another brings the actor, for whatever reason, self-satisfaction.

Recently, more specific attempts have been made to bridge the gap, allowing an explanation of altruistic behavior within the promotion of self-interest. Olson, for instance, has suggested the concept of "hedonic spread"[8] in order to describe how self-interest and self-sacrifice may be seen to be perfectly compatible. In this scheme, pain and pleasure not only relate to the person directly affected, but may be vicariously experienced. Because people are so closely bound up with each other, "the happiness or distress of others soon becomes an immediate object of pleasure or pain for ourselves that we naturally strive to produce or to avert."[9]

He sees people as being possessed by a spirit of benevolence and a sense of duty, which, though sometimes leading to conflicting reactions, more often are combined, together even with "crude self-interest," to make people generous and moral. He concludes that "the greatest non-cognitive factors in the development of moral character are self-love, the spirit of benevolence and the sense of duty. Self-love is a natural tendency of the human animal, whereas the spirit of benevolence and the sense of duty are social products."[10] He accordingly warns against believing that the latter two can be achieved merely by moral exhortation or education; and he sees the possibility of arousing such feelings in the individual as dependent on the "collective wisdom of society."[11]

Olson is of the opinion that such feelings are by no means innate, but must be worked for; "Society must," according to him, "create a harmony of interests between its members such that the well-being more or less crudely conceived of one be favored by the well-being more or less crudely conceived of others."[12]

Nagel, another modern philosopher who has addressed himself to the issue of altruism, goes beyond Olson and argues that there is "such a thing as pure altruism. . . . It is the direct influence of persons interested on the actions of another, simply because in itself the interest of the former provides the latter with a reason to act."[13] He claims that altruism is innate and that "there is a considerateness for others which is beyond the reach of complicated reflections about social advantages."[14]

Altruism cannot be based on emotional explanations but should be explained in terms compatible with the most rigorous standards of logical reasoning. Similar to Olson, Nagel claims that the need for altruism emerges clearly as soon as there is a capability of putting oneself in the other's place. The moment there is a recognition of the reality of other persons, the moment one sees oneself as one person among others, the need for altruism becomes clear; what one desires for oneself (for example, to be helped when in distress) becomes automatically a desire one would have for others also. By contrast, egoism becomes a logical impossibility. Philosophical eogism has no explanation as to why others should help one. The paradoxical situation, which egoism cannot handle, is that often, if no help is forthcoming, then one's own interests can, generally, not be advanced. Conversely, it is difficult to consider negative factors, such as pain, as having only subjective value, of importance only when personally affected, and having no relevance when it is others who are undergoing the suffering.

Philosophers, then, seem to be seeking a consensus where other-oriented and/or sacrificial behavior, in one particular circumstance, is seen as being a contribution to one's own interest in the long run. It is rational self-interest which leads to moral and altruistic behavior.[15]

Work in the Natural Sciences

In contrast to these speculative debates of philosophers, in the natural sciences attempts have been made to examine empirically the nature of helping behavior among animals, and then to extrapolate to human life. Darwin's theory of evolution[16] has provided a working framework for many naturalists to explain processes in society on the basis of similar processes that have been noticed in nature. Darwin had postulated the existence of a struggle for existence based on a scarcity of resources in which the fittest survived; later evolutionists elaborated on the theme and stressed the inevitable egoistic tendencies of animals intent on self-preservation and self-aggrandizement in a hostile environment. One of the notable early writers was Huxley,[17] who described the process of evolution, as it impinged on human society, as a Hobbesian war of all against all.

These basic ideas were later adapted to explain the nature of progress in society, where, in the struggle for existence, the strong would overcome the weak, and would have no obligation to tend to them. The sociologists Spencer in Britain and Sumner[18] in the United States were the foremost proponents of this approach. Hofstadter, in his discussion of Social Darwinism in America,[19] has described how deeply ingrained such ideas were and how they were often exploited to justify the harshest and most selfish measures taken at the expense of others. In such an intellectual atmosphere there was little prospect of cultivating standards of altruistic behavior.

The major reply to these Darwinian works was by Kropotkin, in his classic study of mutual aid.[20] Kropotkin did not deny the basic facts of evolution as set out by Darwin, but claimed that inasmuch as there was a struggle for existence, it was most successfully resolved not by egoistic actions at the expense of others, but by cooperative endeavors. Evolutionary progress—in nature and society—was best assured when mutual aid was practiced.

In developing his argument Kropotkin described instances of mutual aid among animals at all levels of development, and at different stages of human history. While his thesis fitted in well with his overall philosophical stance,[21] the book is far from being a speculative treatise. The empirical evidence is meticulously put together, and many of the examples from the animal world are based on Kropotkin's own personal observations and study in the field, as a zoologist. He writes that "in all these scenes of animal life which passed before my eyes, I saw Mutual Aid and Mutual Support carried on to an extent which made me suspect in it a feature of the greatest importance for the maintenance of life, the preservation of each species, and its further evolution."[22] And in contrary situations where animals were forced to struggle against overwhelming odds on their own, far from being strengthened thereby, they were seriously impoverished. Struggle in such conditions seems to have had a debilitating effect.

Kropotkin notes that the restrictions that Darwin himself had placed on the use of the struggle for existence were often ignored by later evolutionists who "reduced the notion of struggle for its existence to its narrowest limits. They came to conceive the animal world as a world of perpetual struggle among half-starved individuals, thirsting for another's blood. They raised the 'pitiless' struggle for personal advantages to the height of a biological principle which man must submit to as well, under the menace of otherwise succumbing in a world based upon mutual extermination."[23]

Kropotkin's own observations and studies confirmed the existence of a struggle for existence in nature, and a process of natural selection; in addition he conceded that there were many examples of warfare and extermination in human history. The sum total, however, showed that there were at least as many, and possibly more, instances of mutual support, aid, and defense among animals of the same species or, at least of the same society.

Sociality is as much a law of nature as mutual struggle . . . if we . . . ask Nature: "Who are the fittest; those who are continually at war with each other, or those who support one another?" we at once see that those animals which acquire habits of mutual aid are undoubtedly the fittest. They have more chances to survive, and they attain, in their respective classes, the highest development of intelligence and bodily organization . . . we may safely say that mutual aid is as much a law of animal life as mutual struggle, but that, as a factor of evolution, it most probably has a far greater importance, inasmuch as it favors the development of such habits as and characters as insure the maintenance and future development of the species, together with the greatest amount of welfare and enjoyment of life for the individual, with the least waste of energy.[24]

Kroptkin, documenting his thesis with an abundance of examples from his own work and the work of other zoologists, claims that such mutual aid is found at all stages of evolutionary development, even among the lowest animals.

His work is of great importance and provides probably a far more accurate explanation of the manner in which evolution proceeds than some of the works that are ostensibly in the Darwinian tradition, where Darwin's terminology is freely used, but insufficient attention is paid to the restrictions he placed on too liberal or too literal an application of his ideas.

However, the key test for bystander work is found in the examples which Kropotkin provides of mutual aid at work in the historical development of mankind, here presenting a direct contrast to the work of Huxley, his immediate protagonist, and of the Social Darwinists. Relying on contemporary anthropological work (that of Bachofen, Tylor, Maine, and others)[25] Kropotkin argues that, even at the most primitive stage of human development, people have tended to coalesce into communities for mutual protection and mutual benefit.

Kropotkin notes that while historians have catalogued a long list of warfare and oppression, arousing inevitable presumptions as to mankind's negative inclinations, a closer analysis of everyday human affairs, generally ignored by contemporary writers and later historians, indicates tight bonds of solidarity and a constant search for community. Indeed, as family ties broke down, they were replaced by new territorial frameworks, such as the village, based on "a union for common culture, for mutual support in all possible forms, for protection from violence, and for a further development of knowledge, national bonds, and moral conceptions,"[26] with much common activity in hunting, fishing, and agriculture.

Kropotkin finds in the development of the medieval city further expression of mutuality, with protection for all members and the extensive system of professional guilds, based upon close personal contacts.[27]

In dealing with modern society, Kropotkin describes the many examples of mutual aid still extant at the community level, despite the growing power of the state on the one hand and the greater accent on individualism on the other. Of particular significance for bystander consideration are his examples of volunteer groups specifically dedicated to rescue attempts on behalf of unknown strangers, such as the Lifeboard Associations, with their crews of "volunteers, whose readiness to sacrifice their lives for the rescue of absolute strangers to them is put every year to a severe test; every winter the loss of several of the bravest among them stands on record."[28] Kropotkin sees this willingness as the "gist of human psychology."[29] While not all can be heroes, the hero conjures up strong feelings among others that "they ought to have done as well."[30]

Yet, what of those instances where helping behavior is not forthcoming? Kropotkin asks "about those men who were drowned in the Serpentine in the presence of a crowd, out of which no one moved for their rescue"; to which he replies that "the answer is plain enough"[31] —these innate feelings of solidarity may be eroded where, as in cities, for example, "the absence of common interest nurtures indifference, while courage and pluck, which seldom find their opportunities, disappear or take another direction."[32] Even so there are exceptions. People in certain professions, such as miners and seamen, have their feelings of solidarity constantly enhanced through common endeavors and a constant involvement with common dangers, while, more important, at the neighborhood level, there are many examples of mutual aid. Kropotkin concludes that neither the centralization of power in the state, nor the writings of philosophers and sociologists as to the inevitability of competition and struggle, have been able to destroy the feelings of solidarity that have been such an important part of human evolution.

Studies of animals have continued apace in the years since. The most significant attempts to examine their behavior in their natural settings, and to extrapolate from this behavior to human beings, have been in the field of ethology, where attempts have been made to determine the extent to which instinctive behavior has an influence on animal and human behavior. Although the evidence is diverse, the greatest impact on public awareness has been made by the work of those who have stressed the instinctive aggressive tendencies and the drive for territorial control.[33] Although not dealing specifically with altruism, the work of Lorenz and others[34] has tended to reiterate much of the earlier Darwinian approaches to animal and social human living. Even so the aggression described is mainly interspecies; within the species, with only few exceptions, there is little aggression, as members of the same species generally have the capacity to ritualize any conflicts in a nonharmful manner, and there are built-in inhibitions against intraspecies killing. As Kaufman notes,[35] many of Lorenz's arguments to explain the innate tendencies to violence could have been used just as convincingly to explain innate tendencies to altruism.

Some other classic studies of animals[36] in their natural environment have given clear indications of helping behavior and a willingness to share desirable possessions, such as food.[37] Wynne-Edwards[38] has argued that there is an even more subtle capacity to evince overall consideration for the long-term needs of the species. Like Kropotkin, he claims that the principle of natural selection is applicable not on an individual basis, encouraging selfish behavior, but on a group basis. His major concerns are with the problem of animal overpopulation in a limited environment of scarce resources. Through extensive field studies he comes to the conclusion that the groups with the best prospects for survival would be those that have an instinctive capacity to control their reproductive rates in such a way so as to make the final population outcome compatible with the continued welfare of the species as a whole within its ecological surroundings. In effect, each individual animal seems to possess a built-in knowledge of how to accommodate its own reproductive needs to those of the group as a whole. Wynne-Edwards notes that many animals delay their initial reproduction, or alternatively introduce delays between births. This altruistic tendency works to the benefit of the group as a whole.

There has been some confirmation, in a number of laboratory experiments, of this capacity to sense the need of another animal of the same species and to respond constructively. Masserman and colleagues[39] have shown that monkeys consistently refrained from pulling a chain that brought them food in order to avoid giving a shock to partners, and they claim that the monkeys were reacting empathetically to signs of distress.

Research work by Rice and Gainer[40] apparently yielded similar considerate behavior in the albino rat. Where a rat had the capacity to relieve the suffering of another rat by pressing a bar it did so constantly. However, Lavery and Foley,[41] in a later study, showed that the intervention was based more on the annoyance at the squealing of the affected rat than on any desire to terminate the suffering. In their research the tested rat intervened far more to stop a "white noise" than to aid the other rat. Rice himself, in further research,[42] noted that it was quite likely that the intervention was based more on fear, caused by the squealing, than on any desire to help the other rat.

In his comprehensive survey of altruism, Krebs[43] argues that the "infra-human research has failed to supply decisive evidence for the existence of altruism." Hebb,[44] however, challenges this assertion, and argues that at least among the higher primates there is much evidence for altruistic behavior. However difficult it is to know exactly what the motivations are for the behavior of primates, Hebb is of the opinion that such comparative analysis of behavior among the primates may provide better tests for the existence or otherwise of altruism than research among humans since the behavior among primates is less complex than among humans. He writes that the "comparative evidence is crucial," as it "shows that altruism may arise . . . where there has been no training in generosity. On any reasonable view, this requires a reinterpretation of the traditional hedonistic, law-of-effect view of human nature and human motivation."[45]

Additional support for the existence and importance of altruism comes from a key article by Holmes.[46] He notes that those accepting an evolutionary approach to behavior are faced with the challenge of showing that any behavior present in modern times and in advanced species must have had its origins in earlier times and in simpler organisms. Dealing specifically with altruism, he writes that "if genuine altruism exists . . . the evolutionists must look upon it as the product of a long period of development."[4][7] He takes issue with theories that deny altruism in human society, and then claims that the altruism that does exist is the result of "a deep-seated trait resting upon basic instincts that go far down in the animal kingdom. For all social animals altruism has a very real value in the struggle for existence. Animal societies everywhere are mutual benefit associations, and the altruistic instincts which make for social solidarity and effective co-operation would be favored by natural selection. . . . Instincts leading to unselfish behavior are just as basic, therefore, as any other manifestations of life."[4][8]

While echoing much of Kropotkin's ideas, Holmes expands on the theme of mutual cooperation by attributing it to genetic factors. He argues that the origins of such altruism lie in parental sentiments toward their offspring. He sees reproductivity as contributing little direct benefit to the parent, while involving great sacrifices and dangers. It is in this respect that Nature has set up devices for ensuring altruistic behavior by parents, flowing directly from a physiological base.

A Critique of Sociobiology

Recently sociobiologists have picked up some of these ideas, and altruism has become an important factor in this new discipline.[4][9] Their work, which has been accompanied by much controversy and criticism, attempts to explain human behavior on the basis of evolutionary and genetic factors. From this evolutionary and genetic perspective altruism poses a problem of particular concern. Since altruism often involves sacrificial behavior, there is the very real possibility that, through a process of natural selection, the altruistic genes will diminish and, in the course of time, tend to disappear, while conversely, the possessors of the nonaltruistic genes, the beneficiaries of altruistic actions, are liable to increase. The consequence is that the very practice of altruistic behavior should lead to the elimination of altruism.

Thus, for instance, when a predator approaches a group of animals as potential prey, the animal that will cry out the alarm[50] in order to warn the others is the one most likely to attract the attention of the predator and become the victim, while the other animals, suitably forewarned, make their escape. In its most extreme form, among the social insects—bees, wasps, ants, termites—those creatures who are the most hard-working and self-sacrificial on behalf of others have no reproductive capacity, and are thus unable to transfer the genes of their altruistic behavior. By principles of natural selection, the altruistic genes should, in the course of time, become extinct or, at least, of negligible impact. A number of theoretical solutions to this dilemma have been offered.

One of the possibilities is the concept of kin selection,[51] based on the fact that much altruistic behavior is oriented to the needs not just of animals of the same species, but more specifically of those carrying the same genes. Often the degree of other-oriented behavior is in direct proportion to the degree of proximity of the relationship. The caring behavior of many parent animals toward their offspring is the most significant example.

Another key example used by sociobiologists is the behavior of social insects, who labor strenuously on behalf of the reproductive success of their mother, the queen, and the general welfare of the other members of the hive. As Barash notes, for those animals, such as the workers in the hives, who have no reproductive capacity of their own, their "eusociality is . . . a true pinnacle of altruism."[52] Hamilton[53] suggests that the reason for this altruistic behavior is that the workers actually share more genes with other members of the hive, generally their siblings, than they would if they had their own offspring.

Another form of altruism—reciprocal altruism—has been suggested by Trivers,[54] who says the initiation of altruistic activity will, in the long run, bring benefits because it will lead to an altruistic response by the initial beneficiary. This kind of altruistic activity is considered to be more common among the higher animals, including human beings, and Trivers' line of reasoning does indeed bear close resemblance to that of social scientists who see altruism mainly as a reciprocal process, as will be discussed further on in this chapter.

Trivers notes that the prospects for altruism are greatest for those animals or societies which offer the most prospects of benefiting, in the course of time, from reciprocal action by others in response to one's own altruistic act. Altruism is thus most likely where there is a long lifetime, a low dispersal rate, and mutual dependence.

Trivers, in contrast to some of the other sociobiological approaches, notes that altruistic behavior may take place even where there is no genetic connection—in fact, even across species. He describes the process of cleaning symbiosis, where small fish attach themselves to larger "host" fish of another species and clean them of ectoparasites finding their own food in the process. Trivers stresses that the larger fish never exploit the smaller fish, never eat them (even when they enter the mouth to do the cleaning), and tend to return to the same area on a regular basis for further cleaning sessions.

It is not clear to what extent these increasingly extensive writings on altruism by sociobiologists are useful for understanding altruistic behavior among human beings. Sociobiology as an academic discipline has come under a great deal of attack by related disciplines, especially inasmuch as it attempts to seek a genetic bias for human behavior. The existence of an altruistic gene is also a problematical concept. In human behavior the term altruism connotes not merely the helping behavior, but also the empathetic feelings. Among certain animals it is clearly possible that their helping and sharing behavior is based on such feelings—such as in the protective practices of parents, or the group behavior of bands of animals. But to use the term altruism for the instinctive behavior of social insects is to place a different interpretation on the word, since it ignores the sentiment of empathy, which is part of the essence of altruism. Furthermore, the idea of altruism in human society normally excludes helping and caring behavior within family settings, or even among friends. It is the behavior toward strangers that determines whether altruism has been practiced.

From this aspect, Trivers's description of cleaning symbiosis is the most relevant of the sociobiological explanations. However, in this instance, there is no sacrifice, nor even any real danger, once it is clear that the larger fish has no intention of eating the small cleaner. So, in a sense, the summation of sociobiological writing to date indicates, on the one hand, sacrificial behavior (such as in the social insects) without any help to strangers, and, on the other hand, help to strangers, but without any risks or sacrifice. Neither model appears to be compatible with the concept of altruism as commonly understood in the human context. Kin selection and cleaning symbiosis are interesting concepts in their own right, but they fail to explain in any way those key aspects of altruistic behavior that involve sacrifice on behalf of strangers.

In their involvement with altruism, the sociobiologists have tended to ignore the fact that even among animals or insects which share common genes, helping and sharing is not always found. There are instances of animals that neglect or kill their offspring.[55] Certainly, in human society, relations within the family are not always harmonious; they may be hostile and may involve infanticide and child abuse. In human society, the possession of common genes does not provide any guarantee of instinctive love.[56]

I have dealt with the writings of sociobiologists, since the empirical examples they provide form an essential aspect of the total picture of altruistic behavior in nature. However, like other social scientists, I tend to doubt the direct significance of their work for a clearer understanding of human behavior. Human behavior is much too bound up with cultural impressions, with constant learning experiences, with the impact of historical knowledge and comparative awareness, for such a complex phenomenon as helping behavior to be ensconced primarily within a genetic imprint. Yet these examples of altruism do have a value inasmuch as they tend to offset the belief that the instinctive aspect of life—whether human or otherwise—is purely selfish. They also tend to give greater credence to those philosophical and social studies that claim that mutuality is an important part of social life. The importance of their work is not in providing any extrapolation to the instinctive behavior of human beings, but in showing that helping behavior as such is possible, even at the lowest and simplest forms of life. It would perhaps be naive to expect altruistic behavior in humans to flow from genetic bases, as is true of social insects, but it would be foolish to ignore the fact that other-oriented behavior does exist in nature, with beneficial results. In any event, just as in human society, the examples of altruistic behavior are matched by examples of cruel and aggressive behavior. The evidence of nature is not of the inevitability of altruism, but of its possibility.

In one respect, at least, the sociobiologists have provided a challenge for social scientists. Realizing the implications of altruistic behavior for their evolutionary and genetic approach, they have not hesitated to confront this problem directly. In contrast, social scientists have not devoted nearly as much effort proportionately, to an attempt to come to grips with the important question of altruism as a factor in social life. While in social psychology and developmental psychology there has been a significant effort to remedy this lacuna in the past decade, sociology still skirts the issue of altruism.

Sociological Analyses

Altruism may well serve as a key test of many theories of human behavior. Inasmuch as altruism exists it tends to confirm those theories built around the basic premises of the innate good in human nature or the harmonious structure of society, and to undermine those whose premises flow from a conception of human nature as selfish, eogistic, and aggressive, or from the alienating nature of society. Yet, surprisingly, with a few exceptions, sociologists have ignored the concept completely or relegated it to a peripheral aspect of their concern.

As Sorokin has noted,[57] and bemoaned, social science research has concentrated on the negative aspects of society in an attempt to understand what draws out the evil in people, and what are the underlying causes of the various social problems confronting modern societies. But little effort has been made to find out what draws out the best in people. "The criminal has been recorded," writes Sorokin, "incomparably more than the saint or the altruist; the idiot has been studied much more usefully than the genius."[58] The result is that social science knows "little about positive types of persons, their conduct and relationships."[59]

Sorokin saw the slanted nature of much research to be in itself symptomatic of the faults of modern society. In an attempt to rectify the discrepancy of the research he set up a Research Center in Altruistic Integration and Creativity at Harvard;[60] but beyond this, at least in sociology, there has been only minimum response to his call for greater research efforts in the nature of altruistic behavior.

Books on deviance still abound, while those on altruism are rare; despite the wide variety of subsections of professional concern focusing on specific issues, there is as yet no group of scholars working together on the concept of altruism. In their compendium of knowledge about human behavior, Berelson and Steiner[61] have no reference to altruism, nor is there any mention of the topic in most basic textbooks of sociology. Disaster research has, of course, referred to altruism, but this work has not been incorporated into general studies. In criminology the few studies on bystander behavior are entered under the larger rubric of victimology in *Abstracts in Criminology.*

The reluctance of sociologists to examine the concept of altruism becomes all the more intriguing when it is remembered that some of the founders of sociology often used the concept. Durkheim, for instance, in his first major work discussing social solidarity and the collective conscience, stressed that altruism was not "a sort of ornamental aspect of social life, but it will forever be its fundamental basis ... men cannot live together without acknowledging, and consequently making, mutual sacrifices."[62]

Later, in his study on suicide,[63] Durkheim returned to the concept, describing three different types of suicide, each qualitatively different from the other—altruistic, egoistic, anomic. Altruistic suicide was a consequence of a person's deep loyalty and commitment to a person (for example, in India, where the widow would jump onto the funeral pyre of her deceased husband) or to a value (for example, the officer ending his life because of a military failure) or to a culture (for example, suicidal missions carried out in time of war).

Yet, whereas the concept, anomie, has subsequently been developed into a central concept of deviance, even to the use of the term in English,[64] there has been no similar development of research and theory for altruism.

Some parallel work by Mauss,[65] a colleague of Durkheim, also attempted to understand the subtle bonds that hold society together. While Durkheim had shown that the division of labor had sociological meaning no less than economic, Mauss showed that the act of giving has implications far beyond the mere transfer of goods and services, for each such transaction helps to build up a basis of reciprocity within the society and thereby draws its members closer together. Mutual exchanges of gifts, possessions, and services are firmly embedded in social behavior and help to weave together a network of reciprocal obligations. People act for the benefit of others in order to ensure their own welfare in some subsequent transaction. There is an implicit obligation to respond to the benefits that one gains; exchange cannot be understood only in terms of the direct economic interest involved in a particular transaction.

Mauss's work has had much impact on anthropological work,[66] while in sociology it is echoed in a classic article by Gouldner on the norm of reciprocity,[67] where he describes the norm as transcending any cultural traits and being universal in nature—". . . no less universal an element of culture than the incest taboo, although, similarly, its concrete formulations may vary with time and place."[68]

Gouldner sees the norm as being based on two minimal interrelated demands: that people should help those who have helped them, and that people should not injure those who have helped them. He suggests that much utilitarian philosophy flows from the insight that activities "to satisfy the expectations of the other" may often be initiated by egoistic considerations since there is an implied inducement "for the latter to reciprocate and to satisfy his own [expectation]."[69] Helping behavior thus becomes not only morally desirable but expedient. "If you want to be helped by others," Gouldner writes, "you must help them,"[70] and adds, "there is an altruism in egoism, made possible through reciprocity."[71]

Leeds, in a thoughtful analysis of altruism,[72] develops this idea. She stresses not the norm of reciprocity, but the norm of giving. She notes that direct reciprocity may not always come into effect; particularly in true altruistic acts, the altruist might be offended by a reward for his efforts, while in other circumstances the beneficiary of altruistic action might resent having to display gratitude.

Reciprocity cannot be expected only in a dual relationship; its true relevance is within a network of relationships, where through a chain-reaction development, the recipient of altruistic action would be inclined in the future to help others. "This network of altruistic acts . . . cuts across the regular lines of reciprocity."[73] Through experiencing, or even observing, altruistic acts, the beneficiary, or the bystander, would be much more disposed to perform altruistic acts in the future. Thereby an overall atmosphere conducive to altruism would emerge, each additional act enhancing further the emergence, expansion, and stability of the network of altruism.

This is the kind of thinking that permeates also the work of the exchange theorists, particularly Blau.[74] Blau, however, carefully avoids using the word altruism.[75] Since it seems to connote an action devoid of any exchange he uses intrinsic rewards as some sort of synonym for altruism. According to Blau's exchange model, social behavior is based on exchange; where a particular act has no apparent external reward, Blau sees the motivation for action stemming from the internal rewards that accrue to the actor, such as love, gratitude, or self-satisfaction.

But such acts, without an immediate and direct quid pro quo, are themselves premised on the trust that the actor has that others will, in the course of time, reciprocate. In fact, the "gradual expansion of exchange transactions promotes the trust necessary for them. As individuals regularly discharge their obligations, they prove themselves trustworthy of further credit."[76]

Economists too have been puzzled by the existence of altruistic behavior, as it does not fit easily into what Phelps refers to as the "economist's beloved model of utility maximization."[77] Phelps suggests that altruism poses very real problems for economic theory, and that it is time for economists to realize the contribution that altruism can and does make to the functioning of the market. Such considerations are liable to have far-reaching impact on economic thinking, as is shown by some of the articles in the book edited by Phelps.[78]

The converse position, of market considerations being allowed to intrude on basically altruistic actions, has been perceptively analyzed in Titmuss's study of blood donations.[79] This is one of the few sociological studies that has attempted to incorporate the concept of altruism into a study of a particular aspect of social behavior. Titmuss argues that there is a close relationship between the manner used to encourage people to make contributions of blood and the quality of life. He compares situations where blood donors are paid with those where the blood is given voluntarily, and argues against making blood into a commodity, which is bought and sold in a competitive commercial market, with contributions being transformed into a paid service, since the ultimate result will be both an erosion of human values and a diminution of efficiency in providing needed medical services. He notes that, while the book is oriented to issues of social policy such as how best to ensure the ready availability of blood, it is also "... about the role of altruism in modern society. ... It attempts to fuse the politics of welfare and morality of individual wills."[80] In a larger sense Titmuss is examining the limits that have to be placed on the pure form of economic, self-oriented exchange relationships in an impersonal market which characterizes modern society.

From a pragmatic point of view, Titmuss notes that statistics show that a private market in blood entails much greater risks to the recipient of contracting a disease, including risks of death. As the poor, and the unemployed, are often enticed to give blood purely because of the monetary reward, they are then tempted to withhold critical details about their medical history. In many instances, their blood is not suitable because of prior disease.

The impact of the policy adopted for blood donations goes beyond the particular medical service and has overall societal implications. Blood donations serve as a test of people's willingness to provide potential benefits for unknown and unseen strangers, who will never know the source of this life-sustaining material and never be able to express any personal thanks. Of course exchange concepts may be applied where the policy is to allow blood donors and their families free use of blood if the need should subsequently arise. In a sense, then, many blood donors are taking out an insurance policy for their own use of blood in the future. Yet there are always those who give without any regard for such inducements.

Titmuss argues that altruism is an important value that should be fostered, more particularly in modern societies. There is a social need for gift relationships. People have to be made aware of the fact that they cannot limit their interaction with others only to what is demanded by duty or by contract obligations.

Titmuss argues that even in modern societies there is a dependence on others without which even the demands of duty and contractual obligations cannot be met. Thus he notes that, in one of the key aspects of modern society, specialized professionalism, there can be no real progress unless a minimum degree of other-centered activity takes place.

This is of particular pertinence for medicine, where the advance of medical knowledge, and of the individual practitioners, depends partly on the willingness of patients to allow themselves to be "taught on" in teaching hospitals. The situation is similar with sociologists, who "need co-operative field and control material," or "psychologists who need laboratory volunteers."[81]

Many of the advances of modern society are thus not just the product of the innovative ideas of leading scientists, but of the willingness of ordinary members of society to participate in novel experimental situations. Of course, in many instances captive groups are used—prisoners, terminally ill patients, young children at school. In other cases they presume or hope for some benefit to themselves. Yet, beyond all of this, there are those who agree to participate in experimental situations, where the results are problematical, because they are motivated mainly or solely by a desire to be of service to others.

Titmuss is concerned that such willingness be encouraged, and sees in the blood-donor system a crucial test of the validity of altruistic considerations. Social interaction, he argues, cannot be explained only in terms of the economics of marginal utility. There is a need for behavior without any direct, immediate, and tangible return. An awareness of the importance of this factor would help to orient social policy in a direction that would facilitate such behavior. He suggests that ". . . the ways in which society organizes and structures its social institutions—and particularly its health and welfare systems—can encourage or discourage the altruistic in man; such systems can foster integration or alienation; they can allow the 'theme of the gift' (to recall Mauss's words) of generosity towards strangers, to spread among and between social groups and generations."[82]

In granting freedom to individuals which is one of the aims of modern liberal societies, there is a need to ensure that this freedom will not be limited to "consumer choice in material acquisitiveness,"[83] but will also allow ". . . opportunities for ordinary people to articulate giving in morally practical terms outside their own network of family and personal relationships."[84] Such giving to strangers will, in the long run, bring benefit to all the members of society, including the givers themselves. On the other hand, societies that close off options for voluntary other-oriented behavior are adversely affecting the quality of life.

Titmuss concludes that where there is a private market in blood, the consequent "commercialization of blood and donor relationships represses the expression of altruism, erodes the sense of community, lowers scientific standards, limits both personal and professional freedoms . . . places immense social costs on those least able to bear them—the poor, the sick, and the inept. . . ."[85]

While most other writers have accepted altruistic behavior as a fact to be explained—through the intricacies of logical analysis, or the factual description of existing behavior—Titmuss has argued for the positive pursuance of altruism as a desirable aim for a healthy society; to ensure the minimum welfare of society and to enhance the quality of its life. He has reiterated the concerns first expressed by early sociologists, such as Comte and Durkheim, and later developed by Sorokin; in doing so, he has challenged social scientists to contribute to the strengthening of an atmosphere conducive to altruistic behavior.

It is not clear that this challenge will be accepted. While Titmuss's book was received with much acclaim, few other sociologists have shown the willingness to concentrate on this particular form of behavior.[86] Some sociologists seem reluctant to be reminded of their social-reform past, and prefer to concentrate on more solid, objective work. Other sociologists seem more attracted by overall radical critiques of society.

But the challenge of coming to terms with altruism is there and can no longer be evaded. There is a need to develop the theme of altruism expounded by Durkheim, Sorokin, and Titmuss, and to determine whether their thesis of its role in society is correct, and if correct, to determine the means whereby altruistic behavior may be facilitated and encouraged.

Notes

1. Donald Campbell, "Ethocentricism and Other Altruistic Motives," *Nebraska Symposium on Motivation*, 1965 *13*, pp. 305-306.

2. *The Book of Mencius*, II a, b.

3. Friedrich Nietzsche, "Guilt, 'Bad Conscience,' and Related Matters," in Roger W. Smith, ed., *Guilt: Man and Society* (New York: Anchor, 1971), p. 35.

4. Thomas Hobbes, *The Leviathan*, 1651.

5. B. Mandeville, *The Fable of the Bees*, 1734.

6. John Stuart Mill, *Utilitarianism*, see James M. Smith and Ernest Sosa, eds., *Mill's Utilitarianism* (Belmont, Cal.: Wadsworth, 1969), and Jeremy Bentham, *The Principles of Morals and Legislation*, 1789.

7. Adam Smith, *The Theory of Moral Sentiments* (Oxford: Clarendon, 1976), p. 225.

8. Robert G. Olson, *The Morality of Self-Interest* (New York: Harcourt, Brace and World, 1965), p. 37.

9. Ibid., p. 38.

10. Ibid., p. 135.

11. Ibid., p. 134.

12. Ibid., p. 127.

13. Thomas Nagel, *The Possibility of Altruism* (Oxford: Clarendon Press, 1970), p. 80.

14. Ibid., p. 82.

15. For a good selection of articles on philosophical attitudes to moral behavior see David P. Gauthier, ed., *Morality and Rational Self-Interest* (Engle-

wood Cliffs, N.J.: Prentice-Hall, 1970). But for a warning against the dangers of paternalistic attitudes and value coercion, see also L. Dyke, "The Vices of Altruism," *Ethics: International Journal of Social, Political, and Legal Philosophy*, 1971, *81*, pp. 241-252.

16. Charles Darwin, *The Descent of Man*, 1871.

17. Thomas H. Huxley, "The Struggle for Existence in Human Society," *The Nineteenth Century*, Feb. 1888; also in Huxley, *Evolution and Ethics and Other Essays.* For a contemporary critique of this Darwinian approach see J.G. Schurman, *The Ethical Impact of Darwinism*, 1887.

18. Herbert Spencer, *On Social Evolution: Selected Writings* (Chicago: University of Chicago Press, 1972); and William G. Summer, *Folkways* (New York, 1906).

19. Richard Hofstadter, *Social Darwinism in American Thought* (New York: Braziller, 1955). For further views on Social Darwinism, see Michael Banton, ed., *Darwinism and the Study of Society* (Chicago: Quadrangle Books, 1961).

20. Peter A. Kropotkin, *Mutual Aid: A Factor in Evolution* (New York: Garland Publishing, 1972).

21. See his *Memoirs of a Revolutionist.*

22. *Mutual Aid,* "Introduction," p. ix.

23. Ibid., p. 4.

24. Ibid., pp. 5-6.

25. J.J. Bachofen, *Myth, Religion and Mother Right: Selected Writings,* R. Manheim, trans. (Princeton: Princeton University Press, 1967); E.B. Tylor, *Primitive Culture* (New York: Harper, 1958); Sir Henry Maine, *Ancient Law,* 1861.

26. *Mutual Aid,* p. 126.

27. Ibid., chapters 5 and 6.

28. Ibid., p. 275.

29. Ibid., p. 277.

30. Ibid.

31. Ibid.

32. Ibid.

33. For a summary of this field, see Robert Ardrey, *The Territorial Imperative* (New York: Atheneum, 1966).

34. Konrad Lorenz, *On Aggression* (New York: Harcourt, Brace and World, 1966).

35. Harry Kaufman, *Aggression and Altruism: A Psychological Analysis* (New York: Holt, Rinehart and Winston, 1970), p. 98.

36. For some classic studies which contain descriptions of helping behavior see W.N. Kellog, *Porpoises and Sonar* (Chicago: University of Chicago Press, 1961), and W. Kohler, *The Mentality of Apes* (New York: Harcourt, Bruce, 1927); see also W.C. Allee, *The Social Life of Animals* (Boston, Beacon Press, 1958).

37. H.W. Nissen and M.P. Crawford, "A Preliminary Study of Food-sharing Behavior in Young Chimpanzees," *Journal of Comparative Psychology,* 1936, *22* pp. 383-419; see also J.B. Siebenhaler and D.K. Caldwell, "Cooperation Among Adult Dolphins," *Journal of Mammalogy,* 1956, *37*, pp. 126-218.

38. V.C. Wynne-Edwards, *Animal Dispersion in Relation to Social Behavior* (New York: Hafner, 1962); see also his "Self-regulating systems in Populations of Animals," *Science,* 1965, *147*, pp. 1543-1548.

39. J.M. Masserman, S. Wechkin, and W. Terris, " 'Altruistic' Behavior in Rhesus Monkeys," *American Journal of Psychiatry,* 1963, *121* pp. 584-585.

40. George E. Rice, Jr., and Priscilla Gainer, " 'Altruism' in the Albino Rat," *Journal of Comparative and Physiological Psychology,* 1962, *55,* pp. 123-125. For a similar experiment, see E.M. Church, "Emotional Reactions of Rats to the Pain of Others," *Journal of Comparative and Physiological Psychology,* 1959, *52,* pp. 132-134.

41. J.J. Lavery and P.J. Foley, "Altruism or Arousal in the Rat?" *Science,* 1963, *140,* pp. 172-173.

42. George E. Rice, Jr., "Aiding Behavior versus Fear in the Albino Rat," *Psychology Record,* 1964, *14,* pp. 165-170.

43. Dennis L. Krebs, "Altruism: An Examination of the Concept and a Review of the Literature," *Psychological Bulletin,* 1970, *73,* pp. 258-302.

44. D.O. Hebb, "Comment on Altruism: The Comparative Evidence," *Psychological Bulletin,* 1971, *76,* pp. 409-410. For Krebs's reply to this article see D.L. Krebs, "Infrahuman Altruism," *Psychological Bulletin,* 1971, *76,* pp. 411-414.

45. Ibid., p. 410.

46. S.J. Holmes, "The Reproductive Beginnings of Altruism," *Psychological Review,* 1945, *52,* pp. 109-112.

47. Ibid., p. 109.

48. Ibid.

49. See especially Edward O. Wilson, *Sociobiology: The New Synthesis* (Cambridge: Harvard University Press, 1975); and David P. Barash, *Sociobiology and Behavior* (New York: Elsevier, 1977).

50. See, for example, J. Maynard Smith, "The Evolution of Alarm Calls," *American Naturalist,* 1965, *99,* pp. 59-63.

51. W.D. Hamilton, "The Genetical Theory of Social Behavior," *Journal of Theoretical Biology,"* 1964, 7, pp. 1-52, and J. Maynard Smith, "Group Selection and Kin Selection," *Nature,* 1964, *201,* pp. 1145-1147. For a collection of articles dealing with these issues (including these two articles) see George C. Williams, ed., *Group Selection* (Chicago: Aldine-Atherton, 1971).

52. Barash, *Sociobiology and Behavior.*

53. Hamilton, "The genetical Theory. . . ."

54. Robert L. Trivers, "The Evolution of Reciprocal Altruism," *Quarterly Review of Biology,* 1971, *46,* pp. 35-57.

55. See, for example, accounts of such behavior: Alexander Sutherland,

The Origin and Growth of the Moral Instinct (London: Longman's, Green, 1898; reproduced New York: Arno Press, 1974). This book is comprehensive and contains examples of both destructive and nurturant parental behavior in all types of living creatures.

56. See, for example, accounts of child abuse: David G. Gil, *Violence Against Children: Physical Child Abuse in the United States* (Cambridge: Harvard University Press, 1970). See also my discussion of parental and adult hostility, "Beyond the Oedipus Complex: Reflections on the Myth and Reality of Generational Conflict," *Theory and Society,* 1976, *3,* pp. 1-41.

57. See Pitirim A. Sorokin, *Altruistic Love: A Study of American "Good Neighbors" and Christian Saints* (Boston: Beacon Press, 1950).

58. Ibid., p. 4.

59. Ibid.

60. For an anthology of articles published under the auspices of this center see Pitirim A. Sorokin, ed., *Explorations in Altruistic Love and Behavior* (Boston: Beacon Press, 1950).

61. Bernard Berelson and Gary A. Steiner, *Human Behavior: An Inventory of Scientific Findings* (New York: Harcourt, Brace and World, 1964).

62. Emile Durkheim, *The Division of Labor in Society* (Glencoe, Illinois: The Free Press, 1966), p. 228.

63. Emile Durkheim, *Suicide: A Study in Sociology* (Glencoe, Illinois: The Free Press, 1966).

64. See Robert K. Merton, *Social Theory and Social Structure* (Glencoe, Illinois: The Free Press, 1949).

65. Marcel Mauss, *The Gift: Forms and Functions of Exchange in Archaic Societies,* Ian Cunnison, trans. (London: Cohen and West, 1954).

66. See, for instance, the work of Max Gluckman, *Politics, Law and Ritual in Tribal Society* (Chicago: Aldine, 1965); and Bronislaw Malinowski, *Argonauts of the Western Pacific* (New York: Dutton, 1932).

67. Alvin Gouldner, "The Norm of Reciprocity: A Preliminary Statement," *American Sociological Review,* 1960, *25,* pp. 161-178.

68. Ibid., p. 171.

69. Ibid., p. 173.

70. Ibid.

71. Ibid.

72. Ruth Leeds, "Altruism and the Norm of Giving," *Merrill-Palmer Quarterly,* 1963, *9,* p. 229.

73. Ibid., p. 235.

74. Peter M. Blau, *Exchange and Power in Social Life* (New York: John Wiley and Sons, 1964).

75. Although Blau does not use the word altruism in the book, he has an index reference, with cross-references to "intrinsic rewards," "reinforcement," "reverse secondary," and "self-interest."

76. Ibid., p. 98.

77. Edmund S. Phelps, ed., *Altruism, Morality and Economic Theory* (New York: Russel Sage, 1975).

78. For further discussion of altruism and economics, see the articles in the book edited by Phelps.

79. Richard M. Titmuss, *The Gift Relationship: From Human Blood to Social Policy* (New York: Pantheon, 1971).

80. Ibid., p. 12.

81. Ibid., p. 215.

82. Ibid., p. 225.

83. Ibid.

84. Ibid., p. 226.

85. Ibid., p. 245.

86. In the early 1960s a few articles on altriusm appeared in leading sociological journals, but there was no follow up, and these works have been given little attention. In one article, Friedrichs tried to set out a means for rating altruism (Robert W. Friedrichs, "Alter versus Ego: An Exploratory Assessment of Altruism," *American Sociological Review,* 1960, *25*, pp. 496-508); in another article Ribal pointed out that altruism could best be understood in terms of a typology of giving and receiving, in which there were four possibilities—the Altruistic Self, the Selfish Self, the Receptive-Giving Self, and the Inner-Sustaining Self. (Joseph E. Ribal, "Social Character and Meanings of Selfishness and Altruism," *Sociology and Social Research,* 1963, *47,* pp. 311-321); while Sawyer presented an altruism scale (J. Sawyer, "The Altruism Scale: A Measure of Cooperative, Individualistic, and Competitive Interpersonal Orientation," *American Journal of Sociology,* 1966, *71,* pp. 407-416).

9

Encouraging Prosocial Behavior

If altruism is to be considered a desirable trait in people, and if an atmosphere of altruism is to be considered an important, perhaps even essential, ingredient for a healthy society, then ways and means of inculcating such traits and creating such an atmosphere must be given due consideration.

One of the areas of social life that has always addressed itself to the problem of altruism is religion. Almost every major religion devotes at least a part of its teaching to exhortations for greater concern for one's fellow beings. In the Christian tradition the parable of the Good Samaritan has been seen as a major message of the importance and desirability of helping behavior.[1]

In a recent study of the Jewish approach on this topic, Kirschenbaum[2] has shown that the rather cryptic phrase from Leviticus (19:16), "Neither shalt thou stand idly by the blood of one's neighbor," has been used as the basis for extensive writings in the Jewish law to determine the various occasions on which help to a stranger in distress is required, and what degree of risks are to be undertaken.

In Buddhist tradition the concept of giving to others is one of the methods of acquiring merit.[3] While the stress is often on giving for religious purposes—for instance, to monks or to temples—altruistic acts on behalf of others are also considered as constituting a giving act.

From a social science perspective much skepticism has been cast on the capacity of preaching, or even other exhortative devices, to substantively affect people's behavior. One widely quoted field study[4] recorded that seminary students, hurrying on their way to deliver a lecture on the topic of the Good Samaritan, were likely to pass by a stranger lying collapsed on the ground.

Far more significant in examining the role of religion, or even any institution aimed at making good citizens, is the extensive research carried out by Hartshorne and May[5] in the 1920s into the character of young people. In one phase of their research into the degree of cheating shown by their subjects, they found that there was no significant difference in the propensity to cheat when tempted between churchgoers or members of the Scout movement and those who had not come under the educational influence of these institutions. Wright[6] has pointed out that different people are attracted to religion for different reasons, and that this fact constitutes a basic difficulty in trying to assess the positive value of religiosity in encouraging positive modes of conduct.

Law and Morality

Another means of inculcating moral values that has been traditionally considered as effective is the law. There is a limited amount of research to indicate that when laws having moral connotations are changed, the fact of the change may have little influence on people's attitudes.[7] However, the issue of the role of the law in fostering morality has aroused controversy not so much in regard to the *efficacy* of the law, but as to the *desirability* of using the law to further the moral values of the society.

In general, most lawyers incline to the viewpoint that, whereas in ancient times and in simple societies there might well have been a role for law in serving the moral ethos and the religious foundations of the society, such functions are ill-befitting a modern, heterogeneous, and secular state.[8]

While there are voluminous writings among lawyers on this issue, in recent times much of the debate has focused around the opposing stances adopted by two leading British jurists, Hart and Devlin,[9] the former arguing that society has no right to impose its morality on the private behavior of its citizens, for instance in sexual behavior, and the latter arguing that society is obliged, for its well-being and perhaps survival, to use the major instruments at its disposal, the law and education, in order to ensure a level of morality without which the very existence of the society would be placed in jeopardy.

Yet, this debate, for all its richness and provocative ideas, has taken a limited form. While the protagonists argue as to the role of law in preventing the commission of acts considered to be immoral, they have almost completely ignored a no less important issue—whether the law should be used to coerce people to virtuous behavior.

Honoré has concisely spelled out this defect in the debate. Taking issue with both Hart and Devlin, he writes that his

> concern is not only wider but different from that of the jurists by whose brilliant and elevated jousting we have been entertained. They have debated whether some parts of the law which coincide with common morality should be scrapped. We, on the other hand, wish to know whether parts of morality, at present outside the law, should be incorporated in it. . . . Some people feel that the intrusion of law into the private sphere of sex is indecent and dangerous. Others feel outraged by the failure of the law to intercede in relation to rescued and rescuers. . . . Should the law encourage or even insist on Do-goodery? Or would this be an intrusion into yet another private sphere, not of sex, but of conscience?
>
> Clearly we have a moral issue on our hands, and one which is concerned not with the "enforcement" of morals but with its non-enforcement.[10]

Honoré has exposed a clear lacuna in the recent debate on law and morality: the lack of reference to what should be a burning issue—the possibility of using the law in order to increase the prospects of morally desirable behavior. In fact, discussing the obligation to a bystander, Cahn suggests that "in certain important aspects, the fear of law is the beginning of virtue."[11] Fuller has argued that there is a fundamental flaw in the whole array of contending viewpoints because of the "failure to clarify the meaning of morality itself."[12] Fuller posits the existence of two moralities, one which may be related to the law, and one which falls outside the ambit of the law. He defines these two types of moralities as being the morality of aspiration and the morality of duty, the former being a positive exhortation to excellence and perfection in human activities, and the latter being the minimal moral requirements necessary for viable social life. The distinction between these two types of morality is crucial: "Failure to make this distinction has been the cause of much obscurity in discussions of the relations between law and morals."[13]

Fuller emphasizes that generally it is the morality of duty only that is translated into legislative injunctions, while the morality of aspiration cannot be encompassed within a legal system. Yet he notes that "considerations of symmetry would suggest that in a morality of aspiration, which strives toward the superlative, reward and praise should play the role that punishment and disapproval do in the morality of duty."[14] Although there may be a need for the legal system to consider the issue of recognized rewards sanctioned by the law, as was discussed in chapter 7, Fuller discounts this possibility. Indeed he argues further that there is an inherent problem in attaining the symmetry which he poses. "Perfect symmetry," he writes, "is marred by the fact that the closer a man comes to the highest reaches of human achievement, the less competent are others to appraise his performance."[15] Further, coercion to virtue may be seen as undermining the very morality that was desired.

The reluctance to use the legal system in the morality of aspiration is understandable, if nevertheless debatable. It is possible to look upon the right to compensation and the protection of immunity as forms of reward.[16] But the real issue is whether tangible expressions of society's acknowledgment should not be considered. Inasmuch as rewards are given by the police and fire departments, local councils or the mass media for prosocial behavior, they are generally awarded for heroic behavior. The most institutionalized procedure for doing this at a national level in the United States is the Carnegie Hero Fund that was set up by the philanthropist in 1904 as a means of rewarding those who had taken personal risks in order to help others.[17] Since its inception, over 6,000 awards have been made, chosen from over 50,000 cases examined by the commission. The commission provides gold, silver, and bronze medals and also monetary compensation where actual losses or injury have been incurred. But on the whole, the impact of such reward on the public at large is minimal, with little publicity in the mass media, and even little response by public figures or educators.

It may be necessary to give far more consideration to the need not only to recognize altruistic conduct after it has taken place, but also to see such recognition as a statement of intent by society as a whole. For, as many social scientists have been showing, models of behavior are often crucial factors in determining other people's behavior.

Developmental Learning

In the last few years there has been increasing research into the nature of moral ideas, how they are formed, particularly in the young, how they may best be fostered, and to what degree they affect conduct. Many educators and psychologists have been claiming that education cannot be limited, as it often is, to the intellectual faculties, but has to embrace all aspects of life—the physical, artistic, creative, and social capacities, as well as the moral aspects of human behavior and social life.

Some of the leading work has been done by a number of researchers who see the growth of moral perceptions as paralleling the intellectual development of the child. Piaget,[18] one of the dominant figures in this field, has shown how children change their perception of morality and justice from being immutable rules imposed by dominant authority figures (usually true of children about seven and under) to a greater awareness that leads (usually by the age of twelve) to a more creative concept of morality based on overall ideas of justice, and consideration of other's needs. Piaget terms the earlier approach of blind obedience to rules as a morality of constraint, and the later approach of creative awareness as a morality of cooperation.

Piaget's developmental approach to concepts of morality has been expanded by Kohlberg,[19] involving not only the thought processes of the young but also the manner in which adults conceive of the relationships between externally imposed rules and the dictates of a personal conscience. Kohlberg's scheme is based on six stages of possible moral development; while Kohlberg agrees with Piaget that there is a clear cognitive and developmental process, he claims that not all children, or adults, reach the highest levels. Whereas Piaget's work is based on children's reactions to stories involving punishment for harm caused, Kohlberg presents them with stories necessitating a choice between moral dilemmas.

Kohlberg refers to the first two stages as being the premoral or preconventional level; rules are obeyed chiefly for fear of punishment (at the first stage) and for a hedonistic desire to satisfy one's own needs (at the second stage). At the next level, the conventional level, the two stages involve a desire to please others by conforming to their expectations, and a desire to obey rules out of a duty to society as a whole.

It is only at the postconventional or principled level that an inner or autonomous morality emerges, based primarily on self-accepted principles, in which one's conscience takes precedence over the official rules of authority. The fifth stage is based on contractual rights freely entered into between equal individuals, while the sixth and highest stage consists of a morality that transcends immediate societal rules and needs, and is based on a search to implement universalistic principles.

Although Kohlberg's work was originally based only on measuring the nature of moral reasoning and delineating the different sequential stages, it has more recently become directly involved in searching for the means to educate children to move into higher stages through classroom discussions of moral dilemmas. Kohlberg credits[20] one of his students, Blatt, with having perceived the possibilities inherent in using discussions of moral topics as a pedagogical tool for furthering moral values. Instead of merely interviewing pupils for research purposes, Blatt proposed that the same kind of moral dilemmas should be adapted for the purpose of classroom discussions in which conscious efforts would be devoted to raising the moral level of the participants, in the course of debating and attempting to resolve the moral dilemma.

In his original research project Blatt found that many pupils who had taken part in discussion would, in the course of several months, move up to a higher stage in the Kohlberg scheme. Kohlberg has termed this process of change the "Blatt effect."[21] In the last few years several school systems have been using programs based on this approach and aimed at improving the moral judgments and reasoning of the pupils, with a fair degree of success recorded.[22]

Turiel's work[23] is particularly noteworthy. He has shown that when adults use a form of moral thinking one stage above that of the children, it often leads to the children themselves raising their level. He notes that the pupil could even sometimes be raised two stages higher by being exposed to moral reasoning two stages above their own. In addition, he showed that their moral reasoning could also be lowered one stage where they were exposed to lower reasoning processes. Later, LeFurgy and Waloshin[24] showed that an increase in one level would have a greater long-term effect than a decrease in level, suggesting that, once a particular stage had been reached, it would be firmly entrenched, despite temporary variations, thus providing further evidence of the developmental basis for moral reasoning.

Despite the positive response and practical application that Kohlberg's approach has generated, a number of criticisms have been voiced as to its perceived weakness. There has been some objection to the emphasis on a developmental process (criticism to which Piaget has also been subjected); in particular, it has been suggested that often younger people may have advanced concepts of morality, such as consideration for others, but may lack the mental capacity fully to express their ideas or sentiments. It is even possible that their moral perceptions actually precede their cognitive and intellectual capacities.

Fraenkel[25] has questioned the presumed universality of the six stages, and their hierarchical pattern. He criticizes also some of the actual practices used by teachers and experimenters in presenting the moral dilemmas and raises doubt as to the value of discussion alone in improving moral concepts, particularly since many of the dilemmas are deliberately kept simple so as to facilitate discussion, whereas most real-life dilemmas are complex. He claims that the use of models and concrete examples is a far better way of making children more aware of desirable moral behavior.

Sullivan[26] too feels that the discussion method is too far removed from reality, and argues that morality can only be judged in terms of a commitment to action. Often, in fact, the ambiguity of a moral dilemma is resolved through action: "all of us mere humans in many situations must act in ambiguity, and . . . in the process of acting we really begin to clarify how we think."[27]

For all the emphasis that Kohlberg and his associates place on the development of moral concerns, almost no attempt has been made to deal with the specific issue of prosocial and altruistic behavior. This is an aspect that Eisenberg-Berg[28] has been critical of. In her work she has attempted to remedy this defect, and, in the process of doing so, has also developed an alternative theoretical approach to the stages of moral development. In their summary of this work, Mussen and Eisenberg-Berg point out that Piaget and Kohlberg "both deal with a circumscribed domain of moral reasoning. . . . The prosocial domain (the thoughts, concepts, and judgments about issues such as personal sacrifice and conflicts between one's own needs and those of others) is not tapped in Piaget's or Kohlberg's procedures. Consider the moral dilemma of a girl who has to decide between protecting herself and risking her own safety to help someone in distress. There is no a priori reason to believe that the same conceptions, judgments and principles are applied in resolving this dilemma as in dealing with the dilemmas presented by Piaget and Kohlberg."[29]

In her research, Eisenberg-Berg related stories in which children were required to make choices between different moral judgments concerning "prosocial actions and conflicts between one's own and another's desires."[30] She found some similarities in the reasoning process used by her interviewees and those of Piaget and Kohlberg, but also noted a number of major differences. Of particular significance is the fact that although her system is also age-related, she found that "young children's judgments about prosocial moral dilemmas were more advanced than their reasoning about laws, rules, and formal obligations."[31] She noted among her younger subjects a clear tendency to base their judgments on what they considered to be the most desirable behavior required by the exigencies of the situation, without any undue reliance on the expectations of authority figures or the possibility of punishment.

In this connection, Staub's research[32] might be relevant. He found that sometimes younger children offered help more than older children. While there was an increase in helping from kindergarten to second grade, there was a decrease from second grade to sixth grade. He felt that the older children were more aware of possible adult disapproval of initiative by children or unusual behavior on their part.

Eisenberg-Berg suggests that there are four stages of prosocial moral reasoning. Stage one is based on one of two unrelated possibilities—either hedonistic, pragmatic orientation, concerned only with the personal and selfish advantage to be derived, or an outward, expressed concern for the needs of others, though without any attempt truly to empathize with that need on a personal basis.

The second stage involves a readiness for prosocial behavior based mainly on expectations held by others and/or a desire to win their approval. The third stage involves direct empathy for the other person and an ability to relate, at the personal level, to the other's plight. This stage may sometimes be given more sophisticated expression when the prosocial actions are related to internalized values, norms, duties, or responsibilities. The fourth stage is one based on one's own resources, the need to maintain primarily one's own self-respect, and to live up to one's own values.

However, as Mussen and Eisenberg-Berg note, there is only a limited amount of research showing a relationship between the stages of moral development reached, as expressed through verbal tests (in all three systems—those of Piaget, Kohlberg, and Eisenberg-Berg), and the actual predisposition to display prosocial behavior. What little research exists does, however, tend to indicate a correlation between attitudes and behavior.

Another theory that uses a developmental approach to moral behavior is that of Peck and Havighurst,[33] who trace five stages of development which give rise to five types of characters: the amoral person, the expedient person, the conforming person, the irrational conscientious person (who is governed largely by a powerful superego), and the rational-altruistic person. This latter type displays the highest examples of moral conduct, understands the needs of others, shows concern for their welfare, and is willing to make sacrifices on their behalf.

The Impact of Models

In contrast to the approach accentuating developmental stages of moral concepts, other researchers have predicated their work on learning theories, and have stressed the importance of exposure to models of behavior[34] oriented to altruistic norms. An interesting approach to the question of learning through models has been adopted by Kaufman.[35] Although his book is devoted mainly to the manner in which aggressive tendencies are learned, he argues that the same processes that lead to aggressive behavior may, if the content is changed, lead to altruistic behavior. He provides several examples of how exposure to aggressive behavior leads to further aggressive behavior and suggests that exposure to altruistic behavior would have similar results.

Kaufman refers to work done by students of violence to show the importance of learning models, and exposure to symbols of violence. He quotes, inter alia, some of the well-known work by Wertham on the role of the mass media in fostering violence, the work of Bandura and Walters showing that children copy patterns of violent behavior which they see in adult behavior, and the work of Berkowitz and La Page which shows that the mere presence of violent objects may in certain circumstances (for instance, where the subjects are insulted), lead to a greater use of verbal violence in response, even if the weapons themselves are not used.[36]

Having catalogued the many and diverse ways in which models of aggressive behavior have an impact on people's behavior, Kaufman tries to show that models of altruistic behavior could easily have the same effect, although there is one major point of difference between aggression and altruism. On many occasions resorting to aggressive behavior leads to immediate, tangible results, whereas moral, socially responsible, and altruistic behavior does not always bring immediate, perceivable benefits.

Nevertheless, Kaufman's conclusion is that people "can be moved toward good as readily as toward evil. Even small children can learn to behave with consideration, altruism, and even self-sacrifice, toward other individuals."[37]

A similar attitude has been adopted by Hornstein,[38] who argues that the "very psychological structures which make aggression possible inevitably create the basis for altruism."[39] He claims that neither tendency is primary or predominant, and that "both simply exist as part of the human potential. Whether human beings are altruistic or aggressive, benevolent or brutal, selfless or selfish, depends upon surrounding social conditions."[40]

Analyzing the results of his own research, and the research of others, Hornstein concludes that there is a far greater propensity to help than is commonly thought, although altruistic tendencies are often predicated on a capacity to identify with the person in need of help. A key factor is whether strangers are perceived as being part of a we-group or a they-group.

Hornstein emphasizes that the prospect of a we-group identification, leading to prosocial behavior, is greatest when a person has been exposed to prosocial behavioral models, has been the recipient of good news, or has been the participant in a happy event. There is a chain-reaction effect which often causes people to act in a way similar to acts that they have recently taken part in or been aware of. Thus "people who receive, or even witness, simple acts of decency and generosity are themselves stimulated to behave benevolently toward their fellows, even when they could do otherwise with impunity."[41]

These acts may be of only minor import, such as in the report by Isen and Levin[42] that finding a dime in a telephone booth made the recipients far more inclined to render simple aid (help a stranger pick up some paper that had been dropped). Similar positive results have been recorded where a subject has been successful in some prior endeavor or has been in a state of elation.[43]

Hornstein also quotes work done by some of his students and colleagues which shows the impact of news broadcasts on people's capacity to expand or contract their concepts of we-group boundaries. One research project[44] showed that where people had heard a news report on the radio, their attitude to a question probing the moral-ethical dispositions of people in general (as to their decency, honesty, and altruism) was markedly influenced by the nature of the news that they had just heard, whether good or bad.

One of the most striking examples of the impact of news on people's behavior was discovered through serendipity. Hornstein and several of his associates[45] had been testing the likelihood that people would pick up a lost wallet, containing money and personal papers, and return it by mail to the owner. A constant pattern emerged over a period of months; about 45 percent of the "lost" wallets were returned. There was only one exception to the pattern: on the day following the assassination of Senator Robert Kennedy, none of the wallets were returned. Hornstein suggests that this change in behavior was partly because people were upset, but even more significantly, because they had lost faith in the social bonds which bind a community together and which make people inclined to consider the welfare of others.

Both Kaufman and Hornstein have touched on an important aspect of helping behavior, showing that the process by which the norms and behavior patterns of altruism are absorbed follow very similar processes to those which generate negative norms and behavioral patterns. Exposure to positive or negative models, or to positive or negative experiences, or to a positive or negative atmosphere, may be a key element in determining the nature of a bystander's response. From this perspective the role of the usual socializing agencies—family, school, mass media—becomes of major importance. The kind of models they present may determine the degree of antisocial or prosocial behavior in the society.

It would seem that the work of Kohlberg and his colleagues has much to offer in this regard, by trying to absorb moral education into the school curriculum. But some of the evidence would suggest that their approach may be too limited to have an optimal effect. Their work needs an additional orientation toward altruism where the pupils are obliged to make a choice between behavior that is not merely helpful to the other person, but that may be risky or inconvenient to them. It should also expand the use of actual behavioral models, and not rely merely on verbal discussion.

Research in these areas is already available. What is lacking is a commitment of the kind shown by Kohlberg and his colleagues and students. The results of reported research indicate that altruistic behavior is contagious, and that the old adage "one good turn deserves another" has validity; more than this, it leads to a cumulative and expansive series of further good turns. Isen and her colleagues[46] have shown how even a general good feeling, or a feeling of success, can lead to prosocial acts. Conversely, negative feelings or experiences, such as failing in a task, can lead to a lessening of prosocial conduct.

A number of research projects have shown how being a witness to prosocial behavior invariably leads a person to display similar behavior when encountering a similar problematical situation. Bryan and Test[47] showed that a driver on a freeway was more likely to stop to help a fellow driver in a stranded car if, just a few miles before, he had witnessed a similar scene of a driver stopping to help another stranded car. Bryan and his colleagues have carried out several other research projects in which children almost invariably adopt the prosocial behavior of a model. He and Walbeck,[48] in a series of projects, have consistently found that the presence of a generous model increases the generosity of the children, for example, in sharing a desired object. While they note that children seem to accept the norm of the altruistic act, they acknowledge that some of the behavior may be simply imitative and may be lacking in deeper altruistic motivation. In general, their research indicates that behavioral models are far superior to verbal exhortations in eliciting moral behavior.[49]

Similar conclusions have been reached by Staub,[50] but he has also measured some additional variables. In one study[51] he compared the value of role-playing with that of induction. In role-playing, the children enacted situations where one needed help and another provided help, and then later exchanged roles so that both could experience the roles of victim and helper. The second variable, induction, was based on typical child-rearing techniques used by parents, where they point out to their children the consequences that their behavior will have for others. Staub found that the most significant influence on children's prosocial behavior was after they had been exposed to role-playing situations. The effect would even be felt in later situations which bore little resemblance to the role-playing incident, so that the later helping behavior could not be seen as merely imitative, but was probably based on the internalization of values of helping, based on the personal role-playing experience.

In contrast, induction seemed to have little effect, even when accompanied by role-playing. Staub suggests that the children may have felt a resistance to the imposition of adult authority, akin to Brehm's reactance syndrome.[52] Hoffman, however, has found induction to be a useful means of teaching moral behavior, and more effective than most other disciplinary approaches adopted by parents, such as power assertion or love withdrawal.[53]

Staub has also shown that nurturant behavior by a model has an added positive influence on a child's willingness to help.[54] Warm and affective behavior by the model tends to increase the likelihood that the behavior will be repeated by the child. A number of other researchers have also remarked on the importance of nurturance.

Aronfreed, summarizing the research in this area,[55] concludes that there are clear indications that the nurturance of a potential model toward a child increases the likelihood of the child's adopting the model's behavior. In his own work on altruism he has shown the significance of shared feelings of pleasure as a key factor in fostering altruistic behavior. Where a model gave a warm expression to events which caused delight (hugging the child, smiling, and talking in a pleased and excited tone of voice, even though the event itself was trivial—a light being switched on) the child would try to recreate the event (making the light come on) even though it meant foregoing a desirable object, such as candy. The tendency to help was the greatest where the child had received several expressions of the model's delight—both hugging and verbal expressions of pleasure.[56]

One of the most intensive studies of the impact of nurturance models was carried out by Yarrow, Scott, and Waxler,[57] who were critical of some of the earlier studies for not having probed the role of nurturance in a more meaningful manner. In their study the models spent a great deal of time with the children in close interaction, and not merely for a limited period during, or immediately before, the test situation. In addition they criticized the earlier research for not having measured behavior patterns over an extended period of time of at least several months. In their research they demonstrated that where the model consistently practiced nurturant behavior, both before and during the research situation, there was an enhanced prospect of aiding behavior.

They argue that nurturance may well be a key factor in the development of altruism and note that parental nurturance, which is the usual way in which nurturant behavior is encountered, is itself a form of altruism; further, nurturant behavior toward children gives them a feeling of acceptance and ease with themselves, and allows them to give thought to the needs of others. They contend that the optimal conditions for inculcating altruism are when altruistic behavior by models is accompanied by nurturant behavior; either one on its own may not be sufficient to have long-lasting effects.

From a pragmatic point of view they tentatively suggest that "the parent who is an altruist in the world but is cold with his child reaps a small harvest in developing altruism in his child."[58] Taking note of this research, Mussen and Eisenberg-Berg[59] echo the criticism of Yarrow and her colleagues of much of the research on nurturance, and add that research findings on the role of nurturant and affective behavior in the home are limited in number and equivocal in terms of the behavior of children. However, when the family backgrounds of altruistic adults are examined (for example, Christians who saved Jews from the Nazis,[60] or people who participated in freedom rides in the southern states on behalf of civil rights[61]), the research indicates that, in a large percentage of cases, the altruists came from families where there were both a great deal of altruistic ideals and actions, as well as a warm, loving atmosphere in the home.

In fact, the role of nurturance may even be seen in the relatively impersonal mass media. Some research projects have shown that prosocial behavior and a warm, affective atmosphere in the programs may have a significant effect in inculcating altruism among young viewers. Mussen and Eisenberg-Berg, after analyzing several of these studies, come to the conclusion that "the overwhelming weight of the evidence supports the hypothesis that exposure to television programs that model prosocial behavior enhances children's prosocial tendencies."[62]

Such programs form only a small part of the fare on television. It is interesting to note that most of the debate about television and the research into its impact, center almost entirely around the question of whether or not television violence and other antisocial acts have an influence on children's attitudes and behavior. Very rarely does public debate focus on whether or not the mass media have a capacity for positively influencing their young viewers, and whether there is an obligation to search for means for doing so. Recently this has become the focus of concern for PTA groups.

Teaching of Values

As increasingly more psychologists and educators have become involved in prosocial behavior, it is becoming clear that there are many possible ways of furthering prosocial behavior. The evidence is not entirely unequivocal, but several of the summations of the research discussed in this chapter show the emerging trends. The field is relatively new; it is possible that all the evidence is not yet in, and that much has still to be learned as to how prosocial behavior may most effectively be encouraged.

From a pedagogical point of view, there is a need to examine not just the values associated with prosocial behavior, but also the techniques that are required. If a concerted effort is to be made to encourage helping behavior, then thought must be given also to instituting educational programs that will facilitate the successful performance of helping behavior. Linked to the theoretical discussions and the use of models, there is a need for learning projects in the applied aspects of prosocial behavior—first aid, self-defense, and so on. There is, as noted in earlier chapters, research showing the salience of personal competence as a factor making for altruism, and occasional newspaper accounts report that a graduate of such a course has successfully intervened to save a life or prevent a crime.

In addition to values and techniques, greater thought should also be given to the extent to which prosocial behavior may be enhanced when young children are allowed to accept more responsibility in the running of their lives. The socialization of accepting more responsibility is liable to have an important influence on the way in which children relate to the needs of others. Staub[63] has shown that children upon whom responsibility devolves tend to display more consideration for the needs of others. Educational systems based on assigning social responsibility are likely to have a positive effect in increasing the prospects of prosocial conduct. But more research is needed on this aspect of behavior and socialization. In fact, it is possible that part of the absolutist approach of young children to moral values, as noted by Piaget and others, may be a consequence of the authoritarian manner in which the moral values are normally transmitted to them.

Staub[64] has also shown how actual learning experiences may involve prosocial behavior in a natural setting. In one research project he took the pupils to a children's hospital where they offered help to the sick children. There is a possibility of using a wide range of such prosocial programs in the educational system, not just for experimental purposes but for a positive learning experience. It is of interest to note that some juvenile court judges are increasingly using community services as part of their efforts to rehabilitate young people brought before them. But such an approach could be used very effectively not just to rehabilitate delinquents, but to encourage all children. Again there is a need for a judicious interaction between the research and practical aspects, to check the efficacy of such projects.

However, what is lacking is not knowledge, but commitment. There are many other problems of education that, after decades of research and on-the-spot experimentation, have not been resolved. Educators have not solved all the problems relating to the three R's and other basics of education, but they have not stopped teaching for that reason. The impact of television (whether it is basically contagious or cathartic) is not finally determined, but there is no moratorium on violence until all the evidence is in.

What is delaying prosocial programs in the school and in the mass media is not a desire to be more certain of how best to implement such programs, but a lack of will. What is needed is an awareness of the fact that moral education is not a marginal aspect of learning, or a passing fad, or a dispensable luxury. What is needed is a firm commitment to the idea that moral education is of the essence of the learning and socialization experience, and is a fundamental aspect of the trust reposed in those who are to prepare the next generation for a positive role in the community. What is needed is a clear realization that television and the other mass media are not merely cheap and readily available means of entertainment, to titillate and amuse, but powerful educational tools, with performers who often serve as role-models for their impressionable young viewers.

Society—through research, investigatory commissions, laws, institutions—has taken note of the large degree of antisocial behavior, especially among the young. Much of the writing and research on juvenile delinquency deals with the faults of the educational system and the negative influence of the mass media.[65] Is the alternative merely to remedy the faults and eliminate some of the negative features, or is there a need to seek a replacement that will not just prevent antisocial behavior, but promote prosocial behavior?[66] Society must, in the final analysis, decide whether it sees the expression of altruism and the performance of prosocial behavior as desirable qualities which should be cultivated. If so, then there is an obligation to use the resources at its disposal to provide the educative experiences that will enable its members, particularly the young, to learn the values and the behavior patterns of such behavior.

Notes

1. It was this parable that was used in the title of one of the first books in the academic analysis of prosocial behavior. See James M. Ratcliffe, ed., *The Good Samaritan and the Law* (New York: Anchor Books, 1966).

2. Aaron Kirschenbaum, "The 'Good Samaritan' and Jewish Law," *Dine Israel* 1976, 7, pp. 11-85. Also published in a separate publication by The Faculty of Law, Tel Aviv University.

3. See Melford E. Spiro, *Buddhism and Society: A Great Tradition and Its Burmese Vicissitudes* (New York: Harper and Row, 1970).

4. John M. Darley and C. Daniel Batson, " 'From Jerusalem to Jericho': A Study of Situational and Dispositional Variables in Helping Behavior," *Journal of Personality and Social Psychology*, 1973, *27*, pp. 100-108.

5. Hugh Hartshorne and Mark A. May, *Studies in the Nature of Character: Vol. 1—Studies in Deceit* (New York: Macmillan, 1928).

6. Derek Wright, *The Psychology of Moral Behavior* (Harmondsworth, England: Penguin Books, 1971), pp. 229-238 in chapter 10, "Religion, Education and Morality."

7. See, for instance, N. Walker, "Morality and the Criminal Law," *Howard Journal of Penology and Crime Prevention*, 1964, *11*, pp. 209-219. See also Hans Zeisel, "An International Experiment on the Effects of a Good Samaritan Law," in Ratcliffe, pp. 208-212.

8. For a criticism of this approach see Leon S. Sheleff, "Morality, Criminal Law and Politics," *Tel Aviv Studies in Law*, 1977, *2*, pp. 190-228.

9. H.L.A. Hart, *Law, Liberty and Morality* (Stanford: Stanford University Press, 1963); Patrick Devlin, *The Enforcement of Morals* (London: Oxford University Press, 1968).

10. Antony M. Honoré, "Law, Morals and Rescue," in Ratcliffe, p. 226.

11. Edmond Cahn, *The Moral Decision* (Bloomington: Indiana University Press, 1955), p. 190.

12. Lon L. Fuller, *The Morality of Law* (New Haven: Yale University Press, 1964), p. 3.

13. Ibid.

14. Ibid., p. 30.

15. Ibid.

16. As discussed in chapter 7.

17. See the annual reports by the Fund. See also Jack Markowitz, *A Walk on the Crust of Hell* (Brattleboro, Vermont: Stephen Greene Press, 1973).

18. Jean Piaget, *The Moral Judgment of the Child* (London: Kegan, Paul, 1932).

19. Kohlberg's work appears in a number of articles; see especially Lawrence Kohlberg, "The Development of Children's Orientations toward a Moral Order: Sequence in the Development of Human Thought," *Vita Humana*, 1963,

6, pp. 11-33; "Stage and Sequence: The Cognitive-Developmental Approach to Socialization," in D.A. Goslin, ed., *Handbook of Socialization Theory and Research* (Chicago: Rand McNally, 1969), pp. 347-480.

20. Lawrence Kohlberg, "Foreword," in Peter Scharf, ed., *Readings in Moral Education* (Minneapolis: Winston Press, 1968). See Blatt's dissertation study: Moshe Blatt, "Studies on the Effects of Classroom Discussions upon Children's Moral Development," Ph.D. dissertation, University of Chicago, 1970. See also Moshe Blatt and Lawrence Kohlberg, "The Effects of Classroom Moral Discussion Upon Children's Level of Moral Judgment," *Journal of Moral Education,* 1975, *4,* pp. 129-161.

21. See Kohlberg, "Foreword," pp. 3-5.

22. See selection of articles in Scharf: "Part III: Teacher as Moral Educator and School as Social Curriculum," pp. 137-195; Richard H. Hersh and Diana Pritchard Paolitto, "Moral Development: Implications for Pedagogy"; Lawrence Kohlberg, "The Moral Atmosphere of the School"; Elsa R. Wasserman, "Implementing Kohlberg's 'Just Community Concept' in an Alternative High School"; Thomas Lickona, "Creating the Just Community with Children"; and Peter Scharf, "School Democracy: Promise and Paradox."

23. Elliott Turiel, "An Experimental Test of the Sequentiality of Development Stages in the Child's Moral Judgments," *Journal of Personality and Social Psychology,* 1966, *3,* pp. 611-618. See also James Rest, Elliott Turiel, and Lawrence Kohlberg, "Level of Moral Development as a Determinant of Reference and Comprehension of Moral Judgments Made by Others," *Journal of Personality,* 1969, *37,* pp. 225-252.

24. William G. LeFurgy and Gerald W. Waloshin, "Immediate and Long-term Effects of Experimentally Induced Social Influence in the Modification of Adolescent's Moral Judgments," *Journal of Personality and Social Psychology,* 1969, *12,* pp. 104-110.

25. Jack R. Fraenkel, "The Kohlberg Bandwagon: Some Reservations," in Scharf, *Readings in Moral Education,* pp. 250-263.

26. Edmund V. Sullivan, "Structuralism per se When Applied to Moral Ideology," in Scharf, pp. 272-287.

27. Ibid., p. 275.

28. Nancy H. Eisenberg, "The Development of Prosocial Moral Judgment and Its Correlates," Ph.D. Dissertation, University of California, Berkeley, 1976.

29. Paul Mussen and Nancy Eisenberg-Berg, *Roots of Caring, Sharing and Helping: The Development of Prosocial Behavior in Children* (San Francisco: W.H. Freeman and Company, 1977), p. 120.

30. Ibid.

31. Ibid., pp. 121-122.

32. Ervin Staub, "A Child in Distress: The Influence of Age and Number of Witnesses on Children's Attempts to Help," *Journal of Personality and Social Psychology,* 1970, *14,* pp. 130-140.

33. Robert F. Peck and Robert J. Havighurst, *The Psychology of Character Development* (New York: Wiley, 1960).

34. For a general discussion of the impact of modeling see the collection of articles: Albert Bandura, ed., *Psychological Modeling: Conflicting Theories* (Chicago: Aldine, 1971).

35. Harry Kaufman, *Aggression and Altruism* (New York: Holt, Rinehart and Winston, 1970).

36. See F. Wertham, *Seduction of the Innocent* (New York: Holt, Rinehart and Winston, 1954), and *A Sign for Cain* (New York: Macmillan, 1966); A. Bandura and R.H. Walters, *Social Learning and Personality Development* (New York: Holt, Rinehart and Winston, 1963); L. Berkowitz and A. LePage, "Weapons as Aggression-eliciting Stimuli," *Journal of Personality and Social Psychology,* 1967, *7,* pp. 202-207.

37. Kaufman, p. 141.

38. Harvey A. Hornstein, *Cruelty and Kindness: A New Look at Aggression and Altruism* (Englewood Cliffs, N.J.: Prentice-Hall, 1976).

39. Ibid., p. 1.

40. Ibid.

41. Ibid., p. 132.

42. Alice Isen and Paula F. Levin, "Effect of Feeling Good on Helping: Cookies and Goodness," *Journal of Personality and Social Psychology,* 1972, *21,* pp. 384-388.

43. David Aderman, "Elation, Depression, and Helping Behavior," *Journal of Personality and Social Psychology,* 1972, *24,* 91-101.

44. H.A. Hornstein, E. LaKind, G. Frankel, and S. Manne, "The Effects of Knowledge about Remote Social Events on Prosocial Behavior, Social Conception, and Mood," *Journal of Personality and Social Psychology* (to be published). Quoted in Hornstein, *Cruelty and Kindness,* p. 120.

45. See Hornstein, pp. 117-118.

46. Alice Isen and Paula F. Levin, "Effect of Feeling Good . . ."; Alice Isen, "Success, Failure, Attention and Reaction to Others: The Warm Glow of Success," *Journal of Personality and Social Psychology,* 1970, *15,* pp. 294-301; Alice Isen, Nancy Horn, D.L. Rosenhan, "Effects of Success and Failure on Children's Generosity," *Journal of Personality and Social Psychology,* 1973, *27,* pp. 239-247.

47. James H. Bryan and Mary A. Test, "Models and Helping: Naturalistic Studies in Aiding Behavior," *Journal of Personality and Social Psychology,* 1967, *6,* pp. 400-407.

48. James H. Bryan and Nancy H. Walbeck, "The Impact of Words and Deeds Concerning Altruism Upon Children," *Child Development,* 1970, *41,* pp. 747-757.

49. See also Esther R. Greenglass, "Effects of Prior Help and Hindrance on Willingness to Help Another: Reciprocity or Social Responsibility," *Journal of*

Personality and Social Psychology, 1969, *11,* pp. 224-232. For different results see David Rosenhan, Frank Frederick, and Anne Burrowes, "Preaching and Practicing: Effects of Channel Discrepancy on Norm Internalization," *Child Development,* 1968, *39,* pp. 290-301.

50. Ervin Staub, "Child in Distress: The Influence of Modeling and Nurturance on Children's Attempts to Help," *Developmental Psychology,* 1971, *5,* pp. 124-133. For a summary of his research, and a good overview of the field of prosocial behavior, see his "The Development of Prosocial Behavior in Children," *University Programs Modular Studies* (Morristown, N.J.: General Learning Press, 1975).

51. Ervin Staub, "The Use of Role-playing and Induction in Children's Learning of Helping and Sharing Behavior," *Child Development,* 1971, *42,* pp. 805-817.

52. Jack W. Brehm, *A Theory of Psychological Reactance* (New York: Academic Press, 1966). See my reference to this theory in chapter 2.

53. Martin L. Hoffman, "Parent Discipline and the Child's Consideration for Others," *Child Development,* 1963, *34,* pp. 573-588; Martin L. Hoffman and H.D. Saltzstein, "Parent Discipline and the Child's Moral Development," *Journal of Personality and Social Psychology,* 1967, *5,* pp. 45-47.

54. Staub, ". . . The Influence of Modeling and Nurturance . . . ."

55. Justin Aronfreed, *Conduct and Conscience: The Socialization of Internalized Control over Behavior* (New York: Academic Press, 1968), pp. 304-314.

56. Ibid., pp. 143-146. Based on unpublished manuscript, Justin Aronfreed and Vivian Paskal, "Altruism, Empathy, and the Conditioning of Positive Effect," 1965; for a similar research project see Elizabeth Midlarsky and James A. Bryan, "Training Charity in Children," *Journal of Personality and Social Psychology,* 1967, *5,* pp. 408-415.

57. Marian R. Yarrow, Phyllis M. Scott, and Carolyn Zahn Waxler, "Learning Concern for Others," *Developmental Psychology,* 1963, *8,* pp. 240-261; see also Marian R. Yarrow and Phyllis M. Scott, "Imitation of Nurturant and Non-nurturant Models," *Journal of Personality and Social Psychology,* 1972, *21,* pp. 139-148.

58. Ibid., pp. 255-256.

59. Mussen and Eisenberg-Berg, pp. 80-87. See also Salomon Rettig, "An Exploratory Study of Altruism," unpublished Ph.D. dissertation, Ohio State University, 1956.

60. Perry London, "The Rescuers: Motivational Hypotheses About Christians Who Saved Jews from the Nazis," in J. Macaulay and L. Berkowitz, eds., *Altruism and Helping Behavior* (New York: Academic Press, 1970).

61. David Rosenhan, "Some Origins of Concern for Others," in P. Mussen, J. Langer, and M. Covington, eds., *Trends and Issues in Developmental Psychology* (New York: Holt, Rinehart and Winston, 1969), pp. 134-153. See also "The Natural Socialization of Altruistic Autonomy," in Macaulay and Berkowitz, pp. 251-268.

62. Mussen and Eisenberg-Berg, chapter 7, "The Mass Media and Social-izers," pp. 101-118. The research they refer to includes Brian Coates, H. Ellison Pusser, and Irene Goodman, "The Influence of 'Sesame Street' and 'Mister Rogers' Neighborhood' on Children's Social Behavior in Preschool," *Child Development,* 1976, *47,* pp. 138-144; Lynette K. Friedrich and Aletha H. Stein, "Aggressive and Prosocial Television Programs and the Natural Behavior of Preschool Children," *Monographs of the Society for Research in Child Develop-ment,* 1973, *38* Serial No. 151; Lynette K. Friedrich and Aletha H. Stein, "Prosocial Television and Young Children: The Effects of Verbal Labeling and Role Playing on Learning and Behavior," *Child Development,* 1975, *46,* pp. 27-38.

63. Ervin Staub, "A Child in Distress: The Effects of Focusing Responsi-bility on Children on their Attempts to Help," *Developmental Psychology,* 1970, *2,* pp. 152-154. See also the comparative study of different cultures by John M. Whiting and Beatrice B. Whiting, *Children of Six Cultures* (Cambridge: Harvard University Press, 1974), in which they show that the more responsibility given to the child the more likelihood there is of prosocial behavior. See also Elise Boulding, "The Child and Nonviolent Social Change," in Israel W. Charny, ed., *Strategies Against Violence: Design for Nonviolent Change* (Boulder, Col.: Westview Press, 1978), pp. 68-99, especially p. 91.

64. Ervin Staub, "The Effects of Persuasion and Modeling on Delay of Gratification," *Developmental Psychology,* 1972, *6,* pp. 168-177.

65. The 1967 President's Commission on Crime contains an excellent critical review of the degree to which delinquency is related to negative factors in the schools and the mass media. See the report on "Juvenile Delinquency."

66. For good summaries of research and practical work in moral education see the work of A.W. Kay, *Moral Development: A Psychological Study of Moral Growth from Childhood to Adolescence* (New York: Shocken, 1969), and *Moral Education: A Sociological Study of the Influence of Home and School* (London: Allen and Unwin, 1975).

10 Empathy and Humanity

Bystander studies deal primarily with the immediate responses of a person to the distress situation of a stranger. They probe the prospects of aid being forthcoming, the risks that people are likely to assume, the legal rights and obligations of all involved parties, the dimensions of the bonds that hold a community together, and the moral dimensions of altruism. They deal pragmatically with the attitudes and behavior of individuals, groups, and communities in responding to accidents, crimes, and disasters.

Yet, they also transcend the specific crisis situation. They provide a glimpse into the capacity of a person to be aware of a shared humanity with others, to sense their emotions, their anguish, their fears; they show a capacity to reach out beyond the regular bonds of family, community, friendship, and to relate to other people in terms of their needs even when there is no prior personal contact with, or knowledge about, the other person.

Although much of the earlier bystander studies focused on the situational variables, some of the more recent research is dealing with the overall atmosphere of a community, or a culture, and with the bonds of empathy people sense for each other.

Hornstein[1] in particular has stressed this aspect, claiming that the key factor in eliciting a response is whether the other is defined in terms of "we" or "they." Unlike other group categorizations, these categories are based primarily on subjective feelings about external and objective data. It is not the data that determine the response, but the way in which they are interpreted. These subjective feelings may fluctuate, according to passing mood, social influences, and circumstantial factors.

Hornstein notes that there is "nothing inherent in any distinction between human beings that compels us to see others as *they*. Time and circumstance act upon substantive considerations and determine each individual's conception of who is *we* and who is *they*."[2]

It is from such a perspective that the larger implications of bystander behavior become apparent. For in embracing people within an orbit of belonging, a commitment is made to them, an emotional attachment is forged, a willingness to help, perhaps even sacrifice, is assumed. In defining others as "they," in excluding them, the conditions are created for ignoring their plight.

Such differentiation is applicable not only to those in the immediate vicinity. The dilemma of personal responsibility for another's welfare involves not just the chance encounter with the victim of a crime, an accident, or a disaster. These are exceptional events; in fact, only occasionally will the average person encounter situations of this nature.

But there is a larger arena in which we constantly play out bystander roles—in our awareness of the victimization of others, often in places far removed geographically, involving people who are total strangers, no more than anonymous figures in some human drama. Because of the overwhelming role of mass communications in the modern world—both the media for supplying information, and the means of transport for creating mobility—the plight of others refers not only to the neighbor calling for help or the stranger fortuitously drawn into one's vicinity, but also to those victimized wherever they may be and whatever may be the source of their plight. To relate to such victims requires that spatial barriers and social differences be discounted, and that the victims, for all their anonymity and distance, be seen essentially in human terms.

The modern world has no isolated islands in which refuge can be found from the dilemmas caused by victimization, in which the cries of the world's victims can be blocked out. There is a very close connection between the bystander role in a limited face-to-face situation, and the bystander role in large-scale victimization. The detailed reporting, in the electronic and written media, in books and lectures, of the plight of others, is now vividly brought home. For members of the world community, the ongoing plight of the masses of anonymous victims can be as real as the agonizing forty minutes of the Genovese incident. The inescapable dilemma as to whether, and how, to respond is one that confronts us without respite.

In chapter 3 it was shown that, on many occasions, natural disasters in a community tend to strengthen the community bonds as people try to help each other, and as aid from outside, in both personal and material form, converges on the area. What kind of reaction can be anticipated when disaster strikes farther afield? At what point is one entitled to claim that the problem is of no concern, or that distance nullifies any desire to help, or that the sheer enormity of the others' plight renders any effort at the personal level meaningless?

These are issues that are becoming increasingly difficult to avoid. It is not only that the modern world facilitates instant information. We live also in the shadow of a holocaust deliberately and systematically perpetrated with the cognizance of the world at large; we live in the shadow of the horrendous fury of atomic power that has devastated two cities and today has the accumulated power to wreak total destruction on a world scale; we live amidst warnings of ecological disaster that threatens future generations. And we live also amidst the constant barrage of news of millions made homeless by the vicissitudes of war; of children with bloated bellies starving to death from famine in far-off lands; of total cities suddenly destroyed by earthquake; of individuals subjected to torture because of their beliefs; of refugees in overcrowded, decrepit ships seeking sanctuary in other lands.

If altruism consists partly in the ability to enlarge the framework of egoistic concerns, if the socialization process of the child involves accepting consideration for ever larger groups of people—from family to community, and later ever larger social entities—then the ultimate altruism must be the capacity to embrace all of humanity.

Hoffman explains the socialization process of children in these terms. As children grow older, they become increasingly capable of entering into another's place and fully comprehending the nature of the other's distress, until "with further cognitive development the person may also be able to comprehend the plight not only of an individual but also of an entire group or class of people—such as the economically impoverished, politically oppressed, socially outcast, victims of war, or mentally retarded."[3]

There are indeed occasions in which individuals, deeply touched by the plight of particular victims, will offer their personal involvement. For some situations a regular organizational basis is set up to facilitate altruistic action on a larger scale. The Red Cross is one of the dominant organizations of this type, ready at a moment's notice to rush supplies and personnel to the scene of a disaster. The United Nations, too, has set up a number of bodies whose major task is to provide humanitarian aid to children, refugees, famine-stricken areas.

Various other organizations exist which provide a basis for personal involvement. Amnesty International is an outstanding example in this respect. Started in the early 1960s, after a strong personal reaction by a British lawyer to reports of unjust treatment of political prisoners, it has had a phenomenal growth, and today is in the forefront of many legal struggles to alleviate the sufferings meted out to political prisoners and the injustices to which they and their families are subjected.

For some the bonds of concern for the suffering extend beyond the human race and include involvement in the struggle on behalf of animals against their exploitation for commercial purposes, and against their indiscriminate use in scientific research. This struggle has taken on more meaningful dimensions as concern mounts for endangered species, and as evidence accumulates of the intellectual and emotional qualities of some animals closest to homo sapiens: whales, dolphins, apes. In some instances, efforts on behalf of animals involve sacrificial and risk-taking behavior.

Kaufman and Hornstein[4] have shown how closely intertwined are the processes leading to aggression and those leading to altruism. But the connection between them has additional aspects. The possibility of aggression or any other antisocial act being practiced against particular victims may be partly a consequence of the lack of altruistic concern on the part of others in their role as bystanders. It has been said that for evil to succeed it is sufficient that good people do nothing. To quiesce by volition is often to acquiesce by default. The degree of negative phenomena in social life may well be in inverse ratio to the degree of altruism.

Bystanders of the Holocaust

A number of writers who have discussed the Holocaust in Europe in the war years have attached blame to those who failed to respond with sufficient vigor to the crisis situation. Morse sets out what he terms "a Chronicle of American apathy,"[5] dealing with the unsuccessful efforts to save European Jewry. Noting that most studies of that period are "essentially a history of the killers and the killed," he stresses that his own work "concentrates on the bystanders rather than the killers or the killed. It attempts to answer two fundamental questions: "What did the rest of the world and, in particular, the United States and Great Britain, know about Nazi plans for the annihilation of the Jews? What was the reaction to this knowledge?"[6]

Later Morse adds another question, which is crucial for the bystander issue. "Could anything have been done to prevent the murder of six million men, women and children?"[7]

His study concentrates on the plight of the Jews because their destruction was meant to be total, but he takes note of the millions of others who were killed, on a selective basis, by the Nazis: "The Czechs of Lidice, the Yugoslav school children of Kragjeva, the Russians of countless villages, the Polish intellectuals, the gypsies, the Catholic priests imprisoned in Dachau."[8]

Morse divides his book into three parts—the Bystanders, the Victims, and the Rescuers—and documents the lack of concern and the lack of action on the part of those who were, he claims, in a position to offer aid. He notes the barriers put against immigration; sometimes even the quotas themselves were not filled. And he contrasts the strict immigration control at a time of imminent disaster with the generous impulses which characterized the early days of the American republic. He asks:

> "What had happened to George Washington's admonition to his countrymen "humbly and fervently to beseech the kind Author of these blessings . . . to render this country more and more a safe and propitious asylum for the unfortunates of other countries"?

> And what of the Legacy of Thomas Jefferson, who, in 1801, had asked: "Shall we refuse the unhappy fugitives from distress that hospitality which the savages of the wilderness extended to our forefathers arriving in this land? Shall oppressed humanity find no asylum on this globe?"[9]

Morse's conclusion is that the Nazis exploited the initial apathy and inaction as the measures against their victims became more intense and more thorough until, in the course of time, those who had initially been "bystanders to cruelty became bystanders to genocide."[10] Morse's book is not a mere documentation of past atrocities; it is a warning and a plea. "If genocide is to be prevented in the future, we must understand how it happened in the past—not only in terms of the killers and the killed but of the bystanders."[11]

Dadrian's work[12] on the genocide against the Armenians in the First World War also draws attention to the fact that the likelihood of outside intervention is a factor in the calculations of the oppressors. He quotes a report of Hitler's reaction to the protests of some of the German military, when told of the plans for genocide: "Who after all speaks today of the annihilation of the Armenians? . . . The world believes in success alone."[13] Each vicious act accomplished without a determined reaction by others lays the basis for further activities in the future.

Charny's work on the Holocaust[14] hews even closer to the bystander theme. His basic thesis is that it is the indifference to suffering of strangers at the immediate personal level that acts as a cancer eating away at the very fabric of social life and that provides the basic conditions within which wholesale victimization of genocidal dimensions may be committed. The perpetrators rely on the indifference of outsiders, knowing full well that most people will, in any case, choose not to know of the ugly happenings. Yet, he points out that, if there is real concern, it is possible to know what is happening, and that in the final analysis the quality of knowing or unknowing is a function of one's own inner choice to dare to know or not.[15]

While Charny's initial concern is as a response to the Holocaust in Nazi Germany, he intersperses his work with a plethora of events that have taken place in recent years, with the mass media providing full reports of mass slaughter, yet with little effective response at either the personal or the governmental level. He quotes from Wiesel to show how bystanders try to block out the full and cruel implications of that which they are witnessing. The scene conjured up bears close resemblances to the Genovese incident:

> He, standing behind the curtains, watched. The police beat women and children; he did not stir. It was no concern of his. He was neither victim nor executioner; a spectator, that's what he was. He wanted to live in peace and quiet.[16]

Charny, Hornstein, and others have shown how the victimization of total groups is dependent not merely on the way in which the perpetrators relate to their victims but also to the way in which bystanders respond to this action. Both perpetrators and bystanders use a similar means of denial of the humanity of the victim. Once that cognitive and emotional process is complete, the perpetrators may proceed, untrammeled by any intervention by the bystanders. Had the bystanders sensed, and expressed, closer bonds of human contact with the victims, they might have taken more effective action to avoid the catastrophe, and the perpetrators might have hesitated to act.

The research by Milgram[17] is most pertinent in this respect, and has been used by many social scientists as a basis for understanding the sources of inhumane behavior. His research was conducted partly as a response to the atrocities of the Second World War in order to examine the circumstances in which people might be persuaded to execute acts of cruelty against others. The subjects were ordinary people, having no personal or ideological propensities toward dehumanizing behavior. When put into an experimental situation in which they were requested to administer electric shocks to others, some of which were ostensibly of a lethal nature, they showed a greater inclination to obey the directions of the researcher than to desist from the suffering they were, as far as they knew on the basis of what they had been told, inflicting on their unknown victim. It is activities of such a nature, performed by people with no sadistic trends or ideological tendencies, that Milgram sees as being the basis for large-scale oppressive actions based on a blind obedience to authority. Charny sees the indifference to the suffering of a fellow being as also signifying the initial willingness to be a silent spectator of even worse brutalities in the future.]

[Hornstein's analysis of Milgram's series of experiments is more hopeful, for he points out that, in some of the later experiments, in which a number of variations on the basic process were introduced, the number of people willing to administer shock was dramatically reduced when there had been some prior connection between the victim and the subject.[18] Even minimal personal contact was sufficient to prevent the inhumane acts. Tilker's research[19] elicited similar results, this time on the part of bystanders. In his research the subjects were observers at an experiment similar to Milgram's, in which shock was administered. As the experiment progressed, the observers evinced much sympathy for the victim, and often intervened to stop the experiment, especially where they had been assigned some responsibility for what was happening and where they could actually see the suffering of the "victim."]

In recording the Holocaust and the implications it has for the theme of the bystander, it must not be forgotten that while most people were apathetic and governmental bodies lax in their efforts, there were those who struggled to help the victims at considerable and continual risk to themselves and their families. In their book *The Samaritans: Heroes of the Holocaust,* Bartoszewski and Lewine[20] detail some of the dedicated and dangerous work of those who helped, placing "on record some of the finest examples of genuine brotherhood of man, regardless of origin, faith or political belief."[21]

London's research[22] into Christians who saved Jews from the Nazis is an attempt to gain some sociological knowledge on the background and the motivation of these rescuers. He comes to the conclusion that a "zest for adventure and the workings of chance both were important for the initiation of rescue behavior." However, in addition, a "strong identification with a very moralistic parental model and the experience of social marginality gave people the impetus and endurance to continue their rescue activities."[23]

In including the London article in their book on helping behavior, Macaulay and Berkowitz have shown the importance for altruism and bystander behavior in the efforts made by individuals on behalf of the victims of political, racial, and religious persecution. Another study in this book, conducted by Rosenhan, deals with the backgrounds of civil rights workers in the southern states of America.[24] Among the most committed of these workers Rosenhan notes the "altruistic environment" in which they had grown up. They "seemed very much influenced by identificatory learnings from the past. These learnings consisted not merely of moral precepts, but also of percepts. They were taught not only to believe but to do. Such doing often severely stigmatized them, and was costly in terms of personal risk and effort. Their sustained ability to tolerate high costs and low payoffs, all on behalf of others, leads us to believe that theirs was an autonomous altruism."[25]

There is in these studies the beginning of an important and potentially constructive area of research into the backgrounds and characteristics of those who are prepared to identify with the suffering of people from another group, to help others in the struggle against economic deprivation, national humiliation, racial oppression, religious persecution. For many, they must brave the indifference, and sometimes even the opposition, of their immediate environment—family, friends, neighbors—in order to provide help to members of another social group, strangers to them yet linked by the bonds of a shared humanity.

Humanitarian Aid

The personal level is clearly an important one. Yet there are some problems of a basically political nature that can lead to a meaningful response only when action is taken at the governmental level. A recent book[26] dealing with instances of civil strife discusses the circumstances in which relief on an international scale may be anticipated. In separate articles the book discusses fighting that took place in the years 1965-1973 in four different parts of the world: Burundi, East Pakistan/Bangladesh, the Dominican Republic, and Nigeria/Biafra. The writers show the different variables that affect the possibility of international aid being given to alleviate the suffering of those victimized by a war situation. Their conclusions are extremely pessimistic. Davis, in summarizing the lessons of these four efforts, writes that "civil wars . . . have provided harsh political environments for international relief agencies attempting ministrations";[27] yet, even so, there are other situations of mass victimization in which outside aid is even more difficult to perform—where the fighting is between different nations, or where there is internal repression falling short of civil war.

Sometimes in the case of natural disasters, for internal political reasons, the governmental authorities are deliberately recalcitrant in providing relief, even when international efforts are mounted to provide it. Too often even relatively innocent relief functions by nonpolitical humanitarian organizations may have political implications within the specific context of the internal politics of a particular country.

In his review of international disaster relief, Green claims that "national sovereignty—or an interpretation of it which has in fact been shaped by the narrow self-perceived interests of a small group of politicians—has . . . frequently caused thousands of needless deaths and greatly increased the impact of disasters on the 'normal' development process."[28] He argues that normal diplomatic procedures are often futile, and that, in such circumstances, it is only the pressures exerted by the international mass media as proxy bystanders, that may, by arousing world public opinion, force the governments of the disaster area to acknowledge their need for help, as well as activate other governments and private organizations to respond. Green sets out a plan for international action to deal with natural disasters, with the human consequences of violent conflicts (refugees, and so on), and with systematic violations of human rights. "Certain problems," he concludes, "are by definition international."[29]

However, defining the problems as international and eliciting a willingness on the part of the world community to help does not always resolve the issues. Franck and Radley[30] have debated the need and the desirability of allowing states the right to intervene militarily on behalf of a victimized people, and to offer humanitarian aid. They argue strongly against the recognition of any norm of international law allowing intervention—not because they are insensitive to the real needs that often arise, but because historical precedent indicates that, where intervention has taken place, it was usually done to further the political interests of the intervening state, and not the humanitarian needs of the victims. Conversely, many situations of victimization have gone without response from the world community even when, as in the case of the Holocaust, the position of the victims was extreme and their plight was known. As international lawyers, Franck and Radley fear that the granting of an international right of intervention for humanitarian purposes would be exploited for political ends. "A 'right' so little exercised in circumstances where morality . . . most craves its application is rightly suspect."[31] They reluctantly conclude that "a usable general definition of 'humanitarian intervention' would be extremely difficult to formulate and virtually impossible to apply rigorously."[32]

A French writer, Julliard,[33] has recently given expression to the frustration felt at the inability to contribute meaningfully to the plight of martyred people, victimized by what he terms as torturing states. Well aware of the reluctance of governments to act, he calls for an "internationale of human rights," based on people's needs and not national sovereignty. Given the oppressive nature of many states in the modern world, he argues that "to take any other view.is to become the accomplices of butchers."[34]

What, then, is to be done in the face of suffering? The issue of aid at the international level, of help being offered across national borders to the victims of wars, political oppression, physical annihilation, or natural disasters, is a complex one, and a full analysis is beyond the scope of this book. It certainly requires a great deal of consideration, research, and policy formulations, far more than have been accorded it in the past. Social and political scientists would be well advised to devote serious attention to the human and political factors involved in such situations.

In this chapter I have only alluded to some of these human and political problems of a global scale in order to draw attention to some of the ultimate implications of the bystander role, of the full meaning of a willingness to sense empathetic feelings for a stranger, and of an awareness of living in a world where one is regularly confronted by reports of mass suffering. There is, as Milgram, Charny, and Hornstein have suggested, a clear link between the bystander role at different levels, whether face-to-face or on a mass scale, whether in the immediate vicinity or far removed.

In his study of the Holocaust and other examples of extreme situations, Des Pres[35] describes the dedication with which many of the survivors have taken upon themselves the sacred task of bearing witness to the memory and the suffering of those who perished. To a degree, they are driven by feelings of guilt at having survived, knowing full well that, for all the savagery in the camps, "there was also a web of mutual aid and encouragement," and that in a "literal sense, therefore, the survivor owes his life to his comrades."[36]

But they are also determined to ensure that there shall be no forgetting of the horrors, that there shall be a perpetual reminder of what happened. "Confronting radical evil, men and women instinctively feel the desire to call, to warn, to communicate their shock."[37] Discussing the various threats to humanity today, he concludes that "the survivor's scream arises from the deepest fear of all, that mankind, or indeed all life, is now endangered."[38]

We are, in a sense, all survivors of past tragedies; we are all inextricably bound up with each other, dependent upon each other. We are also all potential victims and potential bystanders of political oppression, of natural disasters, of physical violence, of ecological destruction.

For all, the gnawing questions persist: What is our obligation—personal or collective—for the tragedies which take place in our midst? Did we do enough to avert them? Could we have done more? How shall we behave if tested again?

Buber writes of the person who

> through acting or failing to act, has burdened himself with a guilt or has taken part in a community guilt, and now, after years or decades, is again and again visited by the memory of his guilt . . . while the image of action or inaction has remained in the living memory, time and again admonishing, attacking, tormenting.[39]

The Fall, Camus's story[40] of the degeneration of a prominent lawyer after failing to respond to the cries of a drowning woman, serves as an allegory of our times. He is haunted by his sense of failure as he tortures himself with the agonizing recollection of a crisis moment in his life when he ignored the entreaties of an unknown voice crying out to him in the darkness. He is driven by the need to relate his tale of woe; he is obsessed by the wish to have an opportunity to redeem himself; and he is fearful that, given another opportunity, he would be found wanting once again. On the final page the reader takes his leave of Celeste, Camus's antihero, contemplating, as always, the memory of that fateful moment, and muttering, "Oh young woman, throw yourself into the water again so that I may the second time have a chance of saving both of us," and then thinking to himself, "A second time, oh, what a risky suggestion! Just suppose, *cher maitre,* that we should be taken literally? We'd have to go through with it. Brr . . . ! The water's so cold! But let's not worry! It's too late now. It will always be too late. Fortunately!"[41]

Notes

1. Harvey A. Hornstein, *Cruelty and Kindness: A New Look at Aggression and Altruism* (Englewood Cliffs, N.J.: Prentice-Hall, 1976).

2. Ibid., p. 125.

3. Martin L. Hoffman, "Developmental Synthesis of Affect and Cognition and Its Implications for Altruistic Motivation," *Developmental Psychology,* 1975, *11,* p. 617.

4. See the previous chapter for discussions of the work of Kaufman and Hornstein: Harry Kaufman, *Aggression and Altruism: A Psychological Analysis* (New York: Holt, Rinehart and Winston, 1979); Hornstein, *Cruelty and Kindness.*

5. Arthur D. Morse, *While Six Million Died: A Chronicle of American Apathy* (New York: Random House, 1968). See also Henry L. Feingold, *The Policies of Rescue: The Roosevelt Administration and the Holocaust 1938-1945* (New Brunswick, N.J.: Rutgers University Press, 1970). This book, while not ignoring the moral issues, is a more factual and documented account, dealing more with the political and legal dimensions.

6. Ibid. For an analysis of the efforts made in Britain before the war to cope with the problem of refugees, see Ari J. Sherman, *Island Refugee: Britain and Refugees from the Third Reich, 1933-1939* (Berkeley: University of California Press, 1973).

7. Morse, p. x.

8. Ibid.

9. Ibid., p. 131.

10. Ibid., p. 383.

11. Ibid., p. x.

12. Vahakn N. Dadrian, "The Structural-Functional Components of Genocide: A Victimological Approach to the Armenian Case," in I. Drapkin and E. Viano, *Victimology* (Lexington, Mass.: Lexington Books, 1974), pp. 123-136.

13. Ibid., p. 133. The quotation was originally from Majorie Housepian, "The Unremembered Genocide," *Commentary,* Sept. 1966, *42,* pp. 55-62.

14. Israel Charny, unpublished manuscript. See also the article in which Charny raises a number of moral issues connected with the bystander role: "And Abraham Went to Slay Isaac: A Parable of Killer, Victim and Bystander in the Family of Man," *Journal of Ecumenical Studies,* 1973, *10,* pp. 304-318.

15. Ibid., section in chapter 13 of manuscript, "The Bystander Role as Accomplice to Evil."

16. Ibid. The quotation is from Elie Wiesel, *The Town Beyond the Wall* (New York: Atheneum, 1964), p. 150.

17. See Stanley Milgram, *Obedience to Authority* (New York: Harper and Row, 1974).

18. Hornstein, pp. 138-139.

19. Harvey A. Tilker, "Socially Responsible Behavior as a Function of Observer Responsibility and Victim Feedback," *Journal of Personality and Social Psychology,* 1970, *14,* pp. 95-100.

20. Wlasylslaw Bartoszewski and Zofia Lewine, *The Samaritans: Heroes of the Holocaust* (New York: Twayne Publishers, 1970).

21. Ibid., p. 57. See also Philip Friedman, *Their Brothers' Keepers: The Christian Heroes and Heroines Who Helped the Oppressed Escape the Nazi Terror* (New York: Schocken, 1978).

22. Perry London, "The Rescuers: Motivational Hypotheses about Christians Who Saved Jews from the Nazis," in J. Macaulay and L. Berkowitz, eds., *Altruism and Helping Behavior: Some Psychological Studies of Some Antecedents and Consequences* (New York: Academic Press, 1970), pp. 241-250.

23. Ibid., p. 249.

24. David Rosenhan, "The Natural Socialization of Altruistic Autonomy," in Macaulay and Berkowitz, pp. 251-268.

25. Ibid., p. 267.

26. Morris Davis, ed., *Civil Wars and the Politics of International Relief: Africa, South Asia and the Caribbean* (New York: Praeger, 1975).

27. Ibid., p. 93. For further discussion of the human dimensions of internal civil strife, see Leo Kuper, *The Pity of It All: Polarization of Ethnic and Racial Relations* (Minneapolis: University of Minnesota Press, 1977).

28. Stephen Green, *International Disaster Relief: Toward a Responsive System* (New York: McGraw-Hill, 1977), p. 41.

29. Ibid., p. 78.

30. Thomas M. Franck and Nigel S. Radley, "After Bangladesh: The Law of Humanitarian Intervention by Military Force," *American Journal of International Law,* 1973, *67,* pp. 275-305.

31. Ibid., p. 290.

32. Ibid., p. 305.

33. Jacques Julliard, "For a New Internationale," *New York Review of Books,* July 20, 1978, p. 3.

34. Ibid.

35. Terence Des Pres, *The Survivor: An Anatomy of Life in the Death Camps* (New York: Oxford University Press, 1976).

36. Ibid., p. 37.

37. Ibid., p. 33.

38. Ibid., p. 201.

39. Martin Buber, "Guilt and Guilt Feelings," in Maurice Friedman, ed., *The Knowledge of Man: Selected Essays of Martin Buber* (New York: Harper and Row, 1965).

40. Albert Camus, *The Fall,* Justin O'Brien, trans. (New York: Knopf, 1957).

41. Ibid., p. 147.

11 Conclusion: Bystanders and Their Victims

It was the Genovese case in 1964 that set off the train of discussion and research that has formed the basis for much of the material presented in this book. At the time it created a stir and quickly became a cause célèbre, raising questions about the nature of the social bond and the quality of social life. More directly, it questioned the faith people might have that a neighbor or a stranger would recognize one's plight, would appreciate one's agony, and would be willing to render aid.

In retrospect, it is not clear why this specific case made such an impact and became so engraved in the consciousness and memory of so many, inside the United States and beyond. It was neither unique nor representative. It was merely part of a large mosaic of varied reactions by bystanders.

The years of research into bystander behavior have helped to elucidate many aspects of the problem, but a definitive statement encompassing all its ramifications still eludes us. The daily papers continue to apprise us of a wide variety of behavioral patterns: of callous disregard reminiscent of the Genovese case, of helping behavior in natural disasters, of sacrifices which earn rewards, of simple acts of kindness that are ruthlessly exploited, of innocent requests for help that are refused.

Despite the focus that has been placed on the Geneovese case, there are two interesting sidelights connected with the case that have been largely ignored.

Four days after the Genovese murder,[1] a New York resident heard a noise in his neighbor's apartment. He went to investigate and found a strange man removing a television set from the apartment. When questioned, the stranger nonchalantly stated that he was helping the tenants of the apartment to move. The neighbor, not knowing of any such plan, became suspicious and observed the actions of the stranger, who put the television set in a parked car, then returned to the apartment. Although the stranger's bearing seemed to indicate the legitimacy of his actions, the neighbor remained puzzled, and consulted with a friend who lived nearby. They decided to take precautionary measures. While one called the police, the other went to the car, opened the hood, and removed the distributor cap. Both then continued to watch the actions of the stranger as he returned to the car. When he failed to start it, he calmly got out, locked it, and walked away. When the police arrived shortly afterwards, the two involved neighbors were able to point out the stranger in one of the nearby streets and he was apprehended.

The stranger admitted to stealing from the apartment, as well as to several other burglaries. He stated that he had returned to the burglarized apartment to pick up a tool that he had left behind.

After a few hours of further questioning, detectives elicited from the burglar the confession that a few nights earlier he had killed Kitty Genovese, and that he had committed one other rape and murder and made several other attempts. Thus, the actions of two concerned bystanders had led, paradoxically, to the arrest of Kitty Genovese's murderer, and possibly prevented other future murders.

As to the second incident connected with the Genovese case,[2] a little over ten years after that tragedy, another murder was committed in the same neighborhood. A neighbor who had been one of the thirty-eight witnesses to the Genovese murder once again was awakened by cries for help in the early hours of the morning. In a later interview she said that she had heard the voices of a man and a woman in a nearby apartment, the sounds of a struggle, and the screams of a woman. She had interpreted the incident as a lovers' quarrel and so had not called the police. The body of the dead woman was found thirty-six hours later.

Was it really a problem of incorrect perception that caused this particular bystander to fail a second time, as Camus's Celeste feared he might do? Or was it apathy, or fear, or stupidity? How much more do we know about the inaction of this bystander on her own in 1974 than we knew when she, together with thirty-seven other witnesses, had failed to react ten years earlier?

Our knowledge has undoubtedly expanded, and there is a better appreciation of overall social processes. But individual instances will continue to puzzle and amaze, to cause despondency about the human condition, or, conversely, to evoke hope and faith.

As this book was being completed, the press[3] carried an account of the rescue of a woman who had been swept downstream by a strong river current. She was spotted by three teenagers riding their bicycles along the river bank. While one of them went off to fetch help, the other two rode along the bank trying to catch up with the woman struggling in the water. After about a mile they came abreast, then waded into the water and pulled the victim onto the bank. It was only then that one of the boys discovered that he had helped to save his own mother's life.

Although widely reported, this case has not made the same impact as the Genovese case. Yet it is no less pertinent to the study of the bystander.

It serves to remind us that we can never know when we may be bystanders and who our victim will be; or when we may be victims and who our bystander will be.

Notes

1. For a full account of this incident, see Albert A. Seedman and Peter Hellman, *Chief!* (New York: Arthur Fields, 1975), pp. 109-147.

2. Robert D. McFadden, "Dying Screams of Model Are Ignored in House at '64 Genovese Murder Site," *New York Times,* 27 December, 1974, p. 1.

3. See article in *Los Angeles Times,* 5 June, 1978, p. 1: "Boy Races River, Finds He's Saved His Own Mother."

Index of Cases

Index of Cases

Author Index

Author Index

Abbott, D.J., 95
Adelman, L., 122
Aderman, D., 188
Allee, W.C., 168
Allen, C.K., 75, 82
Anderson, C.D., 61
Archer, D., 72
Ardrey, R., 168
Aronfreed, J., 182-183
Ash, M., 60-62

Bachofen, J.J., 156
Bancroft, H.H., 94
Bandura, A., 180, 188
Banfield, L., 61
Banton, M., 168
Barash, D.P., 160
Barbour, J., 70
Barton, A.H., 39, 41
Bartoszewski, W., 196
Bassiouni, M.C., 91, 138
Batson, C.D., 186
Beardsley, R.K., 98
Bell, J., 72
Bell, W.G., 31
Bellamy, J., 87, 91-92
Bentham, J., 113, 153
Berelson, B., 162
Berkowitz, L., 22, 180, 196
Bickman, L., 55
Blackwell, K., 147
Blatt, M., 177
Blau, P.M., 164
Bohlen, F.H., 110
Borofsky, G., 54-55
Boulding, E., 190
Brehm, J.W., 24, 189
Brett, P., 120
Brown, R.M., 8, 72, 93-95
Burrowes, A., 189
Bryan, J.H., 182
Buber, M., 199

Cahn, E., 175
Caldwell, D.K., 169
Calhoun, G.M., 78
Cam, H.M., 87, 97
Campbell, D., 152
Camus, A., 199-200
Cannavale, F.J., 61-62
Cannon, D.A., 55
Cardozo, Justice B., 124
Carlson, R.L., 71
Chadborn, J.H., 99
Charny, I., 195-196, 199
Chiu, T., 84-85, 120
Cizanckas, V., 71
Claiborne, W.L., 72
Clark, R.D., 19-20
Clifford, W., 85-86
Clinard, M.B., 95
Coates, B., 190
Comte, A., 167
Conklin, J.E., 69, 76
Coser, L., 72
Coulton, G.G., 98
Crawford, M.P., 169
Crawshaw, R., 44
Cross, J.C., 147
Crumplar, T., 147
Cutler, J.E., 95

Dadrian, V.N., 195
Darley, J.M., 12-18, 19-21, 24, 53-54, 137, 186
Darwin, C., 154-157
Davis, M., 197
Dawson, J.P., 109, 131-132, 144, 146
Deacon, J.B., 31
Deaux, G., 30-31
Des Pres, T., 199
Devlin, P., 174
Dodd, D.J., 25
Drapkin, I., 8
Dyke, L., 168

Subject Index

Subject Index

About the Author

Leon Shaskolsky Sheleff has a law degree from the University of Cape Town and a Ph.D. in sociology from the Ohio State University. He has a joint appointment as senior lecturer in the Institute of Criminology and Criminal Law and the Department of Sociology at Tel Aviv University. In 1978 he was on sabbatical leave, teaching in the Program in Social Ecology at the University of California, Irvine.